2+2=5

How The Transgender Craze is Redefining Reality

By Katie Roche

First published by Katie Roche in 2020

Copyright © 2020 Katie Roche

All rights reserved

Published by Amazon Kindle Direct Publishing

ISBN: 9798649935074

Contents

1. Introduction 1
   My Peak Trans Story 3
   How did the Transgender Craze Begin? 5
2. What Causes Gender Dysphoria? 16
   Is Gender Dysphoria a Mental Disorder? 16
   Autogynephilia 18
   Social Contagion 20
   Genes 21
   Social Status 21
   Brain Sex 22
   Sex isn't Real Anyway? 24
3. The Truth about Sex Reassignment 28
   Why Do Doctors Perform Sex Reassignment? 28
   Do Sex Changes Work? 29
   "Let me change sex or I'll kill myself"- Why do So Many Transgender People Die of Suicide? 29
   The Downsides of Transitioning 33
   Fertility 37
   No Regrets? 38
4. Neither Male nor Female: Non-Binary Genders 40
   "What are Your Pronouns?" 40
   Am I Non-Binary? 43
   "Non-Binary Identities are Valid" 45
   Identifying out of Privilege 48
   Doublethink- Are Non-Binary People Warriors or Victims? 49
5. Never too Young- Transgenderism and Childhood 53

    Childhood Transitions- Changing sex in childhood 54

    Woke Education 56

    Indoctrination Through Play 57

    Woke Parents 59

6. Transgenderism in Policy 65

    'Equality' Laws 65

    The Ministry of Truth: Changing Records, Re-Writing the Past .. 66

    The Thought Police 68

    "Transgender Rights are Human Rights" 73

7. The Left and Transgenderism 77

    The Terrifying Transgender Rights Activists 82

    "You must have sex with me": The cotton ceiling 85

    Transgender Rights Activists Vs Women 86

8. Trans Inclusionary, Woman Exclusionary- Taking Over Women's Spaces and Rights 90

    Trans-Identified Males in Women's Jobs 90

    Trans-Identified Males in Woman's Spaces 92

    Sport 96

9. Erasing Women 103

    Don't Say Woman! 103

    That's Cissexist! 105

    Trigger Warning: Menstruation 107

    Abolishing Motherhood 110

    'His'story- Transgendering Historical Women 112

10. Not Allowed to Speak Out 115

    "You're Fired!": Transgenderism and Employment 115

    "You're Banned!" Censorship on Social Media 117

    "Get out of My Pub!" 118
    Trans-Exclusionary Arts 118
    Cancel Culture 119
    Suppression of Research 119
    No Platforming 123
    "My Identity is not for Debate" 125
11. Hope? 128
    Will COVID-19 Put Things into Context? 128
    History Repeating Itself? 129
    Fightback on Self-Identification 132
    Keeping Children Safe 133
    Saving Women's Sports 135
    Protecting Women's Spaces 136
    Protection of Free Speech 138
    Progress in Healthcare 139
12. Conclusion 140
References 155
Index 220

1. Introduction

"Anything could be true. The so-called laws of Nature were nonsense. The law of gravity was nonsense. 'If I wished,' O'Brien had said, 'I could float off this floor like a soap bubble.' Winston worked it out. 'If he THINKS he floats off the floor, and if I simultaneously THINK I see him do it, then the thing happens.'

George Orwell, 1984 (1)

When a person changes sex, we are expected to believe that something impossible has occurred: we are expected to believe that a woman has become a man or that a man has become a woman. Like an alchemist believing that a base metal has turned to gold, or a magic show where a magician pulls a rabbit out of a seemingly empty hat, something that defies the laws of nature has supposedly happened. And we are not meant to question it.

We must learn to ignore what we see and hear and indulge the person's fantasy. We must call the burly, deep voiced person 'madam' and the slight-built, soft-faced person 'sir'. We must suppress our horror at the thought of a person having their healthy genitals cut off. Instead, we must be proud. We must celebrate a person's realisation that they have been living as the 'wrong' gender for their whole lives and now they're fixing it. We must pretend it is possible to be neither male nor female. We must entertain calling people 'ze' or 'they' instead of 'he' or 'she'. We must take a three-year-old boy who says he is a girl seriously. We must suppress our knowledge that a person who was born male will be male for all his life, and instead accept that a person has become a different sex. It is one thing to politely call a person by their preferred pronouns and name. It is another thing to accept that the person has literally transformed into a different gender. Or that they never really were the sex they were born as. Yet that is precisely what the legal system, the medical establishment and our politicians are increasingly expecting us to do. So why is this a problem?

Because it is women who are bearing the brunt of the impact of transgenderism. Through transgenderism, the patriarchy has found a new way of oppressing women. It is women who are being forced to let transgender people into our spaces. It is women whose rights are being set aside for transgender people. Sadly, the dangers of transgenderism were not unforeseen. Greer tried to warn us of how the concept of transsexuality reinforces gender roles and how transgender women would use their status to enter female-only spaces. She also warned of how transgender people demand to be treated as normal women at times yet expect special treatment because of their transgender status at other times (2). And she has been ignored. Sadly, much of what she predicted has come true.

Given how women have been oppressed throughout history, the use of transgenderism to oppress women is not surprising. We live in a man's world. Most politicians are men. Most famous historical figures are men. Most big business owners are men. Almost everything is dominated by men. On the other hand, we women are the lesser sex. We are the sex who gets pregnant and has children; we are the ones who have to care for them, when there's plenty of deadbeat dads who turn their back on us. And we earn less; in the UK, men on average earn almost nine percent more than women (3).

We also face a lot of danger. Being physically weaker and smaller than men, we cannot defend ourselves against physical attacks. Men have a punch which is on average 162% more powerful than a woman's punch (4). If a man wants to hurt you, there's little you can do about it. All through our lives, we also face the threat of sexual violence (rape or sexual assault). In England and Wales, one in five women has been the victim of sexual violence, compared to less than one in 20 men (5). Globally, more than one in three women has experienced sexual violence (6). In addition, women are in danger of being murdered because of their sex. In 2018, 149 women were killed in the UK, most by their male partner or ex-partner (7). Around the world, women face even bigger threats. An estimated 5000 women a year are killed in so called 'honour killings', where a woman is murdered by a family member because her behaviour is said to have brought dishonour on the family. For instance, if she has had an affair or become pregnant outside of marriage. Although in some cases, it is used when a woman has been raped or to conceal incest (8). As well as this, in the Indian sub-continent, many women die in dowry-related disputes, where a married woman's in-laws kill her (8). In 2006, 7600 women were reported to have died in this way (8). While it would be easy to assume that women have gained equality and can afford to give some of their rights up for transgender people, this is clearly not the case. Which is why transgenderism is so problematic.

My Peak Trans Story
Gender critical feminists often talk about hitting 'peak trans'- the moment when you realize the truth about transgenderism. Here's my peak trans story.

When the transgender trend started, I tried to believe in it. I really did. Every other left-winger seemed to be embracing transgender rights, so I felt that I should too. I tried to believe that it was possible to change sex. I tried to be happy that countries were passing laws to let transgender people use their bathroom of choice. I tried to be pleased at the growth in people identifying as non-binary. I tried to share in the joy of Caitlyn Jenner coming out. I tried to see two and two making five. But no matter what I did, I just couldn't help but see the truth.

As a child, I had always been taught that even though I was a girl, there was nothing wrong with 'boys' things. It wasn't hair, make-up or clothes that made me a girl. And that it would be okay for me to go into a 'man's' job when I grew up. I played with both soft toys and cars. I played outside in the mud. I wasn't interested in dressing up or doing my hair. But that was fine. I had learned that nobody needed to conform to gender stereotypes and that I was fine as I was.

I was a young adult when the transgender craze began. I was hearing more and more about transgender and non-binary identities and I began to wonder if I was non-binary. I decided to learn more about non-binary identities and then I realised something; all they talked about was gender stereotypes. So often I would read things like "I always knew I was really a boy because I like sport" or "I'm not completely male because I like romantic comedies". This troubled me: these aren't reasons someone isn't really a man or a woman. They are just people who don't fit into the stereotypical gender roles. At that point, I realized that there was no such thing as being non-binary. I was simply a woman who wasn't interested in conforming to gender stereotypes. And that was okay. But if non-binary didn't exist, did transgender identities- where someone was 'born in the wrong body'- really exist? I decided to learn some more. I realized that transgenderism was all about gender stereotypes- that there was no way that someone could be 'born in the wrong body'. I also realized that contrary to what transgender activists claim, identifying as transgender wasn't about breaking the gender binary. I stopped accepting transgenderism.

Was I a bigot? The good left-wingers all support transgender rights. They condemn the wicked TERFs (Trans-Exclusionary Radical Feminists) like Germaine Greer and Julie Burchill for not including transgender people in their feminism. Conversely, the bad right-wingers, who don't support transgender rights are nasty, cruel and responsible for many transgender people's deaths. I don't support any other right-wing views, so this left me feeling confused about my political identity. Then I discovered gender critical feminism. It reminded me of what I knew all along; there's no wrong way or right way to be a woman. There's no need to identify as non-binary or transgender. The transgender trend was all about the gender stereotypes I had always been taught to reject. I wasn't a bigot after all. Nor are all the Big Bad Right-Wingers or the evil TERFs. I am still politically left-wing; I support equality for oppressed people. But transgender people are not an oppressed group. And being a woman isn't a feeling. It's a fact. Feminism isn't about being nice. It's not about making people feel comfortable. It is about gaining rights for women. It can be ugly, rude and sometimes even aggressive. This might make trans-identified people feel uncomfortable. But women have fought hard for their rights. We won't let transgenderism take them away.

I don't hate transgender people. I hate the idea of people having healthy parts of their bodies removed. I hate that children are being rendered infertile when they are too young to make such decisions. I hate the thought of people's bodies being changed irreversibly by hormones given by therapists who are all too ready to go along with their patient's belief that they were 'born in the wrong body'. I hate that women and girls are constantly being usurped by men who identify as women or worse, 'non-binary'. I hate having to pretend that sex isn't real. And I hate that nobody is allowed to speak out against all of this. I have to admit I'm terrified about what will happen to me now I've published this book. So many other people who have questioned the transgender narrative have suffered in many ways. I can't help but worry. Will I be arrested? Will I go to prison? Will I be attacked? What about my family? Will they be safe? Will I be sued? But I feel I must be brave. I must speak out.

How did the Transgender Craze Begin?
Between 0.3% and 0.6% of the UK and US population is estimated to be transgender (9,10). Why has such a small group of people become so prominent?

To understand how we got to this point, it's useful to look at where transgenderism started. Transgenderism came about thanks to the medical innovations that took place in the mid to late 20th century. A very small number of sex reassignment surgeries were carried out prior to 1966. Perhaps the most notable of these was Lili Elbe, who underwent several experimental sex change procedures in the 1930s, the last of which- an attempt to implant a womb- killed her (11). In 1952, Christine Jorgensen was the first person in the USA to have undergone sex reassignment surgery (12). The first known female-to-male sex reassignment surgery was carried out in 1944 in the UK on Michael Dillon (13).

In the USA, Harry Benjamin, an endocrinologist, pioneered the concept of transsexualism. Benjamin took the view that the best treatment for Gender Dysphoria was to perform sex change surgeries. When meeting with Jan Morris, a writer and one of his patients, he said "if we cannot alter the conviction to fit the body, should we not, in certain circumstances, alter the body to fit the conviction?" (14). He claims that sex reassignment surgery started being performed at reputable hospitals as a result of his work (14). In 1966, he published *The Transsexual Phenomenon*, the first major textbook on transgenderism (15). As a result of this, other doctors started to learn about transgenderism and Benjamin's views spread. Benjamin's line of reasoning has now become the mainstream view on treating Gender Dysphoria.

In the same year, Johns Hopkins Hospital set up the first gender identity clinic in the USA, which specialized in performing sex reassignment. However, the clinic shut down in 1979 under the leadership of Dr Paul McHugh, after research found that sex reassignment surgery did not improve the patient's quality of life (16). In spite of this, transgenderism was still gaining acceptance amongst the medical establishment. In 1980, the American Psychological Association recognised Gender Identity Disorder (now known as Gender Dysphoria) as a medical condition (17). This enabled people in the USA to potentially have sex reassignment treatments covered by their health insurance.

While initially healthcare services were reluctant to pay for sex reassignment treatments, providers were later forced to fund surgeries and hormones. In the UK, a legal challenge meant that the NHS was forced to provide sex reassignment surgery on human rights grounds (18). In 2003, the case of Van Kück v. Germany, which was heard at the European Court of Human Rights, ruled that European state healthcare systems were required to pay for sex reassignment (19). In the USA, the 2010 Affordable Care Act banned health insurers from restricting healthcare coverage for sex change treatments (20).

From the 2010s onwards, there has been a big rise in people having sex reassignment surgery. In the UK, between 2006 and 2016, the number of adults seeking sex changes rose by over 300% (21). For children, there has been an even bigger increase. Between 2009/10 and 2017/18, the number of children being referred for treatment for Gender Dysphoria rose 4000% (22). While in the USA, there were four times as many sex change operations performed in 2014 than there were in 2000 (23). While Sweden- a country that has been very tolerant of transgenderism for many years- saw Gender Dysphoria rates rise by 1500% (24). As well as this, the World Health Organization recategorized Gender Dysphoria from being a psychiatric disorder to a 'sexual disorder' (25) - a symbolic victory for many campaigners, who felt stigmatized by being categorized as mentally ill.

There were several reasons why transgenderism grew in the 2010s. The first factor is the media. The media have always been fascinated by transgenderism. Because the notion of a person changing sex defies nature, it attracts attention from the public. Even when Gender Dysphoria was very rare, there were still a lot of trans-identified characters on television and news coverage of transgender issues. Some notable examples of trans-identified characters in fiction include *The Crying Game* and *Boys Don't Cry* (26). There were also influential documentaries, such as *The Pregnant Man,* about trans-identified female Thomas Beatie and his pregnancy, which was released around the world in 2008 (27). Anderson points out that terms like 'her penis' or 'pregnant man' are eye-catching. They get sales, views and clicks (28). And as always, the media don't let the truth get in the way of a good story. Like that the 'pregnant man' is actually a woman.

But in the 2010s, transgenderism started to pop up everywhere. Big celebrities -most notably Caitlyn Jenner- started coming out as transgender. A number of influential pro-transgender television programs were also broadcast during this period, including documentaries such as *My Transsexual Summer* (29) and *Transformation Street* (30) in the UK *and Becoming Chaz* (about Chaz Bono's sex change) and *I am Cait* (about Caitlyn Jenner) in the USA (28). But this hasn't been the only reason why transgenderism took off at this point in time.

The internet has also been a huge driver in the growth of transgenderism. While the internet has been around for many years, in the mid to late 2000s, technological changes let people use the internet in ways that allowed for transgenderism to expand. There were several reasons for this. Firstly, social media has enabled people to learn about transgenderism and also to contact other transgender people. The blogging site Tumblr became particularly notable for its discussions of identity politics, especially gender issues. Many transgender ideas and concepts began there. Haimson *et al.*, (31) found there were several reasons why Tumblr in particular had such a large transgender community. Firstly, unlike other social media sites, Tumblr allowed sexual content before it was taken over by Yahoo! in 2018. This meant that explicit discussions about transitioning were allowed that were not permitted on other platforms. Secondly, Tumblr did not require people to use their real identities, which enabled users to experiment with their identity and use an identity that their offline friends and family were not aware of. As well, Tumblr's format, which allows for people to write lengthy posts and to share photographs, videos and artwork, made it a valued source for finding information about being transgender.

In addition, on social media, transgenderism is often presented as brave and inspirational. If someone doesn't feel that they're any of those things, identifying as transgender could provide this. The sex change process itself is portrayed as an exciting journey of self-discovery. The person transitioning is shown as striving to 'live my best life' or to 'be my most authentic self'. Once they have completed the transition, they will often say how much happier they feel. For a person who feels their life is disappointing, this could lead to them questioning their gender identity and hoping that they too will start to 'live their best life'.

As well as this, innovations in technology enabled people to learn about and discuss transgenderism in a discreet way. In the 1990s and early 2000s, most people who had a computer typically had a desktop computer with wired, dial-up internet which was often shared by the whole family. Everyone in the room could see what you were doing. In most cases, a person simply couldn't spend all day on the computer- internet was expensive and someone else would need the computer soon enough. Under these circumstances, a teenager could hardly make a video in the corner of their living room in front of their whole family about how they are questioning their gender. Or pour their heart out on a blog about their transphobic parents. Nor could they sit and watch videos about how life as a transgender person. Or pictures showing the more intimate aspects of changing sex.

But in the late 2000s, broadband led to much faster internet speeds and computer technology improved. This enabled people to watch videos on their computers and perform more activities online. More importantly, these innovations allowed for people to use the internet in a more private way. Wireless internet (wi-fi) became more widespread, enabling people to use the internet in more varied locations. More portable devices, such as laptops and smartphones, enabled people to use the internet in a more personal way. The portability of these devices, along with the widespread adoption of wi-fi also allows the user to take the device in another room or outside the home. The devices themselves are more discrete than a desktop computer, so nobody can see what you are looking at. This means that people can read and watch videos about gender and sexuality, and record videos or write about their experiences with gender, without their friends and family knowing. However, this comes with several downsides. A person can spend a considerable amount of time learning about gender without others contradicting them. As a result, unconventional views (such as that biological sex doesn't exist) go unchallenged, causing people to become disengaged from reality. People are also able to spend more time on social media, which could jeopardise their real-life relationships with people who are prepared to state their honest opinions about sex and gender. In turn, these relationships are replaced with much looser online relationships, who 'support' a person by providing unconditional validation, even when it is not warranted.

Another change has been the development of algorithms that allow for sites to personalize their content to the user based on their behaviour and preferences. This is known as the filter bubble. Pariser argues that the personalization of social media and search engines means people only hear views that they agree with. As a result, they are no longer used to hearing opposite perspectives or being challenged (32). While television programs and newspapers show multiple viewpoints on certain issues, with the internet, people only see the perspectives they agree with. For people who are questioning their gender identity, being repeatedly told that transgender and non-binary identities are valid, by websites and social media pages that are sympathetic to transgenderism presents several issues. Firstly, it makes it difficult to think critically about their views. They cannot understand why their thoughts make little sense to those outside their online community and assume the only reason others disagree with them is because of bigotry. As well, they cannot evaluate the validity of transgender or non-binary genders. Nor do they get to learn about the negative impacts of transitioning. Although this information is readily available, transgender communities continually emphasize the benefits of transitioning and minimize the disadvantages. In addition, online, nobody hears any doubts about their opinions and experiences from other people in general. This makes it difficult for people to cope with being questioned in real life, and so they perceive their friend's and family's doubts or surprise over their gender identity as a serious act of abuse.

Socio-political factors have also played a part in the growth of transgenderism in the 2010s. Because of neoliberalism, millennials grew up in a very individualized society. As a result, the millennial generation is very self-absorbed. Most millennials grew up either in the Thatcher/Reagan era or in the aftermath of it. This generation grew up learning that there was "no such thing as society" and have been raised to put themselves first. This has affected the left. Combined with the emphasis on lived experience from post-modernism, the focus of left-wing politics has changed to 'me' instead of 'us'. In the past, young left-leaning people were interested in social issues relevant to other people (such as global poverty, HIV, dictatorships and torture) or issues relevant to both themselves and others (such as women's rights). Now, it's all about you. It's about how you're not like other people of my gender. Instead of working with other women to fight women's oppression, it's about you fighting other women to make them recognize that you are more oppressed than them because you're neither male nor female.

There is also an overlap between socio-political factors, the growth of social media and the rise of transgenderism. Young people use social media to learn about social issues. Because of the left's emphasis on discussing personal experience, this is seen as a good place to talk about transgenderism and other social issues. While it's great that young people are so politically engaged, the trouble is that social media is not very representative of real-world social issues. Instead, it is skewed towards the interests of middle-class people, who may be more likely to be interested in identity politics rather than larger issues. As middle-class people don't have the same material worries as other people, they have more time to contemplate identity-related issues.

Privileged people are more able to express their views online because wealthier people are more likely to have a computer and internet access. For instance, in the USA, low income neighbourhoods have much lower rates of people with an internet subscription than higher income neighbourhoods (33). In 2019, 94% of people with an annual income over $100,000 owned a laptop or desktop computer, compared to just 54% of people with an income below $30,000 (34). Therefore, social media is not really getting a fair representation of people's experiences. As a result, left-wingers think they are learning about oppression, but they don't hear about the issues people who are less wealthy face- like not having enough money for basics, living in poor quality housing, or not being able to afford healthcare. This makes it hard to put things in perspective. Their own issues feel huge and so it's easy to think you're seriously oppressed. This is one of the reasons why transgender issues are so greatly overrepresented in online political spaces. The plight of transgender people can easily feel enormous when you don't hear about other issues in the world. And being 'misgendered' or told your identity is not valid can seem like a huge insult.

This book is about the impact transgenderism has had on society. It will look at the dangers of transgenderism- both to transgender people themselves and on society as a whole. It will focus primarily on the UK and the USA, but it will also look at examples of transgenderism in other countries too.

I will use the preferred pronouns and names of any transgender people I write about. Like Sheila Jeffreys (35), I think that using the preferred pronouns implies the person's biological sex has changed. Unlike Sheila Jeffreys, I live in a country where not using a person's preferred pronouns is deemed a 'hate crime' and people have been given heavy fines, community service and even suspended prison sentences for 'misgendering' a transgender person. I don't particularly want to be prosecuted for a hate crime, although I do feel that everything in this book needs to be said.

However, I will refer to transgender people from this point onwards as trans-identified people. Describing someone as a 'transwoman' or a 'transman' implies that they have literally become a member of the opposite sex. A person cannot change sex, so I will not pretend they have done. A trans-identified male is more often known as a transgender woman or a transwoman. It is a male who identifies as a woman. A trans-identified female is what is generally called a transgender man or a transman. These people are females who identify as men.

When the term 'transgender' is used, it will be used in its broadest sense, to refer to anyone who identifies as a different gender to their biological sex, including people who identify as a member of the opposite sex, as gender non-binary, as having multiple genders or as having no gender. 'Transgenderism' will be used to describe an ideological belief that people can be born as a member of the wrong sex, that people are able to change their sex and that a person can be a member of multiple genders, gender non-binary or having no gender. 'Transsexual' will be used to refer to a person who identifies as the opposite sex and have either undergone some type of medical intervention to attempt to change their sex or is in the process of pursuing such treatment.

This book will be structured as follows: chapter 2 will examine the causes of Gender Dysphoria. Nobody has ever found what causes people to identify as transgender. Many theories exist. Some theories have become very popular with the transgender community, while other theories have been buried by transgender rights activists. This chapter will present the most prominent theories and assess their credibility.

Chapter 3 will look at the realities of the sex reassignment process and ask if the so-called 'gender-affirming' approach is the best way to deal with Gender Dysphoria. It will critically assess the claims made by transgender rights activists that sex reassignment surgery is life saving and extremely effective in treating Gender Dysphoria.

This chapter will then explore the side effects of sex reassignment surgery and cross-sex hormones, including infertility, and consider if these treatments genuinely do improve the patient's quality of life. The chapter will also look at the phenomenon of detransitioners; trans-identified people who return to living as their original gender.

Chapter 4 will discuss the growth of non-binary genders, and assess the validity of these genders. It will look at the history of non-binary genders and examine the claim that non-binary genders have existed throughout human history. It will also look at the impact of non-binary genders on wider society, including the use of non-binary pronouns and how the non-binary movement may compromise women's rights.

Chapter 5 will explore the phenomenon of transgenderism in childhood. This chapter will look at the medical treatments used for transgender children. The chapter will also explore the impact that transgenderism has on childhood in general, such as the effect of transgenderism on education and the ways that activists are trying to indoctrinate children. As well, the book will look at what causes children to identify as transgender, including parents who are attempting to raise their children without a gender.

Chapter 6 will look at the effect of transgenderism on policy-making, including how policy makers are forcing the general public to accept transgender people as members of their chosen gender, and how transgenderism is being used to restrict freedom of expression. This chapter will also assess how transgender people's concerns are taking over from other political issues under the guise of 'human rights', and the impact this has on society.

Chapter 7 will examine the impact of transgenderism on politics more generally, including how politicians are devoting more time to transgender issues, at the expense of other groups, especially women. It will also look at tactics used by transgender-rights activists. Many of these cause physical and emotional harm to the people targeted, yet these attacks are often condoned by many people, including the legal system. It also looks at the unreasonable demands that transgender activists make, and how transgender rights activists disproportionately target women.

Chapter 8 will explore how transgender inclusivity is impacting on women. Trans-identified males are now often classed as women for many purposes. This chapter will look at some of the ways that women are being put at a detriment, including how allowing trans-identified males to be considered women is depriving women of opportunities to succeed. It will also assess how allowing trans-identified males into women's spaces may be putting women's safety at risk.

Chapter 9 will analyse how transgender rights activists are trying to erase the very existence of the female sex. Many people and organizations are going to great lengths to avoid saying the word 'woman', and instead are coining new phrases that focus on either female body parts or bodily functions. As well, women's concerns are increasingly being overtaken by fears around 'cissexism'. Women are also being airbrushed away from history. Yet women's concerns about being erased are being suppressed in order to placate transgender people. This chapter will also examine the implications of female erasure.

Chapter 10 will look at how people are increasingly being forced to avoid criticizing transgenderism, through various means, including the legal system, through social media censorship, from no-platforming speakers who question transgenderism and through suppressing controversial academic research. It will also assess the impact of this on the individual's freedom of expression, for trans-identified people and on society as a whole.

Finally, chapter 11 will explore some of the signs of hope that the tide is turning back against transgenderism. For instance, how the legal system is starting to recognise the importance of protecting women's spaces and fighting the illogical phenomenon of amending legal documents to reflect a person's gender identity. Other issues covered will include how measures are being taken to protect children from transgenderism and to prevent trans-identified males participating in women's sports. This chapter will also look at social issues that could force people to reconsider transgenderism, including the 2019-2020 Coronavirus pandemic (COVID-19) and how previous similar crazes have been ended.

2. What Causes Gender Dysphoria?

Gender Dysphoria is the clinical term for being transgender. It is defined by the American Psychiatric Association as a disorder where a person feels extreme distress with their biological sex (36). Nobody knows exactly why some people identify as transgender. But there are many theories. It is important to examine these theories because the whole premise of transgenderism is based on the idea that transitioning is about someone living as their 'true' self. If that's not really the case, then this undermines the whole principle of transgenderism.

Is Gender Dysphoria a Mental Disorder?

Many doctors feel that Gender Dysphoria is a psychiatric disorder that causes a delusional belief that someone is the wrong sex. Paediatric endocrinologist, Quentin Van Meter, who trained at the infamous Johns Hopkins Gender Identity clinic in the 1960s and 70s (37) is among the many doctors who believes that Gender Dysphoria is a delusion (38). He reports that every patient he has seen with Gender Dysphoria has grown up in a dysfunctional family and experienced severe emotional trauma. He believes these patients develop Gender Dysphoria as a way of coping with this trauma (37). Another doctor who believes Gender Dysphoria is a mental illness, is psychiatrist Richard Corradi. To explain this, he draws parallels between Gender Dysphoria and Anorexia. According to Corradi, Anorexia -like Gender Dysphoria- is a disorder that causes a distorted body image. But unlike with patients with Gender Dysphoria, medical practitioners do not try to validate an Anorexic person's delusion that they need to continue to lose weight, but rather they aim to correct this delusion and help the person return to good health (39). Contrast this with the gender-affirming approach taken with people with Gender Dysphoria, where the medical profession attempts to make the person into their desired sex (which is not actually possible).

The theory that Gender Dysphoria is a mental illness is supported by the high rate of other serious psychiatric disorders in this population.

Gender Dysphoria has a high co-morbidity with personality disorder- 81% of Iranian Gender Dysphoria patients (40), and nearly 50% of Italian Gender Dysphoria patients (41) has a personality disorder. Personality disorders are thought to be caused at least in part by a person's upbringing (42). In addition, people with Gender Dysphoria are more likely to have other disorders that cause delusions. Between five to eight percent of people with Gender Dysphoria have Schizophrenia, compared to just 0.1 to 0.8% of the general population (43). Schizophrenia and Gender Dysphoria have both been linked to childhood trauma, and it has been suggested that this might be why these conditions commonly occur together (43). This supports Van Meter's position that childhood trauma contributes to the development of Gender Dysphoria.

It's important to note that when doctors say that Gender Dysphoria is a delusion, this doesn't mean people with Gender Dysphoria are 'crazy'. Although the word 'delusion' evokes the image of someone who has completely lost touch with reality, a delusion is simply a belief that doesn't match with the truth (44). Many common mental health conditions, including most anxiety disorders, cause delusions. For instance, when a person has a panic attack, they are often experiencing a belief that the physical sensations they experience represent some life-threatening or life-changing event (such as a heart attack or some type of break-down). This is a delusion because they believe something that is very unlikely to be true (44). Phobias are also a form of a delusion, because the fear that people with phobias experience results from exaggerated ideas about the dangers posed by the thing they are phobic of (44). Perhaps almost everyone experiences a delusion at some point in their lives.

Admittedly, a significant weakness of this theory is that is has not been studied as much as other theories of Gender Dysphoria. Regardless of this, it still is a very credible perspective. But it is not the only theory of value. Nonetheless, if this theory is correct, it raises some worrying issues. The general aim of psychiatric care is not to change the patient's circumstances but to help them to cope with life as it is. For instance, if a person were suicidal because they were in serious debt, healthcare systems wouldn't go and pay all the debts off to make them feel better. Instead, they would provide medication and talking therapies so that the person could cope with being in debt and deal with it themselves. The same is true of practically any person and any set of circumstances. But transgenderism does the precise opposite- it tries to change a person's circumstances when this is unrealistic and leaves the person without any coping skills. More alarmingly, the treatment often leaves patients with serious and permanent damage to their bodies- something that would normally be seen as a great tragedy.

Autogynephilia

Another high-profile theory is Blanchard's transsexual types (45). Richard Blanchard sets out two types of men who transition to living as women; androphilic transsexuals and autogynephilic transsexuals. Androphilic transsexuals are homosexual men who have always been very effeminate and who typically transition before the age of 30. These people tend to live in homophobic communities and transition because it is safer to live as a trans-identified male than as a gay man. The second type are autogynephilic transsexuals, who are sexually attracted to the idea of themselves as a woman. They commonly report having sexual fantasies about being a woman, including helping a maid to clean their house, menstruating, and using a vaginal douche. Additionally, many autogynephiles report involuntary erections when dressed as women. Autogynephiles also often have a history of using female clothing-especially underwear- to masturbate.

Why would someone be sexually interested in being a woman? The answer is that autogynephilia is a form of masochism. Bailey and Triea found that trans-identified males have a very high rate of sexual fetishes, especially fetishes of a masochistic nature (46). Because women are seen as the lesser sex, trans-identified males are aroused by the thought of being a woman; as trans-identified males have a masochistic desire to be humiliated and dominated over, the thought of being a woman achieves this. Furthermore, there is a possibility that being transgender in itself might also provide this arousal. After all, if someone is attracted to the idea of having a low social status, and they are always hearing that transgender people are extremely vulnerable, then a person might also be aroused by transitioning. Is this why transgender people talk about being so vulnerable? Do they find the idea that everyone hates them exciting? This book can't answer these questions, but they do pose a troubling possible explanation for why transgender people behave as they do.

Nevertheless, many transgender activists deny the existence of autogynephilia, and often react very strongly when this subject is discussed. Dreger describes the backlash both she and others received for writing about autogynephilia; both she and colleagues have received personal letters and emails attacking them and their families (47). She claims that there are two reasons why transgender activists reject the concept of autogynephilia. Firstly, it makes transgender people come across as sexually perverted, which would give them a bad public image, delegitimizing their cause. Furthermore, she also theorizes that the acknowledgement that trans-identified males are aroused by imagining themselves as a woman invalidates their identity, by reminding them that their fantasy that they are a real woman is just that; a fantasy (47).

Conversely, other transgender people claim that many non-transgender women experience autogynephilia too, so autogynephilia is not the cause of Gender Dysphoria, but a manifestation of the person's femininity (45). Blanchard says this is not correct. He claims that the study where this claim comes from included many poorly-worded questions and an unrepresentative sample (45). On the contrary, Blanchard states that he does not believe that biological females experience autogynephilia (45).

While autogynephilia is a largely convincing explanation for many cases of Gender Dysphoria, there are several things that it does not explain. Firstly, why do prepubescent children experience Gender

Dysphoria? Small children don't generally have sexual fantasies, so they are unlikely to experience autogynephilia. Also, why do people identify as non-binary? It is possible that many effeminate people who identify as non-binary experience autogynephilia, but on the other hand, many don't seem to display the same sexual interest in femininity (many aspire to be androgynous or even retain the appearance associated with their natal sex). Furthermore, why are so many more people now identifying as transgender, especially women?

Blanchard proposes that more people are identifying as transgender because it is now more socially acceptable to transition (45). This might explain some of the growth in people transitioning, but it does not explain why this has grown so much. Nor does it explain why more women and girls are identifying as transgender. Traditionally, most trans-identified people were males. But in recent years, there has been a huge growth in females identifying as transgender. In the UK, in 2007, 75% of children referred to the Tavistock and Portman Gender Identity clinic were males seeking to transition to female, but in 2017, 70% of patients were females who wished to transition to male (48). Why is this?

Social Contagion
A more probable reason for the major growth in people with Gender Dysphoria is social contagion. Lisa Littman, a professor at Brown University, wrote a paper describing Rapid-Onset Gender Dysphoria (ROGD) (49). The paper described children (overwhelmingly teenage girls) who were suddenly becoming transgender when they had no history of Gender Dysphoria or gender non-conforming behaviour. The paper attributed this phenomenon to social contagion, especially from the use of social media sites which featured many high-profile transgender users (49). This theory is supported by instances where clusters of people have started identifying as transgender. For example, a secondary school in Brighton in the UK has 76 children identifying as transgender(50). As well, there is the Rogers family in the UK, where the stepfather Greg Rogers and his

5-year-old stepdaughter Jayden are both transgender (51). They are not blood relatives, so there cannot be a genetic explanation for this. In these cases, there is almost certainly an element of social contagion. Furthermore, Veissière argues that the growth in women and girls with Gender Dysphoria is because women are more prone to social contagion in general, pointing out that incidents of mass sociogenic illnesses disproportionately affect women (52). This supports Littman's theory.

Genes

Genetics have also been suggested as a cause of Gender Dysphoria. There are many families with more than one member with Gender Dysphoria. Perhaps the most famous example of two people in the same family transitioning is the film and television directing duo, the Wachowskis. Famous for directing *The Matrix* film series, Larry Wachowski came out as transgender in 2012 and changed her name to Lana, while Andy Wachowski came out four years later and is now known as Lilly (53). But they aren't the only family with more than one transgender member. For instance, there's the Harrots family in the USA (54), where the father, Daniel Harrots, his two biological children, Mason and Joshua and their stepmother, Shirley Austin are all transgender. Does that mean there's a genetic element to transgenderism? Some scientists think so (55). Indeed, Gender Dysphoria has a 20% concordance amongst identical twins (56). This means that in 20% of cases where one twin was transgender, the other one was too. This suggests there may be some genetic element to transgenderism, but that it is not totally genetic.

However, this doesn't necessarily mean that Gender Dysphoria is caused by a mismatch in brain sex or that sex reassignment surgery is the best treatment for it. There are genetic elements to many other mental illnesses, including Schizophrenia (57), Depression (58), Anxiety (59) Bipolar Disorder (60) and Anorexia (61). Even though these disorders have a biological basis, they are still mental illnesses. To treat them, doctors aim to correct inaccurate beliefs caused by these conditions, rather than to validate them.

Social Status
Another theory is that women transition to live as males to escape the oppression that comes from femininity. Researcher Anna M. Kłonkowska points out that as males have a higher social standing than females, many women's desire to become male is rooted in a wish to be treated with the respect that being male commands (48). This is an interesting theory, and it may account for some cases of Gender Dysphoria, but it does not explain why so many men transition to living as women.

Brain Sex
Perhaps the most prominent theory of Gender Dysphoria is that trans-identified people have a brain sex which is disparate to their biological sex. The claim is that males typically have a male brain and females have a female brain, but a transgender person is a male born with a female brain or a female born with a male brain. As a result, they feel as if they are the opposite sex. To fix this discrepancy, the person must be treated as if they were their brain sex, or else they will experience severe distress. According to transgender rights activists, the only reasons that transgender people have such a high rate of mental illness are because they are distressed by their biological sex not matching their gender identity (which can be alleviated by gender-affirming medical care) and because society fails to accept transgender people for who they are. This phenomenon has been termed 'minority stress' (35). This theory used to be very popular with trans-identified people, and it has become so entrenched in society that even many trans-sceptical people accept the brain sex theory. On the face of it, this is a credible explanation for Gender Dysphoria. Indeed, many brain scan studies claim to show that transgender people have the brain of the opposite sex. There have even been promises of brain scans for diagnosing Gender Dysphoria in the future (62). These studies have been well-publicised in the media, but there are many problems with this theory.

The first problem is that the results of these studies are inconsistent. Although many studies have found differences in the brains of trans-identified and non-trans-identified people, overall, these studies have not found any consistent differences (63). This means that when a study has been reproduced, different studies have found different results- some studies have found that some areas of the brain are different in transgender people, but other studies have not found this.

Secondly, the existence of a brain sex is in itself controversial. Unlike with the other sex characteristics in the body, there's no absolute differences between the brains of men and women (64,65). Instead, there are some brain features that are more commonly found in men and features that are more commonly found in women (65). It's not possible for a doctor to look at a brain scan and say "that's a male brain" or "it's a female brain", like it is with other parts of the body (64). Hence, it's difficult to say for certain that brain sex is real. We are certainly nowhere near a point where a transgender person could have a brain scan that would confirm that they have a brain sex which is different to their biological sex.

Third, even if brain sex does exist, it might be caused by environmental factors, rather than biology. The brain is malleable, so differences in the brain don't necessarily mean sex differences are innate. It's hard to know what's caused by nature and what's caused by nurture in these studies, as gender is so pervasive (64,66). To put this into context, studies have shown that the brain changes because of the way it is used. London taxi drivers have proportionately larger hippocampuses (the part of the brain responsible for long-term memory) compared to other people with a similar level of education and intelligence. Furthermore, another study of trainee taxi drivers found that their hippocampuses got larger as the training progressed (67). This shows that the brain changes in response to the way it is used. As well, there are neurological differences between many groups of people, including people who are politically left-wing and politically right-wing (68). Does that mean political ideology is innate?

This malleability could mean that a man with a woman's brain has developed this brain because of how he uses his brain (for example, through his occupation and his hobbies). His brain could become more masculine if he used his brain in a more masculine way (not that he should have to!) This raises a worrying possibility- when someone has sex reassignment surgery, are they having their body changed to match their personality? This undermines the idea that the sex reassignment process is about making someone's body match with their innate brain sex.

Another issue is that it's not clear what people mean when they say they feel that they are the wrong sex. Anderson raises an important question: what does it mean to feel like a man or a woman? Nobody truly knows what a person of the opposite gender feels like (28). For most people, their gender is a fact of life. So when a trans-identified person says they feel male or they feel female, what is it that they are actually experiencing?

Sex isn't Real Anyway?
While the brain sex theory of Gender Dysphoria has enjoyed many years of popularity, it has begun to fall out of favour with transgender people. The latest claim that transgender people now often make is that biological sex is a social construct. Basically, they say that there is no such thing as being a man or being a woman at all. Everyone's real sex is whatever sex they wish to be. Multiple transgender rights activists have made this claim.

Perhaps the most infamous case of this was when *Scientific American* published an article in the opinion section, by neuroscientist and PhD student, Simón(e) D Sun, called 'Stop Using Phony Science to Justify Transphobia', which makes the claim that "sex is anything but binary" (69). In a major departure from what other transgender rights activists have said for many years, Sun claims that brain sex is also a myth. Unfortunately, much of what

Sun says is either factually inaccurate or seriously misrepresents the science.

The first claim that Sun makes is that both men and women can have XX or XY chromosomes. Sun says that some people with XY chromosomes have ovaries. This is correct. But these women have a condition called XY Gonadal Dysgenesis, or Swyer Syndrome. They are unable to produce eggs and need hormone replacement therapy from adolescence onwards (70). This condition also often occurs alongside neuropathy and Campomelic Dysplasia- an extremely serious disorder that causes severe skeletal abnormalities (70). Few people with Campomelic Dysplasia live past infancy (71). 75% of people with Campomelic Dysplasia have either female or ambiguous genitalia but have XY chromosomes (71). Hence, having XY Gonadal Dysgenesis is not a small quirk of nature. Sun also says that some people with XX chromosomes have testicles. This is also true, but like women with XY chromosomes, these men are also infertile and require hormone replacement therapy (72). It certainly isn't the case that a healthy, fertile adult could find out by chance that they have the sex chromosomes of the opposite sex.

Sun also argues that the concept of sex hormones is a myth because both men and women make oestrogen and testosterone. While it's true that both sexes make both kinds of hormones, women's bodies produce much less testosterone than men. The average man produces 35 nmol/L of testosterone, while the typical woman's body produces less than three nmol/L (73). As well, men produce much less oestrogen than women. Pre-menopausal women produce between 15-350 pg/mL of oestradiol (the main type of oestrogen), while adult men produce just 10-40 pg/mL (74). There is some overlap- a man at the top range of oestradiol production will make as much as a woman at the bottom of the range. But on average, men produce much more testosterone than women, and women produce much more oestrogen than men. Therefore, Sun's claim that there are no sex hormones is vastly over simplistic.

Many transgender rights activists cite this article as evidence that sex isn't real. However, there are many reasons why Sun's article doesn't prove this. Firstly, it's an opinion piece from a column "exploring and celebrating diversity in science". Most of the articles published under this column are about the experiences of scientists from underrepresented groups. These articles don't make the same kind of bold claims as Sun's article does. Moreover, it isn't a peer-reviewed journal article or showing incontrovertible proof that biological sex is not real. It certainly does not represent the scientific consensus on sex.

More importantly, most scientists do accept that sex is real. Anderson (28) quotes epidemiologist Lawrence Mayer's statement given to a North Carolina court, where he states that sex is defined by reproduction and that no other definition of sex exists within medical or biological literature. Anderson also makes the point that the existence of biological sex is not disputed in other species of animal. If you want further proof that most scientists accept the existence of biological sex, look at the Nettie Project, which lists scientists who have signed a declaration stating that biological sex is real (75).

A big issue that Sun also hasn't addressed is reproduction. If there are no males or females, how do people reproduce? Every adult knows how humans reproduce and how this is the main defining characteristic of sex differences. What sex was Sun's dad? Did he have XY chromosomes, testicles and a penis? He must have had, or else Sun would never have been conceived. What about Sun's mum? Was she biologically female? Did she have XX chromosomes? Did she have ovaries, a uterus and a vagina? Sun couldn't have been born if their mum didn't have those.

It might be comforting for trans-identified people to tell themselves that sex doesn't exist. After all, if there is no such thing as a real man or a real woman, then transgender people are no different from anyone else. But this notion simply doesn't stand up to rigorous analysis. As well, the idea that sex isn't real ultimately undermines the case for being transgender and changing sex. If sex isn't real, why do trans-identified people go through painful, complex surgeries and take dangerous cross-sex hormones?

Overall, Gender Dysphoria probably has different causes in different people. The most convincing theories are that it is a psychiatric disorder for some people, a fetish for others and more recently, sociogenic for many people. Some people with Gender Dysphoria probably experience sexual arousal by imagining themselves as a woman. Other people seem deeply unhappy with their natal sex. As Gender Dysphoria is different for different people, it most likely has multiple underlying causes. It may have a genetic or biological component, as well as psychosocial factors. The cause of Gender Dysphoria matters because the sex reassignment process is so extreme. If Gender Dysphoria is purely a psychological disorder with no biological underpinnings, would it not be better to treat it with psychological therapies? It also matters for the way that wider society treats Gender Dysphoria. If Gender Dysphoria is caused by autogynephilia, is helping someone to live out their sexual fantasy on a daily basis a social justice issue? The problem isn't that people with Gender Dysphoria exist. Sadly, people with psychiatric disorders will always exist until a cure is found. However, it is a problem that society is going to great lengths to validate this delusion.

3. The Truth about Sex Reassignment

Many transgender people undergo various surgeries and hormone treatments to try to change their sex. Treatment for transsexual people has a high cost to the taxpayer. In 2014, the NHS spent £17.13 million (around $21.3 million) on treatment for Gender Dysphoria (76). In the US, the military spent $8.4 million (£6.93 million) on treating transgender troops and veterans (77). In spite of these costs, transgender rights activists say that sex reassignment is necessary for their mental health, and that sex change procedures actually save money by reducing spending on psychiatric care for trans-identified people (78). But is this actually the case?

Why Do Doctors Perform Sex Reassignment?

In keeping with the 'brain sex' theory of Gender Dysphoria, the aim of sex reassignment is to make the trans-identified person into the 'correct' sex. Pro-transgender doctors say this treatment is vital. The World Professional Association for Transgender Health (WPATH) claims that sex reassignment surgery is "effective and medically necessary" (79). But are they correct? The effectiveness of Gender Dysphoria treatment is measured in terms of patient's reported quality of life after the surgery. WPATH say that surgery has huge benefits because the majority of patients say their quality of life improved, and they cite multiple studies where all the participants report that they were happier after the surgery (79). But is quality of life the best way to measure the success of the treatment? This isn't the way that the success of most treatments is assessed. As well, validating someone's delusion might well make them happy- at least in the short-term. After all, what would a person with Anorexia say about their quality of life if they were given a gastric bypass? As we will see in the next section, other studies that don't rely on patient satisfaction have shown much less positive results.

Do Sex Changes Work?

There are very few high-quality studies that support the current treatment protocols for Gender Dysphoria. Paul McHugh, has found that much of the evidence supporting the gender-affirming approach is rated by medical evidence review company Hayes Inc. as low-quality (80). Other reports have also found limited evidence supporting the gender-affirming approach. In 2004, the University of Birmingham's Aggressive Research Intelligence Facility (Arif) conducted a review of 100 medical studies on Gender Dysphoria, and identified no evidence to prove that Sex Reassignment Surgery is effective (81,82). The analysis found that most studies were poorly designed. For instance, the Arif review found that many studies had a very high rate of participants dropping out. One longitudinal study that was analysed had nearly 70% of its participants drop out, which could indicate that the participants were not satisfied with their surgery, or even that they had died by suicide (81). Another issue with many studies was that there were no control groups and had small sample sizes (82). Chris Hyde, the director of Arif, said that these flaws meant that the results of these studies were more likely to find that sex reassignment was beneficial, when this was not necessarily true (81).

That such major treatment is carried out without good evidence is worrying. In medicine more generally, surgery is usually only used as a last resort after other treatments have either failed or would be insufficient to treat the problem. Yet sex reassignment surgery is used as the main treatment for Gender Dysphoria.

"Let me change sex or I'll kill myself"- Why do So Many Transgender People Die of Suicide?

One claim that many transgender rights activists make is that trans-identified people are so unhappy with their natal sex because it does not fit with their 'true' sex, so they feel driven to suicide. British sex reassignment surgeon, James Bellringer says "You either have an operation or suffer a miserable life. A fifth of those who don't get treatment commit suicide." (81). The idea behind performing a medical sex change is that the person will feel happier, and their mental health will improve, reducing the likelihood that they will die of suicide. However, research doesn't support that. A large study in Sweden, which compared transgender people with controls from the general population, who were matched based on their year of birth and natural sex. The study found that transgender people who had undergone gender re-assignment were 19 times more likely to die of suicide than the matched controls, and nearly five times more likely to attempt suicide (83).

The study also found that aside from their mental health, transgender people had more physical health problems than non-transgender individuals. In the study, transgender people were nearly three times more likely to die than the matched controls. They were also twice as likely to die from cardiovascular disease or cancer. Additionally, the study noted that many of the transgender people had received inpatient psychiatric care and had other mental health conditions unrelated to their Gender Dysphoria (83). This does not sound like the gender-affirming approach is beneficial for a person's mental or physical health.

Admittedly, there are no studies comparing the suicide rates of people who have not medically transitioned with those who have transitioned, but this would be difficult to study. The best way to research the effect of medical sex changes would be to withhold treatment from a group of transgender people who were under the care of a gender identity clinic, and compare it to the suicide rate of another group who were allowed to transition in the same period. Unfortunately, this type of study would be unlikely to gain ethics approval in the current climate. Hence, we may never know if medical sex changes reduce the likelihood of a transgender person committing suicide.

So why do so many trans-identified people kill themselves? Transgender rights activists claim that transgender people are more likely to die of suicide because they are oppressed. These activists argue that society does not see transgender people as their chosen gender, discriminates against them and generally doesn't understand transgender people. As a result, this causes transgender people to develop mental health problems and occasionally drives them to suicide (84). However, this perspective is very flawed as other oppressed groups don't have high rates of suicide. For instance, men are more likely than women to commit suicide (85). Yet men are not more oppressed than women. As well as this, ethnic minorities also have a lower suicide rate than white people. Payne (86) points out that white people in the USA have the highest suicide rate of any ethnic group. If oppression were a major factor in suicide, the suicide rate for ethnic minorities would likely be higher than it is for white people and for woman than it is for men. it is hugely over-simplistic to say transgender people kill themselves because of oppression.

The fact that many trans-identified people are more likely to have a serious mental illness than other people is also something that must be considered. Jeffreys raises the point that nobody knows if transgender people are more likely to have Depression or another mental illness because of the impact of their Gender Dysphoria, or if people who already have Depression or another mental illness are more likely to identify as transgender and pursue a medical sex transition, perhaps in an attempt to improve their lives (35). This would mean that the real reason trans-identified people are more likely to die of suicide is because of their Depression or other mental illnesses, not because of the way society treats them. If this was true, then it would be better to treat the Depression, not offer sex-change treatments. As the overwhelming majority of people who die of suicide have a mental health condition (87), this is likely to be one of the reasons why so many trans-identified people kill themselves.

Furthermore, telling trans-identified people that they are more likely to die by suicide might actually be encouraging suicides. There's a lot of evidence that suicide is contagious. For example, studies have found that showing television programs or newspaper articles about suicide cause an increase in suicides (88). This is known as the

'Werther Effect', after the 18th century novel *The Sorrows of Young Werther,* by Johann Wolfgang von Goethe, which inspired many suicides at the time. For transgender people, hearing that they have a high likelihood of killing themselves may be a self-fulfilling prophecy (89). Chalk also highlights that transgender children and young people are learning from the media that suicide is a valid response to their personal problems (89).

An example of how the media's reporting of suicide might inspire others to kill themselves is the case of Leelah Alcorn. Alcorn was a 17-year-old trans-identified male from Ohio, who died of suicide in 2014. Alcorn had written a suicide note and posted it to Tumblr. The note called for greater acceptance for transgender people and she said that she wanted her "death to mean something". It quickly went viral. And with that, Alcorn was turned into a transgender martyr. The problem is, the way that Alcorn's death was reported could encourage other transgender people to follow suit. Ditum describes how Alcorns' widely-reported death was reported in a way that could encourage other people to copy the suicide (90). The Samaritans publish a set of guidelines on how the media should report suicides to avoid encouraging other suicides. Ditum describes how the media routinely flouted the rules when reporting Alcorn's death. For instance, many reports implied that Alcorn's death would help advance transgender rights, with one article describing the death as a "wake-up call" (90). As well, most articles referred heavily to Alcorn's transgender identity being the cause of the suicide, but the Samaritans say to avoid this (90). The Samaritans also advise not emphasizing the public response to the death. However, many articles included extensive portrayals of memorials and public vigils (90). Whereas Samaritans say to show how death impacted negatively on the person's family, the media vilified Alcorn's parents, by saying Alcorn's death was caused by them not accepting her gender identity (90). Worryingly, many articles also described how Alcorn died, which also contravenes the Samaritan's guidelines and could be copied by others (90).

A young person could easily identify with Alcorn. Most people won't immediately decide to kill themselves upon hearing about another transgender person's death. But perhaps if you already have Depression, and you're not sure that life is worth living, hearing about how your death could help other transgender people could give you that final push to kill yourself. It seems that the media took the view that because Alcorn was transgender, it was okay to violate the guidelines, and use Alcorn's death to promote transgender rights, even if that would put others at risk. They did not care about how their reporting could harm others. But how many more martyrs will transgenderism create?

When it comes to using sex-reassignment to prevent suicides, gender-affirming care is promising something that doctors can't give; no amount of hormones or surgery can ever truly change a person's sex. High suicide rates of post-operative transsexuals show there's more reasons for the suicide rate other than that trans-identified people are 'born in the wrong body'. This could mean that sex reassignment is not effective in preventing suicide in people with Gender Dysphoria.

The Downsides of Transitioning
One thing that is often overlooked by transgender rights activists is that transgender treatments themselves can have serious health consequences. The dangers of these treatments are rarely discussed. Furthermore, even if a transgender person no longer feels suicidal after transitioning, their life expectancy may still be reduced by the treatments. This is something that needs to be considered when looking at the impact of transitioning.

Cross- Sex Hormones
Many trans-identified people use cross-sex hormones- it is normally the first type of medical treatment given to trans-identified people. For a man wishing to become a woman, this means taking oestrogen, while a woman wishing to become a man takes testosterone. Although these make the person's appearance closer to that of their

chosen gender, cross-sex hormones also have many adverse effects. In a study of people using cross-sex hormones as part of a medical transition, a number of negative side-effects were noted. For people transitioning from male to female, these side effects include increased risk of blood clots and gallstones (91). For people transitioning from female to the male gender role, side effects include decreased bone density, making the bones more likely to break, weight gain and high lipids (fat) in the blood, which increases the risk of cardiovascular disease (91). For both genders, the hormones cause decreased insulin sensitivity, which is often a precursor to developing Type Two Diabetes (91). Both male-to-female and female-to-male trans-identified people using hormones also have a heightened risk of some types of cancer (91). This demonstrates that hormones are not a benign intervention; they can seriously and irreversibly damage a person's health.

The Surgeries
A trans-identified patient typically undergoes at least two procedures: 'top surgery' which is performed on the chest and 'bottom surgery', where the genitals are modified. In many cases for bottom surgery, multiple surgeries are required. Like all surgeries, these procedures carry risks. Some risks include developing an infection, having a bad reaction to the anaesthesia, allergies to the materials used in the surgery and developing blood clots (92). There are also additional risks specific to each type of surgery.

Male-to-female
The most common surgery for trans-identified male is penile inversion, where the testicles are removed, the penis is cut up, and the remaining tissue is sewn up to look like a vulva, including creating a vaginal canal (93). The person must regularly dilate their neovagina for their rest of their lives to stop the cavity from healing up (94). This involves inserting a plastic tube into the cavity on a regular basis.

Complications of penile inversion affect over 50% of patients. They include urinary incontinence, pain when urinating, and having to urinate frequently (95). These occurred for up to one year after the procedure (95). In some cases, there is insufficient tissue to make a neovagina. This is especially common where puberty blockers have been used (96). In these cases, a procedure called a colon vaginoplasty is performed, where surgeons use pieces of intestine to construct the neovagina. This procedure also has many unpleasant complications. 10% of patients experience a bad odour from their neovagina. More serious complications include fistulas (an abnormal passage that forms from inflammation, which in some cases resulted in the colon having to be removed), difficulty passing urine and surgical wounds not healing properly (97). More alarmingly, in one study of 12 patients who had undergone this procedure, one died from complications. Astoundingly, the author still concluded this is a safe procedure (96).

Female-to-Male
The procedure for women wishing to become male is called a phalloplasty. For the phalloplasty, the surgeon takes grafts from various body parts, including the arms and the legs. These are then sewn to make a neo penis, and a device is placed in the neopenis that allows the person to have an erection (98). The phalloplasty typically needs four operations (98). As with male-to-female surgery, there are high risks of complications. Sometimes, the grafts fail, and if this happens, the scarring means the process cannot be repeated. In between 10-64% of cases, a fistula forms. Strictures (when the urethra is scarred and becomes very narrow) form at a similar rate (99).

Top Surgery
Another surgery that most trans-identified people will undergo is 'top surgery', to make the chest area appearance closer to that of the sex the person is transitioning to.

For trans-identified males, silicone breast implants are placed in the chest, similar to a breast augmentation ('boob job') for women who want larger breasts. The most serious complication that can arise from breast augmentation is a form of cancer called Breast Implant Associated Lymphoma. This disease- which is a cancer of the immune system- develops around the breast implant and the scar tissue. Although it is rare, it can be fatal (100). Other serious complications include necrosis (where the tissue dies), or rupture of the implant (101). More common complications include extrusion (where the implant comes through the skin), seromas (fluid collecting around the implant, which sometimes has to be surgically drained) and haematomas (blood around the implant, which also may need to be drained) (100). In addition, breast augmentation has been linked to Breast Implant Illness- a collection of symptoms including fatigue, impaired memory and joint pain. While this illness is not well understood, and indeed, it may not actually be caused by breast augmentation, it is still another potential risk of having this surgery (101).

For trans-identified females, the breast tissue is removed to reduce the size of the breasts, similar to a mastectomy for women with breast cancer. Some complications of breast reduction surgery include haematosis and tissue necrosis, as well as excessive skin around the scar, which often needs to be removed in an additional procedure (92). Less serious complications include obvious scarring, uneven nipple position, loss of sensation in the nipples and being unable to breastfeed (92).

Other Treatments
Even after a person has had these surgeries and hormone treatments, they often still look like their biological sex. Many trans-identified people undergo other surgical procedures to achieve their desired appearance (79). Trans-identified males may have facial feminization surgery. Facial feminization surgery combines multiple cosmetic procedures depending on the patient, including a hair transplant, a rhinoplasty ('nose job'), forehead reconstruction and a lip lift (102).

Trans-identified females may also undergo body masculinization surgeries, which include pectoral implants ('six pack implant'), liposuction and lipofilling (79). While these surgeries may be less invasive than the other procedures used for Gender Dysphoria, and many people who are not transgender undergo these procedures, the more surgeries a person goes through, the more risks they are exposed to.

In addition, many trans-identified males undergo voice training. While in trans-identified females, testosterone makes the voice deeper, trans-identified males must have either surgery or training to make their voice higher pitched. How effectiveness is this treatment? There's not a lot of research into the success of this treatment (103), but trans-identified males report that it is difficult to speak in a high voice all the time (104). Furthermore, regularly speaking in a voice that is higher than natural can cause vocal hyperfunction, which can lead to voice disorders, although being taught certain techniques may reduce this risk (103).

Fertility
To preserve the loss of fertility after transitioning, it is possible to freeze gametes (egg or sperm cells) and have a baby via in-vitro fertilization (IVF) later in life. Many people mistakenly believe that this will mean they will definitely be able to have biological children in the future. In reality, this couldn't be further from the truth. The first problem is that IVF has a high failure rate- each round of IVF as a 29% success rate for a woman under 35. This gets lower as a woman ages, falling to just 2% for women over 44 (105). It is also expensive. It costs on average £5000 (around $6050) per round of IVF in the UK (105). Additionally, for trans-identified males in a relationship with a non-transgender male or another transsexual person, they would need to find a surrogate to carry the baby. As well as being ethically dubious, finding a surrogate is difficult, as few women are willing to do it and it can also be expensive. As well as this, people often run out of frozen gametes. The chances of having a baby using a frozen egg are between two and 12% for each

individual egg cell. While doctors harvest multiple eggs, the odds of having a baby in the end are still relatively low. Women under 35 who have had their frozen eggs thawed and fertilized have a 42% chance of giving birth. The odds are even lower for women who are older than this, regardless of the age they were when the eggs were frozen (106). This means that if a trans-identified female has eggs frozen before having a hysterectomy, at best, they have less than a 1 in 2 chance of having a baby with their eggs. Furthermore, there have also been times when freezing facilities have malfunctioned and gametes or embryos have been unintentionally destroyed (107). Therefore, egg and sperm freezing are no guarantee of getting a baby.

No Regrets?

Nobody ever regrets transitioning. Ever. That's what transgender rights activists will tell you. They claim that those who return to living as their original gender are driven to do so by society's transphobia, and that they are actually still transgender (108). But that's not true. There are many people who do regret transitioning. Detransitioning is when a trans-identified person returns to their original gender identity. The transgender community is very reluctant to discuss detransitioning and often claims that it is vanishingly rare or even that it simply doesn't exist. On the contrary, as more people are changing sex, sex-change regret is becoming more prevalent (109). This has become so common that a detransitioner's network has been set up in the UK (110).

One of the most prominent detransitioners is Walt Heyer. Heyer started living as a woman in the 1980s, but a few years later, he returned to identifying as a man. He now campaigns for more rigorous checks before people are allowed to medically transition (111). Heyer describes having a difficult childhood (112). As a small child, his grandmother would put him in a dress and treat him as a girl. He started wearing a dress at his home in private, until his parents found out and stopped him (112). Heyer was also sexually abused by his uncle. He believes these traumas led to his Gender

Dysphoria (112). Heyer later discovered he had mental health issues and when he underwent treatment for this, he returned to living as a man. Heyer believes that the psychologist who diagnosed him with Gender Dysphoria should have identified his other mental health problems and not allowed him to undergo any 'gender affirming' therapies (112).

Many trans-identified people report being given gender-affirming therapies very quickly. In the case of Elan Anthony, who transitioned from male to female, he was given oestrogen after just two sessions with a psychologist (113). Anthony went on to have sex reassignment surgery, but 20 years later, he detransitioned. He has been left infertile and has difficulties with romantic relationships because of the surgery. Like Heyer, Anthony feels the psychologist too readily affirmed his gender identity and did not probe into any underlying reasons for his Gender Dysphoria.

It's not just trans-identified males who experience sex change regret. The BBC reported the story of Ellie and Nele, two trans-identified females who both went back to identifying as women. Both have taken testosterone and had a mastectomy. Although neither had any surgery on their genitals, they have both still been left with permanent effects from their transition. For instance, their voices have broken and they are often perceived as male during phone calls (114).

Sadly, many changes that result from transitioning are irreversible. If the person has a hysterectomy or castration, as well as being infertile, they will always need hormone replacement therapy (114). Genital surgery is also difficult to reverse. It is possible to undergo surgery to try to restore the original genitals, but it is a complex and expensive procedure that very few surgeons can perform (115). This is a tragedy. Doctors are rushing to affirm people's gender identity and leaving them permanently defaced.

Ultimately, no amount of surgery, hormones or other kind of medical treatment will truly change someone's sex. The best that medical science has managed to achieve is to create the appearance that someone is a member of the opposite sex, which works to varying degrees. It is cruel to pretend that a person can genuinely transition to a different gender. Given how weak the evidence is for the benefits of sex changes, it is astounding that so many doctors are willing to perform them. Are sex changes tomorrow's huge medical scandal, similar to lobotomies? Will we look back in 50 years or so and say: 'what on earth were we thinking?' We won't know for many years, but it is clear that sex reassignment is no panacea.

4. Neither Male nor Female: Non-Binary Genders

How many genders are there? Did you say 2? Not anymore. Here's a clue: it's a lot more than you think. Facebook allows users to choose from 70 options (116). But some people say there are hundreds of genders (117).

What are non-binary genders? A non-binary person identifies as neither male nor female. It is also called NB, enby, genderqueer, gender creative or gender expansive. Some people even identify as multiple genders at the same time (known as bigender or polygender), as different genders at different times (known as gender-fluid), or as having no gender at all (called agender). The concept of non-binary genders is very vague and it's difficult to establish what non-binary identities are without looking at gender stereotypes- after all, what makes a 'binary' man or a 'binary' woman? Nevertheless, non-binary people deny that their identity has anything to do with gender stereotypes. They claim it is a feeling of not being either gender (118). Some practices that non-binary people engage in include using non-binary pronouns, dressing and styling themselves to look androgynous and changing their name to an androgynous name or a name typically given to the opposite gender (119). Some companies and organizations, such as banks, are now letting customers choose to be addressed by non-binary titles, such as Mx. (120).

"What are Your Pronouns?"

Just as there are said to be many genders, there are now at least 29 different gender pronouns aside from 'he' or 'she' (121). Some examples include 'ze/zir', 'co/cos' and the singular 'they'. Explicitly stating your pronouns has become commonplace in certain environments. In many universities, lecturers will ask students to announce their pronouns when they introduce themselves at the start of the course (122). People have also started adding their pronouns to their email signatures in workplaces (123). Some universities, including Edinburgh University (124) and Durham University (125), have even given students pronoun badges to wear during fresher's week.

Non-binary people are very insistent on their preferred pronouns being used. Being misgendered (called by the wrong pronoun) is apparently deeply hurtful. In an article published in *Vice* (126), one interviewee, named Winnie, describes being close to tears after repeatedly being referred to as 'she/her' rather than 'they/them' at a work party. Given that Winnie appears female on the photograph included in the article and has a typically female name, it is easy to see why people would refer to them as 'she'. Another interviewee, Imani, who works as an actor and musician, and uses 'they/them' pronouns said "it makes me feel absolutely invisible and disrespected" when people at work do not use their preferred pronouns. Imani also complains that their colleagues "are not putting in the effort to change how they perceive me" when they call them by the wrong pronoun. On a personal level, there is something very narcistic about this. Perhaps people don't put the effort in to changing how they perceive someone because they have other more important things going on in their lives, along with the needs of their other employees, colleagues and customers to worry about. It always comes as a huge shock to non-binary that nobody else is as interested in their identity as they themselves are.

You might think that the goal of using non-binary pronouns is to abolish gender. On the face of it, that doesn't seem completely unreasonable. After all, gender inequality is a major issue and aiming to abolish gender could theoretically help women. An article in *Scientific American* proposed the abolition of gendered pronouns for this reason (127). But sadly, this is not the case. In response to the article, a group of non-binary people (128) said:

> *"For many trans[gender]/GNC [gender non-conforming] people, gender is an important part of their identity and actively avoiding the act of*

> *gendering manifests as another form of violence—a violence that trans/GNC people have been fighting against throughout the long history of lesbian, gay, bisexual, transgender, queer, intersex, asexual and two-spirit (LGBTQIA2S) experience."*

This quote shows that non-binary genders and pronouns aren't about fighting patriarchy or the gender divide. If anything, it is about reinforcing the concept of gender. The argument is that gender is so important that avoiding emphasising it is "violence". This is the exact opposite of what most feminists believe. This attitude ignores gender inequalities and puts trans-identified people on a pedestal above women.

In addition, the insistence that people never call a non-binary person by a gendered pronoun is ultimately setting themselves up for failure. Generally, when we use pronouns, we make assumptions. We tend to use pronouns when we talk about people whose name we don't know. For instance, we see the person at the reception desk has long hair, a soft face, a high-pitched voice and breasts. Based on that, we assume that person is a woman and use 'she' pronouns to refer to her. Or when we see the person stacking shelves in the supermarket is tall, has narrow hips, a flat chest and an Adam's apple, we assume they are male and call him 'he'. People do not routinely ask for people's pronouns. With a transsexual person who has adopted the appearance of the opposite gender, most people deduce that they want to be called by the pronouns of the gender they are presenting as. But with non-binary people, it is impossible to know their pronouns without asking. How do we know the receptionist doesn't actually use 'ze' pronouns or the shelf stacker prefers to be referred to as 'co'? We don't know these people. We wouldn't go up to them and say, "what are your pronouns?" when we do not plan to have any further interactions with them. It would be very difficult to change this- calling someone 'he' or 'she' is a quick way to refer to someone you don't know. For that reason, it's unrealistic to expect people to stop automatically using 'she' and 'he' pronouns.

Another problem is that the use of non-binary pronouns in conversation can be confusing. The singular 'they' is particularly unclear. When we refer to 'they', are we talking about one person or two or more people? Here's a hypothetical example of a conversation involving someone who uses the singular 'they' pronoun:

Luke: "When is Jane coming?"
Chloe: "They are coming in an hour."

Is it just Jane who is coming, or is Jane bringing someone else with them? If Luke was not aware that Jane uses the singular 'they' pronoun, the next question might be "what do you mean 'they'?" Meaning "Is it just Jane who's coming, or is someone else coming with her?" If Chloe had said "she is coming later", it would immediately be clear that Jane is coming by herself. This is why the singular 'they' is not routinely used.

It's not just the ambiguity that's the issue with non-binary pronouns either. Kerr makes the apt comparison with the Stroop test (129). Like with the Stroop test, where the test-taker must say the colour of the writing, rather than the colour the word spells, when we use a trans-identified person's preferred pronouns, we are forced to deny what we see- that a person with a male appearance is to be referred to as 'she' or 'ze' or vice versa. Kerr argues that like with the Stroop test, using different pronouns blunts our mental agility, and in turn, reduces our ability to question transgenderism.

Am I Non-Binary?

How does a person know that they are non-binary? The intersectional feminist website *Everyday Feminism* has produced a handy guide which helps you work it out (130)! Towards the beginning of the article, there are a set of questions to ask yourself to determine if you're non-binary. One of which is:

> *"Do I feel confined by my assigned gender? Do I feel limited by it, or anxious about it?"*

And another is:

> *"Does it feel like my assigned gender doesn't quite fit with who I really am?"*

These questions are quite alarming. Nobody needs to feel limited by their gender. You are who you are, regardless of your gender. Do all women obsess over clothes, shoes and make-up? Do all women watch soap operas and romantic comedies? Do all women chat with their friends about celebrity gossip? That seems to be what the definition of a woman is to a non-binary person. What about men? Do all men enjoy watching sports with a beer? Do they love talking about cars and technology? The truth is that every man and every woman is unique. There's no right way to be a man and there's no right way to be a woman.

Once you've decided that you are non-binary, this guide recommends "trying out" new names, pronouns and clothing. The trouble with this is that it's not names, pronouns and clothing that makes a person a man or a woman. For one thing, gender stereotypes change over time. For instance, in clothing, pink used to be for boys, while blue was for girls (131). Apart from men's and women's clothes being made for different body shapes, there is no reason for a certain style of clothing to be women's clothing or men's clothing. As well, many names have gone from being boy's names to girls names; Shirley, Shannon and Beverly are some of the many names that used to be boy's names but are now mainly used for girls (132).

The other thing to bear in mind is that we learn gender roles in childhood (133). Right from birth, there are boy's toys and girl's toys. When a child shows an interest in a toy or activity that is not associated with their gender, many parents will say "You can't play with that. That's a boy's toy" or "only girls are supposed to play with those". Shops gender toys as well. These toys reinforce gender roles, because they promote gendered activities. For instance, toys typically aimed at boys, such as Lego, teach visuospatial skills, while toys marketed for girls, such as dolls, promote language skills and empathy (134). We also observe adults behaving in a gendered way. We might hear our mothers talking to her female friends and family about what happened in the soaps last night, or our fathers talking about last night's football match with his male friends. We will then learn that soaps are for women and football is for men. A child will then emulate this with their own friends. And this continues into adulthood. The solution to this is not to identify as non-binary. It is to do whatever you feel comfortable with regardless of your gender and to allow your children to do the same.

Maybe at this point you're still not convinced. Maybe you've always been happy with your gender. Whereas non-binary people are supposedly deeply uncomfortable with their gender. That proves people are non-binary, right? Actually, no. Here's a little experiment to try: set a timer for one minute and think about your little finger on your left hand. Look at it. Touch it. Move it. Focus on nothing but your little finger. Does your finger feel funny now? Maybe it feels different from the rest of your fingers, or even the rest of your body. Perhaps you've even noticed things you've never seen or felt before. Even if your finger doesn't normally feel odd, it probably does now. That's what happens if you focus a lot on something. It's the same if you think about your gender identity. If you focus on it a lot, you'll spot things you haven't noticed before and find it doesn't feel quite right. You might have been happily identifying as a woman, but then you might realize you don't like make-up as much as other women do, or you sometimes played with your brother's toy cars when you were a child, so maybe you're not really a woman after all. Or perhaps you're a man, but you don't like watching sports like other men and as a child, you were never into the same rough-and-tumble play that other boys liked. So perhaps you're partly female. And if you read about what 'non-binary' feels like, it's easy to think you are non-binary.

"Non-Binary Identities are Valid"
Something that seriously undermines the validity of the non-binary movement is that hardly anyone was openly non-binary before the 2010s. When challenged about the fact that non-binary genders were virtually unheard of a decade ago, activists claim non-binary people have always been (135). A commonly cited example is that some Native American tribes had what are known as two-spirit people. Two-spirit people are said to have both male and female spirits. The term 'two-spirit' was coined in 1990 at a Native American history conference (136), although most tribes had their own words for two-spirit. Before this, the word most scholars used was 'berdache', which implied that two spirit people were homosexual. It is now considered offensive (137). Two-spirit people were often assigned special roles within the tribes, such as healers and visionaries (138). While on the face of it there are many similarities between non-binary genders today and two-spirit, there are some key differences. Firstly, unlike with non-binary genders, a person couldn't simply identify as two-spirit in most tribes. Most two-spirits were identified as such as a small child, using a ceremony or other type of ritual (138). Secondly, the term two-spirit is also sometimes used to refer to gay, lesbian and bisexual Native Americans (139). Hence, two-spirit is not the same as non-binary, and it does not necessarily demonstrate that non-binary genders have always existed.

Additionally, the Native American community have condemned white people for calling themselves two-spirit. For instance, the singer Jason Mraz was accused of cultural appropriation when he came out as two-spirit (140). As people do not identify as two spirit in the same way they would identify as transgender, this shows a poor understanding of two-spirit. These non-binary activists don't show any other interest in Native American history or their lives. They have cherry-picked an aspect of Native American mythology for their own use.

There are other examples of third genders from different cultures and different periods in history (138). Most of these examples are specific to one sex- for instance, the Muxes in Mexico are biological males who look and act effeminate. Are they really a third gender? They are certainly not non-binary in the sense that many western non-binary people claim to be. In fact, most of the examples of third genders - such as Hijras in India and Kokec in Turkey, are effeminate men. As these third genders are only applicable to a certain sex, they are not truly defying the gender binary. Perhaps it is like Greer said about how women are seen as defective men, and so 'defective' men (such as transgender people and intersex people) are classed as woman (2). In some cultures, these 'defective' men, who are not considered masculine enough to be classed as men, are relegated to a third gender. This is not progressive. In contrast, the concept of these other genders reinforces masculine and feminine gender roles.

The current non-binary movement started in the early 1990s. It was during this period that the term 'transgender' was broadened to include people who felt neither male nor female. The term 'genderqueer' was also coined at this time. The growth of the internet spread the concept, but it did not enter mainstream usage until the 2010s (141). The term 'non-binary' is thought to have been coined on Tumblr (142). Nearly 30 years ago isn't exactly forever, as transgender activists claim. Where were all these people before? How would they have coped for all this time when not being recognised as non-binary is apparently so devastating? And even if non-binary genders had always existed, why are so many people now distraught at the prospect of being called 'he' or 'she' or referred to as male or female?

The existence of third gender groups in other cultures or historical periods does not prove that non-binary people have always been around. It just proves that some other cultures had the construct of non-binary genders. None of these are the same as modern non-binary genders. Nor do they prove that non-binary identities are valid. Indeed, it's difficult to say what makes an identity valid. We all have many identities, many of which are self-selected (for instance, our political affiliation, membership of a certain organization or religious beliefs) in that sense, non-binary identities could be considered valid. If we assume that valid means that someone has an innate sense of being neither male nor female, then non-binary genders are not valid.

Identifying out of Privilege

When he first started identifying as non-binary, James Shupe -the first person in the USA to be officially recognized as non-binary- claimed he had renounced his male privilege and become "one of the most hated minorities in America", showing perfectly how non-binary people see themselves as extremely oppressed. But is that really the case? (Interestingly, Shupe later abandoned his non-binary identity, describing it as a "sham") (143).

The growth of non-binary genders means that in socially liberal circles, women who are not trans-identified (cisgender women) now have 'cis privilege'. Cis privilege is when it is assumed that everyone is either male or female. According to *Everyday Feminism*, examples of cis privilege include only having male/female boxes on forms, seeing only male and female characters on television and even that major religious texts only feature men and women (144). This version of gender makes women the privileged class. A man who identifies as non-binary is now less privileged than a woman because nobody will indulge him. He is having his cake and eating it, so to speak. He can have male privilege when he is walking through the street and being much less vulnerable to attack than a woman and when he doesn't have to go through pregnancy and childbirth. Conversely, he can be oppressed when it comes to positive discrimination programs and in 'progressive' circles he can claim victim status when he would have previously been seen as privileged.

Why would someone try to give up their privilege? Among left-wing circles nowadays, the worst thing a person can be is privileged. Bell describes how left-leaning groups put minorities on a pedestal- there is always a lot of talk of privilege and the importance of listening to minority voices (145). One group who is particularly maligned are 'cis-hets' (or cishets), meaning someone who is both cisgender and heterosexual. Especially cis-het men. So how does a person stop being a cis-het? By identifying as transgender or non-binary! When a man identifies as non-binary, he can switch from being the least oppressed to the most oppressed in society. Then, instead of having to listen to women because he has male privilege, women have to listen to him, because they have cis privilege. That way, he can be both privileged in wider society because he is male, and also privileged in left-wing circles because he is non-binary. It is also a handy way of oppressing women. By making it so that men who identify as non-binary are valued over women, women's voices are drowned out in progressive circles.

The reason why this is particularly problematic is that a person can identify as non-binary without making the same kind of dramatic changes as a person who identifies as transsexual must make. A man who starts identifying as a woman would typically change their name, their clothing and hair style, start using make-up and later in the transition process, start taking female hormones, have sex reassignment surgeries and legally change their gender. These would be big changes from both a practical and social point of view. However, a man could simply say he is non-binary, without changing any other aspect of his life, and he is immediately a minority. While it's a good thing that people are avoiding making the life-altering changes that transsexuals make, it is not acceptable for people to wriggle out of their privilege when it suits them.

Doublethink- Are Non-Binary People Warriors or Victims?

Some people say that they identify as non-binary as a political statement, and by doing so, they are actively choosing to defy the harms caused by the gender binary (146). In a piece on non-binary people published in the *New York Times*, interviewee Kai says "we're all born nonbinary. We learn gender. And at some point, some of us can't stand it anymore" (146). Kai is right that we all learn gender. But is identifying as non-binary the solution? There's a kind of arrogance in saying that you are non-binary because you feel confined by your gender. It sounds like non-binary people have figured out something that ordinary people are not intelligent enough to realize; that people do not have to be men or women, but instead they have the choice to be some other kind of category. It also implies that all us 'binary' people are happy with the current state of gender.

Also, non-binary identities are not treated like any other political belief. Firstly, we don't generally go to great lengths to accommodate people's political views in any other context.
When a person asks to be called by a non-binary pronoun, they are asking to be treated differently than others because of their political views. In most situations, we don't know a person's political views. It's rather odd to say someone requires special treatment because of their opinions. Furthermore, political views can be discussed and challenged. Most people are perfectly comfortable with being told their political beliefs are wrong, even when they don't agree. And people debate politics all the time. But when it comes to non-binary people, it is seen as unacceptable to question their views on gender.

Then there's the view that non-binary people are a minority group. It is implied that non-binary gender identities have a biological aspect. This version is much like the brain sex concept of transgenderism, except instead of having a woman's brain in a male body or vice versa, a person has a brain that is neither a man's brain nor a woman's brain. For this, they face a lot of oppression. As one non-binary blogger put it: "why would someone risk facing that kind of hate and cruelty just so they could get attention and seem special?" (147). It is precisely because of this 'oppression' that people identify as non-binary. Like being transsexual, being non-binary is presented on social media and in liberal publications as brave. For someone who feels otherwise overlooked or that they have no special qualities, it can be easy to see why they would be drawn to identifying as non-binary. In addition, while non-binary people can try and deny that they identify as non-binary for attention, being called by a special pronoun, having an unusual name and dressing in a unique way makes a person be noticed. For someone who is very extraverted, this would bring them the attention they craved. Thus, it's hard to see how being noticed isn't a factor in some people identifying as non-binary. Furthermore, Anderson (28) points out that if non-binary identity is innate, it would be impossible for someone to be innately gender fluid- the person's gender identity would not be able to change on a regular basis if they had a male brain or a female brain.

Non-binary people seem to have it both ways; that they are engaging in a radical political act and at the same time, that they gender is innate and so they need special treatment to accommodate them. Many will say that they are fighting the gender binary by identifying outside of it. Meanwhile, they will say they need forms that include other gender options and special titles or else they can't fill them out. And they will talk about feeling 'unsafe' when they are not called by their preferred pronouns. This is more to do with feeling unique than fighting patriarchy. What about non-binary people who say that they are distressed at not being called by their preferred pronoun or gender? In these cases, there is likely a sociogenic cause- they have learned from social media non-binary communities that being 'misgendered' is deeply distressing and act accordingly when this occurs.

You could say that it's nobody else's business what gender someone identifies as. So why are non-binary genders such a big problem? Rea (148) points out that identifying as non-binary implies that everyone else is quite content to conform to gender stereotypes. In reality, non-binary people don't generally think too deeply into their identity. Or else they would quickly see the contradictions in their identity, and then they wouldn't identify as non-binary. The non-binary people have a very conservative idea of gender; men do men's things, women do women's things and if you're not into men's or women's things, you're neither a man nor a woman. They don't want to abolish gender. They allow everyone else to suffer because of gender roles while they pretend that they have opted out.

The reality is we are all non-binary. Nobody fits perfectly with the gender binary; people are not gender stereotypes and a special word or pronoun is not needed for people who don't fit perfectly with gender stereotypes. If someone doesn't 'feel' male or female, it is because male and female are not feelings, but biological facts. The goal should not be to invent new words and pronouns for people who don't see themselves as male or female. Rather, it should be to release everyone from the confines of gender roles.

5. Never too Young- Transgenderism and Childhood

Transgenderism isn't just for adults. Children can change sex too! Transgender activists claim that a child is certain of their gender identity between the ages of two and three (28). As a result, children as young as three are being classed as having Gender Dysphoria (149). What's particularly alarming about this is that most children under the age of five do not understand sex permanence; it's perfectly normal for a child to think they will be a member of the opposite sex when they grow up (150). Thus, a small child who proclaims they are a member of the opposite gender is unlikely to be coming out as transgender but to simply not understand that they will always be a member of their biological sex.

You could argue that an adult is free to make their own choices about their body. After all, many people have cosmetic surgery because they are unhappy with their appearance or get a piercing or tattoo to make them stand out. But a child does not have the insight or life experience to make these kind of decisions. Furthermore, trans-identified children have much higher rates of developmental and psychiatric disorders such as Autism (24,151), ADHD, Depression and Anxiety (24) than the general population. This raises a serious concern that the children are expressing unhappiness with their gender because of their other difficulties. It could be that these children think changing sex will solve the problems that result from these conditions. For instance, a girl with Autism might think she would find it easier to make friends if she were a boy, or a boy with Depression might think his life would be better if he were a girl. It also raises the issue of capacity; should a child with a mental illness or developmental disorder be allowed to make a life-changing decision that will affect them for the rest of their lives?

More worryingly, parents often have no choice but to go along with their child's sex change plans. In the USA, child services can remove a child from their family if they won't let them transition (28). And in the UK, there have been at least three cases where the parent's objecting to their child changing sex was a factor in the child being taken into local authority care (152). Parents are faced with a stark choice; let your child transition, even when you know they're far too immature to make such a big decision, or have your child taken away from you, where they'll be allowed to change sex anyway.

Furthermore, there is evidence that some children who wish to transition do not have a good understanding of gender and the reasons for wishing to change sex are based on either misconceptions about sex, or other unrealistic beliefs. Zucker et al., (153) found many such instances, including one child who said he wanted to be a girl so he wouldn't sweat. Another child said he wanted to be a girl so his parents and teachers would treat him better. A third boy started experiencing Gender Dysphoria after his younger sister was born, perceiving that she received more attention from adults because she was a girl, rather than because she was a baby. In this case, the boy's mother also had narcistic personality traits and was very volatile, which Zucker felt contributed to the development of his Gender Dysphoria. This shows that children do not always have a good reason for wanting to change sex. Instead, their desire to change gender may stem from other issues, and so it is unwise to take them seriously when they express unhappiness with their sex.

Childhood Transitions- Changing sex in childhood
In the past, the majority of trans-identified children did not grow to be trans-identified adults. Without so-called 'gender-affirming' treatment (where the child is allowed to live as their preferred gender), 75 to 95% prepubescent children outgrow Gender Dysphoria. However, with gender-affirming treatment, almost 100% of children continue to experience Gender Dysphoria into adulthood (154). This gives the impression that the current treatment of trans-identified children stops them from outgrowing their Gender Dysphoria.

Children as young as 10 years old may start puberty blockers, which are meant to give them time to make a decision on their sex (155), but in practice are used to make the medical transition easier (156). Leuprorelin (marketed as Lupron), which is the drug given to suppress puberty, has many side effects, some of which may not be fully reversable. Although little is known about the long-tern effects of leuprorelin in transgender children, in adults who took leuprorelin in childhood for precocious puberty, there have been many negative effects. Many now suffer from weak bones and teeth, degenerative joint diseases and severe mental illnesses. There are also some indications that the drugs increase the risk of developing Epilepsy (157). In addition, scientists do not know exactly what effect leuprorelin has specifically on trans-identified children, including the impact blocking puberty has on brain development (158). It is deeply worrying that children are being given these drugs, when the effects may last a lifetime.

As with adults, the rationale for transitioning children is to prevent suicide. Although adults with Gender Dysphoria are more likely to commit suicide, the same is not true of children. According to transgender rights activists, one in two young trans-identified people have attempted suicide. This statistic comes from a study undertaken by PACE, an LGBT charity (159). If this is correct, this is comparable with the suicide attempt rate of many serious mental illnesses. 50% of people with Bipolar Disorder (160), 39% of people with Schizophrenia (161) and 16% of people with Depression have attempted suicide (87), compared to three percent of the general population (161). Based on these figures, either trans-identified young people are very seriously mentally ill, or the statistic is wildly inaccurate. Fortunately, the latter appears to be correct. This statistic is not supported by evidence from trans-identified patient's medical records. The UK's Tavistock and Portman Clinic, the only clinic for trans-identified children in the UK, said that less than one percent of its patients have attempted suicide (162). In addition, an analysis published by Transgender Trend revealed that only 27 trans-identified people were included in the PACE study. The author of the analysis, who wishes to remain anonymous, also notes that selection bias may have affected the results. Trans-identified young people with mental health problems may have been more inclined to complete the survey because they wished to share their experiences, so the results have inflated the number of trans-identified people who attempt suicide (163). As trans-identified children are no more likely to kill themselves than other children, this begs the question of why clinicians are so keen to transition children when the main reason for gender changes is to reduce suicide rates.

Even many doctors treating trans-identified children are unhappy at how many children are changing gender. Over the past three years, the Tavistock and Portman clinic has had 35 staff resign in protest over the clinic's practices. Staff have said they resigned over fears of being branded transphobic if they did not agree to allow children to transition, even when they did not think it was appropriate (164). One unnamed psychologist describes how any concerns about allowing a child to transition were often dismissed by other members of staff. It is terrible that even medical professionals are forced to go along with transgenderism, even when they have concerns.

Children are making huge life-changing decisions, when they are considered too immature to make any other major choices. A child under 18 can't get a tattoo, buy cigarettes or alcohol, buy a knife, vote in an election, or do many other things. Legally, they aren't considered responsible enough to make important decisions over their life. Yet they are able to consent to have irreversible damage done to their bodies.

Woke Education
Transgenderism isn't confined to a small number of families where children have changed sex. Transgender ideology has also begun to infiltrate the education system. In the UK, Brighton and Hove Council have approved guidelines for teaching about menstruation in schools, which include teaching that boys can have periods too (165). How do you explain menstruation without talking about biological

sex? A boy with a penis and testicles will never have a period. It is physiologically impossible. Only a girl with a vagina and a uterus can have a period. Teaching that boys can have periods will make it difficult for children to understand sexual relations and reproduction. How will a child understand where babies come from if they are learning that girls can have a penis or boys can have a vagina? Can a girl with a penis get pregnant? Can boys get pregnant? And how does a man with a penis impregnate a woman with a penis? It could be especially confusing for children with special educational needs such as intellectual disabilities and Autism, who are more likely to misinterpret what they are being told. In the near future, there's going to be a lot of confused children out there. All for the sake of transgender inclusivity.

But that's not all. In the USA, a set of guidelines named *Schools in Transition* have been produced jointly by several transgender rights groups and teaching organizations. It makes many troubling recommendations, including that children be allowed to transition at school without their parent's knowledge. The guidelines even recommend that school staff make a plan to ensure that the child's parents don't find out about their child's transgender identity (166). This is very alarming. If a child is seriously in danger, (meaning their parents are likely to be abusive if they found out that their child was transgender), then child protection services should be involved. However, if- as in most cases- the parents may not necessarily embrace the child's gender identity but will not harm the child, then the parents have a right to know. In any case, it is not right for the teachers to hide such a major thing from any other responsible adults in the child's life.

Indoctrination Through Play
It's not just at school where children are being indoctrinated with transgender ideology. Books and toys are also being produced to teach children about transgenderism. There's now several picture books for small children about changing sex. *Introducing Teddy* by Jessica Walton is about a teddy bear named Thomas who decides he

is actually a girl. He wants to be called Tilly, wear a pink bow and be referred to by she/her pronouns. Errol, Thomas/Tilly's owner, embraces the change (167). This isn't a little self-published book being marketed to a very specialist audience. It has been found being sold on an educational supplier's website, in a pack marketed as diversity books, aimed at children aged four to seven (168). Another children's book, *Peanut goes for the Gold* by television presenter Jonathan van Ness, is about a non-binary guinea pig who becomes a rhythmic gymnast (169). This book is also marketed to children aged four and up (170). While children can't be hidden from uncomfortable aspects of life forever, a small child is too young to grasp the complexities of changing sex or the concept of gender identity. At the ages these books are being aimed at, most children are just learning about gender. At four years old, many children won't know what makes a boy a boy and a girl a girl. It is far too early to talk about changing sex without confusing them.

Another book, *Can I Tell You About Gender Diversity?* by CJ Atkinson is targeted toward older primary school children. It is about a 12-year-old trans-identified female. The protagonist talks about how he didn't enjoy playing with dolls as a child and how he is taking puberty blockers and will start taking testosterone when he is 16 (171). While a child at this age might have a reasonable understanding of sex and gender, and be able to understand the concept of transgender, they are still very susceptible to suggestion and may come to believe that they are transgender.

As well as there being books about transgenderism, to teach small children about transgenderism, a transgender toy has been designed. Sam is a transgender Russian nesting doll. Each doll represents a 'stage' in Sam's gender development, starting with Sam as a baby girl who does not know about gender and finishing with Sam living happily as a boy (172). This toy relies on gender stereotypes to illustrate what Gender Dysphoria is. For example, one of the dolls is of Sam pretending to be a construction worker. Why does this mean Sam is a boy? Women can be construction workers too. This toy reinforces gender stereotypes and shows how transgenderism is about nothing more than the failure to live up to the typical norms for the child's gender.

Woke Parents

While many parents express reasonable concerns about their child changing sex, other parents embrace their child's claims that they are transgender, or even encourage their children to identify as transgender.

Jazz Jennings

One of the most famous trans-identified children is Jazz Jennings, from the USA. Jennings first appeared in the public eye in 2007, when she featured on the current affairs program, *20/20* at the age of six with her parents, in an item about trans-identified children (173). Jennings started identifying as a girl as a toddler. She claims to remember being two years old and having dreams about having her penis transformed into a vagina. She was diagnosed with Gender Dysphoria at the age of three (174). A long-running reality series named *I am Jazz* has been running for many years on the digital channel *TLC*. Jennings started hormone blockers at 11 years old and oestrogen at 12. She then underwent sex reassignment surgery at 17 years old. She has suffered many complications from this and has had two additional procedures (175). Because she had received puberty blockers, her penis was not large enough for a conventional penile inversion, so grafts were taken from other parts of her body (176). Her long-running television program has made Jazz a celebrity. She has featured in an advertising campaign for Gillette Venus razors (177). She has also written two books, one of which is a picture book for children (178). A toy doll based on Jennings's appearance has also been sold (179).

Jazz Jennings's case raises a number of concerns. Firstly, Jazz often sounds as if she is repeating what her parents have told her. It's rather suspicious that Jennings claims to remember a dream she had when she was two or being diagnosed with Gender Dysphoria at three years old. It seems more likely that Jazz's parents told her the stories about being a toddler who wanted to be a girl. It's also rather difficult to believe that a two-year-old would know about genitals, sex and gender. It's fair to assume that Jazz's parents must have had a huge influence on Jazz's Gender Dysphoria. It raises the possibility that Jazz's parents encouraged her to transition.

In addition, the ethics of making the reality television program are also questionable. Jazz has had her private life televised for many years without being old enough to make an informed decision. Doctors' appointments where Jazz's genitals and surgery were discussed, along with other personal issues, have been broadcast on television all around the world. Jazz has a right to privacy and it's easy to imagine that having such intimate issues shown in public could have a detrimental effect on her wellbeing. It is an unethical program that shows the greed of the media at its worst. Moreover, it is difficult to understand why any responsible parents would agree to let their child participate in a television program of this nature.

They-Bys and Non-Binary Children
As well as parents letting their child change sex, some parents are starting to identify their child as non-binary right from the beginning. Theybys or they-bys (a portmanteau of 'they' and 'baby') are when a parent decides to raise their child as neither male nor female from birth. They typically do this by choosing a gender-neutral name for the baby, refusing to use gendered pronouns to refer to the child, or even avoiding telling their friends and families the baby's sex (180).

One notable child been raised as non-binary is Zoomer Myers, a child from the USA. They are being raised as non-binary because their family do not wish to impose a gender on Zoomer. The family call Zoomer by they/them pronouns, and say they will continue to do this until Zoomer is old enough to say otherwise (181). The family also buys both boy's and girl's clothes for Zoomer and even refers to Zoomer's toys as 'they'. The Myers have even gone as far as to refuse to tell Zoomer's grandparent's the baby's biological sex so that they would have no choice other than to use they/them pronouns. According to their Instagram account, the Myers have also made cards to give to adults around Zoomer explaining that Zoomer is 'gender creative' (182). They also refuse to select Zoomer's gender on forms when asked (183). What impact will this have on Zoomer? Does Zoomer know why they are being raised in this way? Zoomer is going to go through life wondering why their parents made them into a social outcast. The measures taken to uphold Zoomer's gender-neutral identity are closer to those used for parents of a child with some kind of serious illness or disability (such as making information cards and contacting venues in advance to tell them about Zoomer's pronouns). There is no need to treat this child in this way. Zoomer's parents are drawing attention to Zoomer all the time in the way they treat them. It's easy to imagine that this will do a lot of psychological harm to Zoomer. After all, Zoomer doesn't understand why they are different from other children. They haven't chosen to identify as non-binary. It has been forced on them.

As well as this, some parents are also encouraging older children to identify as non-binary. On the BBC, a radio program was made about a non-binary 10-year-old. 'Leo', who was born female, states that with help from his mother, he discovered that he was non-binary, and wished to be known by male pronouns. Leo started identifying as non-binary after an older family member came out as transgender. In the interview, Leo mentions that his mother is very supportive. His mother talks a lot about how she helped him learn about non-binary genders and to try out pronouns at home (184). At first glance, Leo's mother is being a caring parent. But when you look more deeply, you realise there is something rather odd about the whole situation. Firstly, Leo's mother treats Leo like an adult. At one point, Leo mentions that she asked: "You've always been more attracted to boys, would you be a gay man or a straight man?" (185) This is a very odd question to ask such a young child. She seems to be approaching Leo's gender identity as if he were a friend rather than her child. While Leo sounds very articulate, it is doubtful that he is mature enough to make such big decisions about his gender. He does not need automatic validation from his mother; he needs questioning.

Other times, she sounds more like she is representing Leo in a professional capacity rather than as his mother. Much of what she says is about non-binary identities in general rather than about Leo- the interview doesn't give much of a sense of what Leo is like as a person or why Leo feels he is non-binary. Much of what Leo says also sounds rigid, as if he had learnt it from a script. He doesn't sound like he is expressing his personal thoughts. All of this gives the impression that Leo's mother is the driving force behind Leo identifying as non-binary.

The speed at which Leo and his mother have pursued Leo's non-binary identity is also concerning. The radio program mentions that Leo only started identifying as non-binary two months prior. In that time, Leo has changed his name, his pronouns, is identified as non-binary at school and has participated in extra-curricular activities under his new gender identity (184). Leo and his mother have jumped into this very quickly. If anything, it feels as if Leo's mother is excited to have a unique child rather than that she is helping her distressed child.

Pushing Children to Transition
At first glance, it's hard to see why a parent would want their child to transition, but there are at least two cases where this has occurred. According to Dreger, parents whose children transition are seen as woke and tolerant. Conversely, parents who refuse to let their child transition are perceived to be transphobic conservatives who don't accept their child for who they are (186). This might explain why some parents seemingly push their child to identify as transgender.

In the UK, there was a High Court case of a seven-year-old boy who was forced to live as a girl by his mother (the family can't be named for legal reasons). The case came about after concerns were raised about his abnormal interest in touching other people's genitals. More worryingly, he would often describe the appearance and texture of his mother's breasts and genitals, suggesting he may have been sexually abused (187). Fortunately, the judge realized that the boy did not have Gender Dysphoria. He was removed from his mother's custody and allowed to live with his father. The boy now lives as a boy full-time and shows no interest in being a girl (188).

There has also been a similar case in the USA. James Younger, who was also seven years old, was also told he was a girl by his mother from an early age. James told his father that his mother would put him in dresses and paint his nails. Because of this, his father does not believe that James has Gender Dysphoria, but the court has ruled that James should continue to live as a girl and may begin taking puberty blockers in the future (189).

It's not clear why these particular parents wanted their sons to live as girls. In the former case, Lewis suggests that something akin to Munchausen Syndrome by Proxy may have been at play (187). Perhaps it is to feel woke -after all, transgenderism is celebrated so much in the liberal media, it almost seems exciting and courageous to have a transgender child. Maybe there are deeper-seated reasons, such as disappointment about their child's natural sex (wanting to have a boy when they had a girl or vice versa), or fears that the child might be gay or lesbian and that having a child being the member of the opposite sex would be preferable to having a homosexual child.

Overall, the phenomenon of transgender children is very concerning. Small children say and do all kinds of bizarre things. Everyone must remember being a small child themselves and all the madcap things they got up to. It is quite alarming that anyone would take a small child saying they want to be the opposite gender seriously. Even when a child is older, they still don't always know what they want. Teens experiment with their identity. Most of us remember fighting against our parents by doing all kinds of things. We might have had crazy haircuts and piercings, worn the most outrageous clothes and make-up and listened to controversial music. All of these things can be changed when the teen grows up. Yet many teens are changing sex as part of their teenage rebellion. This cannot be reversed easily. There will be many adults in the future who will live with the effects of their childhood sex changes for the rest of their lives.

6. Transgenderism in Policy

Laws and policies are increasingly forcing people to accept transgenderism. There are now laws treating transgender people as if they have literally changed their biological sex and making it illegal for people to not accept this. In addition, even questioning transgenderism is increasingly being criminalized as 'hate speech'. This chapter will cover policy around transgenderism in governments at all levels, including central or federal governments and state and regional governments.

'Equality' Laws

Anti-discrimination laws are pushing transgenderism on to the public. In the UK (apart from Northern Ireland), gender reassignment is one of the nine protected characteristics of the Equality Act 2010. This means that most forms of discrimination against transgender people are illegal. Fortunately, the law does allow people to treat transgender people differently from non-transgender people if they can show a good reason for this. For instance, refusing to allow a trans-identified male to compete in a women's sports event is allowed to ensure fair competition (190). The intention behind this law -to promote equality- is wonderful. But when it comes to transgenderism, many relatively trivial things are now illegal. For instance, the Equality and Human Rights Commission (the UK's human rights watchdog) states that misgendering a trans-identified person is harassment under the Equality Act (190). Is it unkind to call a trans-identified male 'he' or a trans-identified female 'she'? Yes. But should it be illegal? This certainly sounds extreme. The law is telling us that we must accept something that is not scientifically possible; that a person has transformed into a member of the opposite sex.

The US Senate is also debating bringing in its own Equality Act. Like the UK's Equality Act, it would make discrimination on the basis of gender identity illegal. But unlike the UK's Equality Act, the current bill does not have any protections for sex-based rights. As a result, if this bill were to be passed, people would be forced to let trans-identified people into women's spaces, including women's sports (191). It has already passed through the House of Representatives, so it has a realistic prospect of becoming law. Furthermore, this bill has enjoyed considerable support on the left, with all the Democrat presidential primary candidates stating that they support the bill. The presidential candidate, Joe Biden has promised to make it his top legislative priority if he were to be elected as president (191). This is a greatly worrying step that will have a major, adverse effect on women. It is not promoting equality; it is promoting inequality, with trans-identified people being placed above women.

The Ministry of Truth: Changing Records, Re-Writing the Past

Another way the law is forcing people to accept transgenderism is through the changing of birth certificates and other legal documents. It is possible to change sex in official records and documentation in a third of countries (192). By letting people change their birth certificate, they are effectively trying to change the past. It is denying that they were ever born as their biological sex. Brendan O'Neill (193) makes an apt comparison with the character Winston Smith from the novel *1984*, whose job is to 'rectify' historical documents for the Ministry of Truth. Just as Oceania had always been at war with Eurasia, trans-identified people were always the sex they identify as now. They always have been and always will be- or so they want us to believe.

In the UK, the Gender Recognition Act 2004 lets people change their sex on legal documents. The law was introduced after a 2002 case heard in the European Court of Human Rights, which ruled that not allowing transsexuals to change their birth certificate was a breach of their right to privacy (194). To be allowed to change sex under this law, the person has to be assessed by panel of medical and legal experts. They must also have a diagnosis of Gender Dysphoria and evidence that they have been living as a member of the opposite gender for two years (194). In the USA, it's possible to change the sex on a birth certificate in all but two states- Ohio and Tennessee. The process varies in each state (195).

Some countries are now going even further. While most countries that allow changing sex on official records require the person to have gone through a medical transition, some now let people legally change their sex without any kind of medical intervention. You can simply tell the authorities you're now a member of the opposite sex and they will change your records. It's that simple. Countries that allow self-determination include The Republic of Ireland, Malta and Denmark (196). Non-binary genders have also started to get some legal recognition in some territories; 11 states in the USA allow people to identify as non-binary on official documents such as driving licenses or birth certificates (197). Many countries also let people legally identify as non-binary, including Argentina, most regions of Australia, Canada, Iceland, India, Malta, Nepal, New Zealand, Pakistan and Uruguay (198).

Why is letting people change their sex on their birth certificate a problem? Fair Play for Women points out that this compromises women's sex-based rights. Legally, it will be impossible to distinguish a biological male or female from a trans-identified male or female. This will make it difficult to protect women's sex-based rights because there will be no legal grounds to exclude a person from a single-sex space (199). For instance, if a man legally changes sex, what is to stop him from going into changing rooms? Or being held in a women's prison? What would stop him from being classed as female in healthcare settings? And with self-identification, even if he does not live as a woman, he could still be legally female. And that puts women at risk. Furthermore, a man who has no interest in living as a woman could legally identify as female, and then he would be able to access women-only spaces and abuse women.

Of course, many activists claim they should have the right to change their sex on their birth certificate. Transgender rights activist Simona

Castricum (200) says that not allowing this is "administrative violence" and that "Sex identification is forced upon us as we are all coercively assigned gender at birth without consent". Castricum is wrong for two reasons. First, the birth certificate shows sex -not gender or gender identity. Secondly, as biology chooses your sex for you, nobody has the right to choose their own sex. We don't consent to anything else when we are born. Biology assigns us many things without our consent. We are assigned an ethnicity, our appearance and our parents. For some of us, we are assigned an illness or disability too. We don't get to choose our genes. The birth certificate merely reflects a biological reality.

Furthermore, we can't change any other details on our birth certificates. We couldn't, for instance, be able to decide we were born in a different country, or on a different date, or to different parents. Additionally, a person cannot be biologically non-binary. Apart from some people born with rare variants of intersex conditions, everyone is either biologically male or biologically female. Letting someone change their sex to non-binary would be like letting people change their birth certificate to say they were born in an imaginary town, or on a non-existent date. So why should a person be allowed to change their sex on their birth certificate?

The Thought Police

Laws are increasingly restricting what we can say about transgenderism. Our rights to free speech are gradually being taken away and we can no longer question transgenderism without the threat of serious repercussions.

The Scottish devolved parliament is currently debating a new hate crime bill. In addition to the UK's existing hate crime laws, this new law would make 'stirring up hatred' against transgender people illegal (201). In the current draft of the bill, communicating "insulting" content will be illegal, if it could result in hate being "stirred up" against transgender people. By "displaying, publishing or distributing the material", including on social media, you could be breaking the law. The bill proposes a maximum penalty of seven years in prison for breaking this law. Unlike current hate crime laws, there is no requirement for there to be an intention to upset transgender people. Possessing material that stirs up hatred will also be illegal. So, the threshold for something being illegal under the new law is simply that transgender people find it insulting and it might influence other people to dislike transgender people. It will basically make questioning transgenderism illegal. That means, that if this book were being written and published in Scotland, it would be illegal. So will publishing many other books, blogs, social media posts and articles. It could also be illegal for Scottish people to buy this book, or other books that criticize transgenderism, including many of the sources cited in this book. How frightening is this? It certainly doesn't sound like the type of law you'd typically see in a democratic society. It is attempting to criminalize even thinking about transgenderism in a way other than that prescribed by the Scottish government.

Thoughtcrimes
Existing laws are also being used for restricting freedom of speech. One of the biggest areas affected by this is on the internet. We do so much online now. Online spaces have replaced many real-life social interactions. If you called a trans-identified male 'he' with a friend in a face-to-face conversation or during a phone call, legally speaking, there would be no issues. But if you do it online, you could be prosecuted.

In the UK, the Malicious Communications Act 1988 is being used to prosecute people for what they say online about transgenderism. There are numerous high-profile cases where people have either been arrested, questioned by the police or prosecuted for either misgendering trans-identified people, for 'deadnaming' people (calling them the name they were known as prior to their transition) or for making other comments that implied that trans-identified people were not the gender they identify as.

The police have contacted many people about what they have said online. In Ipswich, police made a phone call to Margaret Nelson- a 74-year-old woman- for her blog posts and Tweets on transgenderism. In her social media posts, she had criticized the notion that biological sex doesn't exist (202). She was told to tone down her comments about transgender people because the posts were upsetting. Fortunately, the police later apologised for the way they had treated her (203,204).

The infamous Stephanie Hayden is also notorious for reporting people to the police for 'hate speech'. Television writer Graham Lineham was given a police caution for misgendering Hayden and referring to her by her old name on Twitter (205). The police also ordered Lineham not to contact Hayden, even though he had never actually directly contacted her. Furthermore, Hayden had posted Lineham's personal details on social media, but she did not get into any trouble (205).

In another case, Kate Scottow, a postgraduate student, was arrested in front of her two young children, for calling Hayden by her old name on Twitter (206). Like Lineham, she was initially released with a caution and also given a court order forbidding her from referring to Hayden as a man. After this, Scottow was later prosecuted under the Malicious Communications Act and given a conditional discharge and a £1000 (around $1240) fine for misgendering Hayden and calling her "a pig in a wig" on Twitter (207). It's difficult to understand why such a mild insult should be dealt with so harshly. In any other circumstances, the police wouldn't even get involved.

You can also find yourself having a visit from the police because of what you say on television. Journalist Caroline Farrow was questioned under caution by the police because of her conduct on *Good Morning Britain,* a national breakfast television program. During a debate with transgender rights campaigner Susan Green, on whether trans-identified males should be allowed to join the Girl

Guides, Farrow had referred to Jackie Green- the trans-identified male child of Green, as 'he' (208). (Susan Green is the founder of Mermaids, a campaign group for trans-identified children and their families).

If that weren't bad enough, you can be prosecuted for what you say in the street too. Declan Armstrong, an Autistic 19-year-old man, was convicted of using abusive or insulting words to cause harassment for saying "is it a boy or a girl?" loudly to his friend, in front of a trans-identified female PCSO (209) (PCSO stands for Police Community Support Officer. They are not police officers, but they can deal with minor crimes). Armstrong was fined £590 ($715) and given a 12-week night-time curfew. What Armstrong said was rude, but given his disability, that is to be expected. Autistic people often have difficulty knowing if a comment is appropriate and can have a tendency to be rude without meaning to be. This could easily have been intended as an innocent question rather than as an insult. But that didn't matter in the eyes of the judge or the Crown Prosecution Service (CPS). The CPS have made an example of Armstrong. In a press report written by the CPS, Greg George, the head of diversity for North Wales Police said: "The sentence reflects the importance of holding individuals to account when they commit hate crime" (210). The prosecution and penalty are hugely disproportionate. All the man had really done was say something impolite, and given his disability, allowances could (and should) have been made. Even if Armstrong were not Autistic, the conviction and sentence are very extreme for something rather trivial.

To put this into context, compare the cases of Scottow and Armstrong to the case of Tara Wolf, a trans-identified male who punched Maria MacLachlan, a 60-year-old gender critical feminist, while she was giving a speech at Speaker's Corner in Hyde Park. For this, Wolf was fined just £150 ($181) (211). It's difficult to see why Scottow and Armstrong both got much bigger fines than Wolf, when Wolf had actually harmed someone but neither Scottow nor Armstrong did. This shows how transgender rights are put above the rights of others. It's frightening that the law forces people to accept the transgender dogma. Innocent remarks and comments are now criminalized. Yes, trans-identified people should be protected from violence and harassment, just as everyone else should be. But people still have the right to question transgenderism.

It's not just in the UK where people can be punished for their views on transgenderism. Some US states are now bringing in their own draconian transgender speech laws. Employers in New York can be fined up to $25,000 (£20,650) for misgendering trans-identified employees (193). And in California, a law makes it illegal for a healthcare worker to not use the preferred pronouns of a trans-identified patient (212). What's alarming about these laws is that it's easy to accidentally misgender a trans-identified person- especially if you've known them as their biological gender for a long time. Now, a person could be criminalized for a simple slip of the tongue.

No Right to Protest
Expressing a dissenting opinion about transgenderism is now not allowed either. Look at the case of the sticker protests in Oxford. To protest transgenderism, feminist groups placed stickers with the dictionary definition of women in Oxford city centre, along with other stickers with the phrase "women don't have penises". This was deemed to be a hate crime. In response to this, transgender activists then put up their own stickers, espousing the validity of transgender identities, with phrases such as "trans women are women" and "support trans people". Incidentally, these were not a crime (213). Putting up these stickers could be seen as vandalism, in which case police should have pursued both the feminists and the transgender rights activists. Tellingly, only the feminists were targeted by the police. But this isn't the only time the police have targeted feminists protesting transgenderism. In Liverpool, a billboard with the dictionary definition of the word 'woman' was also removed because it was considered to be a hate crime (214).

Why do the police spend so much time dealing with comments and stickers when people are dying? It's not as if the police don't have anything else to do. For instance, there is a knife crime epidemic in the UK, which is killing many young people, and injuring many more (215). Yet the police are not dealing with this or any other serious issues. In some instances, police forces are actually seeking out reports of hate crimes. In one case, South Yorkshire Police posted on Twitter asking the public to report "offensive or insulting comments" (216).

It's not only trans-sceptical people who are affected by this. Even the police themselves complain that they can't fight serious crime because they are busy dealing with these trivial matters (208). Chief Constable Sara Thornton, the chair of the National Police Chief's Council says police should focus their time and resources on serious crimes rather than hate incidents. She says that this is not the best use of police time and resources. She also points out that arrests have halved in the past 10 years (217), suggesting that the police are ignoring serious incidents and instead dealing with minor disputes. As a result of the police's heavy-handedness over transgender issues, every single member of the public is suffering.

"Transgender Rights are Human Rights"
When we think of human rights abuses, most people imagine someone living in some horrific dictatorship, being tortured for privately criticizing their leader. Or being imprisoned without trial. Or enduring some other kind of terrible suffering. But what we often don't think of is transgenderism. Yet human rights legislation is increasingly being used to 'protect' transgender people.

The Right to Have Children?
'Compulsory sterilization' evokes an image of people being forcibly dragged away and operated on against their will. But apparently, choosing to be sterilized as part of the legal sex reassignment process is also a form of compulsory sterilization. The United Nations and The European Court of Human Rights (218) classes this as a human

rights abuse (219). Amnesty International also campaigns on this issue (220). In Sweden, the European Court of Human Rights' ruling has been taken particularly seriously. The Swedish government have paid compensation of 225,000 SEK, (equivalent to £18,600 or $25,000) to trans-identified people who underwent sterilization so that they could legally change their sex (221). Approximately 800 people were eligible to be paid compensation (219). What makes this judgement particularly ludicrous is that cross-sex hormones generally cause infertility while the person is taking them. Therefore, the issue of having children is largely moot for any transgender person who has undergone any kind of medical transition (222).

It's not just sterilisation that's a human rights violation. Even when a trans-identified person has been voluntarily sterilized or made infertile by cross-sex hormones, it's their human right to have their gametes preserved so they can have children later in life. In the UK, the NHS was taken to court by the Equality and Human Rights Commission for not providing egg or sperm freezing for trans-identified people (223). The watchdog said that this was discrimination, because non-transgender people undergoing treatment for other disorders that cause infertility are offered this treatment. The difference is that a transgender person has the option to delay their medical transition until after they have had children, whereas other people undergoing medical treatment that causes infertility generally do not have this choice. Also, given that storing gametes and in-vitro fertilization is expensive and has a poor success rate, is it right to ask the NHS to provide this service for transgender people?

The Right to Evade Punishment
To protect their human rights, there have been cases where transgender people have completely escaped a prison sentence because of their gender identity. In the UK, Leila Le Fey, a trans-identified male, was originally sentenced to six months in prison for robbery after stealing wine from an off-license and threatening the shop manager with a claw hammer. An hour after the sentence was

passed, she returned to court. The judge who passed the sentence said that Le Fey could not be sent to a women's prison because she did not have a sex change certificate, but she was deemed too vulnerable to go to a male prison because she is trans-identified. The sentence was changed to a suspended sentence and rehabilitation order (224). It is very unfair that someone can avoid prison because they are trans-identified, even though they have committed a serious crime. It is another example of how trans-identified people's feelings are placed ahead of everyone else's rights and personal safety.

The Right to Serve in the Army

Transgender rights activists claim that banning transsexual people from serving in the army is a violation of their human rights. Many organizations, including the American Civil Liberties Union, say that transsexual people have the right to join the army (225).

From a practical perspective, it's difficult to see how a person who has undergone medical transition can serve in the army and maintain their medical transition. They would need a regular supply of cross-sex hormones, dilators for trans-identified males who have undergone sex reassignment surgery and possibly treatments for any complications arising from the surgery or hormone treatments. These are difficult to arrange in a warzone. Shupe (226) (who detransitioned two years after writing this article) points out that it would be difficult to provide the healthcare typically given to trans-identified people while they are serving. He also notes that hormones and surgeries can have side effects which require specialized medical care, which could be difficult to obtain in a warzone, jeopardizing the person's safety.

Yes, there are many countries that do allow transsexual people to serve in the military, including the UK (227). Although it's rather difficult to understand how or why this is allowed. The British Army won't let many people with medical conditions join. According to the British Army's website, a person may not be able to join if they need regular medication for any medical condition. Even people with relatively manageable medical conditions, such as food allergies and eczema, may not be allowed to serve (228). The website also warns that it would be difficult to obtain medication in many places where the army is deployed. Given that many transgender people say they are so distressed by not having their gender affirmed that they become suicidal, how would they cope if they could not have their hormones or other medical supplies in the army? Also, most transsexual people have their treatment monitored by specialists from gender identity clinics. Wouldn't this be impossible to provide in the army? And couldn't this put the transsexual person's health in danger? It's not prejudice that is the reason trans-identified people can't serve; there are very good reasons for not allowing transsexual people to join the army.

Allowing transsexual people to serve in the army has worrying implications. The worthiness of war aside, having a transsexual soldier who can't fight because they are unable to access their hormones or because of health issues relating to their sex change treatment will stop a unit working as effectively as it should. This will ultimately compromise the army's ability to fight. If a transsexual person suffers serious complications (for instance, an infection or a blood clot), it may not be possible for them to receive adequate medical care. They could suffer serious harms from not receiving rapid treatment, or even die.

The way that transgenderism has taken over policy is terrifying. It is to the detriment of women, and of wider society. For everyone, there are higher healthcare costs and compromised national security. Furthermore, the attitude towards transgender offenders, and the way that so-called 'hate speech' is prioritized over more serious crimes puts society in danger. As well, by lumping transgenderism in with human rights, this ultimately weakens the case for human rights and detracts more serious human rights violations.

7. The Left and Transgenderism

To understand why transgenderism has become such an enormous issue in policymaking, it's important to understand how transgenderism has influenced political discourse. Across the globe, transgenderism has become a big issue in politics, especially in left-wing politics. The political agenda is increasingly being reshaped to fit the needs of the transgender community.

Transgenderism is wonderful. Transgender people are incredibly brave. We're all so proud of transgender people. Everyone who doesn't accept transgenderism is selfish, bigoted and cruel. And everyone who is not transgender needs to do more to help transgender people. Or at least that's what the liberal press tells us. Every day, liberal news sites like *Indy100, Buzzfeed* and *Huffington Post* have articles celebrating someone who is transgender, advising how to be a better transgender ally or reporting of some supposed bigotry against transgender people. Left-wing public figures (such as Laurie Penny and Jack Monroe) and entertainers (for example, Sam Smith and Mylie Cyrus), have all began declaring themselves to be non-binary. If you're a left-winger today, you can't go for very long without hearing about transgenderism.

So why has the left become so entranced by transgenderism? Left-wingers have always been focused on helping oppressed people. And transgender people are frequently described as the most oppressed people in society. As well as the high suicide rates for transgender people, this concern is partly spurred on by the claims that transgender people are extremely vulnerable to abuse. There is an annual Transgender Day of Remembrance, held on the 20th November, to commemorate transgender murder victims, along with transgender people who died by suicide. But are transgender people as vulnerable as we a led to believe? Transgender rights organizations and activists push many questionable statistics about the dangers faced by transgender people. For instance, there is a widely circulated claim that one in 12 transgender people are murdered, rising to one in eight for non-white transgender people. Even though the statistic comes from the USA, it has been posted on social media by Cliff Goodwin (229), a high-ranking British police officer. This murder rate was estimated 15 years ago by Kay Brown, a transgender rights activist (230). However, evidence shows that this estimate is wildly inaccurate. In the UK, a transgender person is actually half as likely to be murdered as a non-transgender person (231). While In the USA, the transgender murder rate is a quarter of that for the general population (232). Furthermore, in the USA, transgender people are no more likely to be a victim of a violent crime than a non-transgender person (233). Therefore, the claim that transgender people are extremely vulnerable to violence is a myth.

A failing of the left is that we put our instinctive urge to help the oppressed before the facts. We want to be kind and don't always look at the deeper issues or question what we are being told, even when we have an inkling that something isn't quite right. This stops the left asking uncomfortable questions about issues and rethinking their initial instincts.

The New Civil Rights Frontier?
According to Helen Lewis (234), transgender rights are seen as next big civil rights issue by left-wingers. But there are several key differences between transgender rights and previous civil rights movements that mean it should not be considered a civil rights issue.

The biggest issue is that transgender rights undermine women's rights. Transgender people are encroaching on the category of 'woman'. Now that women have greater rights and greater equality, trans-identified males are happy to be identified as women. The trouble is, women are oppressed because of their sex, not their gender identity. Rea (148) points out that women were not allowed to vote in elections because they were biologically female, not because they identified as female. They couldn't simply identify as male and get the vote. The same is true of many other issues that affect women.

This matters because in every other civil rights movements, the oppressed group was taking power from their oppressor. In every other civil rights struggle, there was the privileged group (men, white people, heterosexual people, nondisabled people) and the less privileged group (women, ethnic minorities, homosexual people, disabled people). When women gained equal rights in the eyes of the law (such as when they were given the vote or equal pay) men lost out. But because men are the privileged group, losing some of their privileges has served for the good of society. There was no good reason for women to be not allowed to vote or to be paid less than men for an identical job. The same was true of when other oppressed groups gained rights- privileges have been redistributed from the more advantaged group to the less advantaged group. But with transgenderism, the privileged group they seek to gain power from is 'cisgender' women, who themselves are oppressed by men, and to some extent, from lesbian and gay people, who are oppressed by straight people. This is problematic because it takes hard-earned rights away from other groups.

In addition, transgenderism is a relatively new phenomenon. Whereas all the other minorities involved in previous civil rights movements have been around for all of human history, the concept of transgenderism only developed in the early to mid-20th century (15). Gender Dysphoria may have existed for many years, but the notion that a person can change sex only came about recently. Transsexual surgery and cross-sex hormone treatments have only come about in the past 100 years, and the concept of non-binary genders only really started in the 21st century. It's difficult to see how something that has only come into existence relatively recently needs so much effort to be accommodated. For those reasons, transgenderism is not the latest civil rights issue.

British Politics
In the UK, transgenderism has become a major political issue that has gained increasing prominence in political organizations and events.

In the 2019 General Election, Labour said that if they won, they would legally recognize non-binary genders and allow people to legally self-define their gender. However, they also promised to protect sex-based rights (235). The Liberal Democrats said much the same as Labour, but they did not make the same promise on safeguarding woman's rights (236) (The Liberal Democrats have not won a general election since before the second world war and have far fewer MPs than Labour or the Conservatives, so they have no realistic chance of winning. However, they have been part of pacts and coalitions when no party has an overall majority.) On the other hand, the Conservatives, the UK's other main political party, seemingly didn't have to do anything for transgender rights. They won the election with a landslide anyway.

The focus on transgender rights isn't why Labour lost the 2019 election, but it probably didn't help. The former British prime minister, Tony Blair, who was the last Labour leader to win a general election, recently said that Labour won't win the next election if it becomes a transgender rights group, pointing out that transgender issues are not of much interest to the typical voter (237). By focusing on transgender issues, Labour is spending less time connecting with voters on issues that matter to them. Very few people are directly affected by transgender issues, but most people are affected by issues like the economy, education or healthcare. Those are the issues that win elections.

But it didn't end there. In the 2020 Labour leadership election, the party leadership candidates were asked by the campaign group Labour for Trans to sign a transgender rights pledge card. These pledge cards contained vows to expel 'transphobic' party members and to fight against certain trans-sceptical women's rights groups, such as Woman's Place UK and LGB Alliance. Woman's Place UK campaigns for women's rights and protection of women-only spaces (238), while the LGB Alliance aims to renew the LGBT movement's focus on sexual orientation as opposed to transgender issues (239). Two of the three candidates, Rebecca Long-Baily and Lisa Nandy, signed the pledge card (240).

As always, it's women who are hit worse by this. Trade unionist Mark Serwotka, the partner of Ruth Serwotka who runs Woman's Place UK, describes how transgenderism is driving women away from the Labour party. He says it is mostly women who are targeted for being transphobic, when often all they have done is try and protect their sex-based rights. Furthermore, he says that women are regularly being harassed by other Labour activists (241). This is yet another example of how transgenderism hurts women. Transgender rights must take precedent over women's rights, and women are forced to accept it or leave the party.

Fortunately, the pledge did not go down well with many Labour members. The hashtag #expelme started trending on Twitter in protest of the move, where people posted that their trans-sceptical views and challenged Labour to force them to leave the party for being transphobic (242). Kier Starmer, the only male candidate, did not signed the pledge. He won the leadership election, in a bittersweet victory for women's rights. The way that the party members responded shows how strongly people feel about being forced to accept transgenderism. Unfortunately, the party's focus on transgenderism has created serious disharmony with the party, which may carry on damaging Labour's chances of winning the next general election.

US Politics
Transgenderism has impacted on US politics too. The Democrats have been very supportive of transgenderism. Biden has described transgenderism as "the civil rights issue of our time" (243). During the primaries, many of the other candidates expressed similar

attitudes. Prior to leaving the race for the Democratic presidential nominee in the 2020 election, Elizabeth Warren said that if she became president, Jacob Lemay, a nine-year-old trans-identified child, would help her to select the secretary of state for education (244). As well, Warren pledged to make it simpler for transgender people to change their sex on legal documents (245). Other candidates went even further; Michael Bloomberg promised federally-funded sex reassignment surgery and cross-sex hormones. Bloomberg also said that trans-identified males would have the right to stay in women's shelters and that police officers and healthcare professionals would have to undergo implicit bias training to counter transphobia (246).

The Terrifying Transgender Rights Activists

Despite being a very small -albeit vocal- minority, transgender rights activists yield a lot of power. The way that these activists behave is unbelievable. What's even more shocking is that misguided woke left-wingers happily go along with transgender rights activists and turn a blind eye to anything bad they do. These activists- and the wokesters who defend them- are the reason why it is so difficult to speak out against transgenderism. There is no room for dissenting voices with these woke left-wingers. In their view, doing something bad to people who do not support transgenderism is absolutely fine.

Violence

One of the biggest tools used by transgender rights activists is violence. When Tara Wolf attacked Maria MacLachlan, instead of denouncing the violence, multiple trans-identified people's groups came and supported the attack (247). One trans-rights group, Action Trans Health Edinburgh posted a series of Tweets justifying the use of violence. The Tweets equated punching a 'TERF' to punching a Nazi and one tweet stated that "we must be radically and transformatively [sic] violent". That this attack happened in the first place is terrible, but for trans-identified people's rights groups to condone violence is outrageous.

Transgender activists also often threaten violence. Posters saying "There are girls with dicks, guys with vaginas and transphobes without teeth" have begun to appear in cities around the world (248). Other messages, including graffiti calling for TERFs to be burned at the stake, have also been displayed in public (248). Bear in mind that no 'TERFs' are routinely threatening to hurt trans-identified people. Simon Fanshawe, the co-founder of the gay rights group, Stonewall has said "I have never seen a feminist placard that says, 'Death to trans people' but I have seen many placards that say, 'Death to Terfs' or 'Punch a Terf'" (249). Gender critical feminists, on the other hand, are regularly being threatened with violence and being physically attacked.

Even if transgender rights activists had a point, two wrongs don't make a right. The world is a complex place and there are multiple perspectives on transgenderism -and many other issues. Nobody will agree with anyone all the time. It's also interesting that no other minority group act in the same way as transgender rights activists do. For example, you don't see people posting "punch racists" on social media or gay rights organizations endorsing violence against homophobes.

Emotional Blackmail
Transgender people will often say people who disagree with them are trying to kill them by encouraging them to kill themselves. It's unclear if they genuinely feel this way or are simply saying this to try and make people feel guilty. Trans-identified people will often threaten suicide to manipulate people. The feminist academic and campaigner Louise Moody was sent a photograph of a transgender rights activist holding a large pile of tablets. The picture was accompanied by a caption saying, "let the world know that this was [Caroline] Farrow and Moody and 'Belinda'". Moody told this activist to contact The Samaritans, a British suicide prevention charity. However, several other activists posted comments that Moody would be responsible for the activist's death if she killed

herself (250). Given this activist is still regularly posting on social media, presumably she did not follow through with her threat.

Why did the activist tell Moody and others she was suicidal? Most people who are suicidal will reach out to a sympathetic friend or family member, not a stranger who they have been arguing with or an activist who they have an ideological opposition to. On the other hand, it might be hard to believe, but some people with personality disorders actually *do* think that if someone upsets them, it is because that person wants them to kill themselves. They also often will harm themselves to try and make people feel guilty. Of course, the only person responsible for a person's suicide is the person themselves. The problem isn't that mentally ill people threaten to kill themselves because people disagree with them. After all, this is part of their illness. The problem is that other activists happily play along with the emotional blackmail.

Smears
Another tactic used by transgender rights activists is smearing others. Natacha Kennedy (who also uses the name Mark Hellen and has written papers using both of these names at the same time), a trans-identified male lecturer at Goldsmiths, University of London, smeared other academics (251). She made a Facebook group called Trans Rights UK, which featured a list of academics and departments with staff who questioned transgenderism and were 'unsafe' for trans-identified students. Members of the group were encouraged to report these academics for hate crime, with the intention of getting them dismissed from their jobs. Tellingly, all of the academics featured on the list were women.

Litigation
Litigation has become another one of the tools used by the transgender rights activists. Sadly, threatening to sue is a good way of silencing critics. Litigation can get very expensive. Even if you don't lose, you would have to pay for a solicitor to defend the case.

For that reason, most people cave in to the demands of the person bringing the case, even if the case is very weak.

Canadian transgender activist Jessica Yaniv is perhaps the most notorious user of litigation as a campaign tactic. In 2018, Yaniv took five female home beauticians to court for human rights violations for refusing to wax her genitals. Yaniv has not undergone sex reassignment surgery, and still has male genitalia (252). None of the beauticians were trained in waxing male genitals and they argued that it could be dangerous if they attempted to do so. Some of the beauticians also said that they felt uncomfortable with touching male genitals. Others cited religious objections to performing this type of waxing. Yaniv was suing each beautician for up to CA$15,000 ($10630 US dollars or £8800 each). Fortunately, the beauticians won their case and the judge ruled that Yaniv was acting inappropriately in filing the case. Yaniv was ordered to pay all the defendants CA$2000 (£1170 or $1400) each.

Yaniv isn't the only trans-identified person to use litigation against trans-sceptical people. If you live in the UK and you publicly question the transgender narrative, it won't be long until you'll be getting a writ from Stephanie Hayden. Hayden has attempted to sue many people and organizations for transphobia. Mumsnet, Graham Lineham, Kate Scottow, (253) Caroline Farrow, Louise Moody and historian Helena Wojtczak (254) are just some of the many people who have had a case brought against them by Hayden. Many of these cases have either been withdrawn or struck out, but even so, these people have experienced a lot of needless stress.

"You must have sex with me": The cotton ceiling
Transgender rights activists also try to police people sex lives. The phrase 'cotton ceiling' is a term coined for when lesbian women will accept trans-identified males as women in most areas of life, but won't have sex with them (255). It is a play on the term "glass ceiling", with cotton referring to underwear (255). As always, it's women- specifically lesbians- who are to blame for this. After all,

why is there no similar term for heterosexual men who refuse to have sex with trans-identified males? Or gay men who refuse to have sex with trans-identified females? Men are free to choose who they have sex with, but women must learn to accept trans-identified people as romantic and sexual partners. Of course, most people understand that you cannot simply demand that someone find you attractive and want to have sex with you. But not trans-identified people.

Apparently, people must find a way to change their genital preferences for the good of transgender people. In a study conducted into how willing members of the general population would be to date trans-identified people, it was found that the vast majority of people were unwilling to date trans-identified people (256). Worryingly, the last line of the abstract of this study is: "The results are discussed within the context of the implications for trans persons seeking romantic relationships and the pervasiveness of cisgenderism and transmisogyny". The implication seems to be if you don't want to date a trans-identified person, you're a bigot. Interestingly, most transgender people report they are not attracted to other transgender people. In a different survey of trans-identified people, which was undertaken by the University of Hawaii, as part of a larger study, only five percent of participants reported an attraction to transsexual or non-binary people (257). If transgender people aren't attracted to other transgender people, why do they expect non-transgender people to find transgender people attractive?

As the key defining characteristic of sex, genitals are the starkest reminder that a transgender person is not the sex that they identify with. It is difficult to change genitals, and so the closest thing to making them go away is to pretend they don't matter. That people won't have sex with a transgender person because of their genitals makes them feel invalidated. Conversely, a person having sex with them is validating their belief that they are the gender they identify as (i.e. a lesbian woman having sex with a lesbian trans-identified male is showing the trans-identified male that she is seen as a real woman). The problem is, for most non-transgender people, genitals matter a lot in a sexual relationship. It is unreasonable to expect people to pretend otherwise.

Transgender Rights Activists Vs Women

Women's rights are under threat. And women must fight for them. But transgender activists are getting in the way by insisting that they are represented. According to transgender rights activists, women's rights are too focus on…women. The trouble is, being a woman isn't some fun club that mean old 'cis-women' won't let trans-identified people join. We have real issues that we need to fight.

Many transgender rights campaigners are unhappy with how much feminism focuses on women's genitalia. Solis (258) criticizes the Women's March events for the placards that had slogans that, as one interviewee says "equate womanhood with having a vagina". But one of the biggest controversies was the wearing of pussyhats. Pussyhats are pink knitted hats that resemble a vulva, and were worn at feminist events in protest of Trump's infamous "grab 'em by the pussy" comment. But according to transgender-rights activists, these hats are oppressive to trans-identified males who don't have a vulva because they are "reproductive-system focused", and could alienate trans-identified people (259). However, feminism often excludes transgender women because sexism excludes transgender women. Trump didn't say "grab 'em by the dick". To be grabbed by the pussy, you have to have a pussy. And that excludes transgender women.

Furthermore, Ferguson (260) says that feminist activists are often guilty of failing to include trans-identified people. For instance, referring to "women's reproductive rights" excludes trans-identified people, because "it assumes that the only people who need abortions are women". In another case, Irish transgender activists campaigning for the legalization of abortion from the group, Trans Voices for Repeal have demanded that the main campaign body, Together for Yes, issue an apology for failing to include transgender people in their campaign materials. Trans Voices for Repeal claim that this exclusion has had an adverse impact on transgender people's mental health (261). But only women *do* have abortions. It might be hard for trans-identified females to hear that they are female, but people who are biologically male never need abortions. And as testosterone given as part of the sex reassignment process usually causes infertility, it can be assumed that the cases where a transgender man has experienced an unintentional pregnancy must be very rare.

Another thing that these activists overlook is that being a feminist activist is optional. A lot of women give up their own time and money to fight for feminist causes. It can be hard work. But they do it because they believe in the cause. It's frustrating to be told the thing you're doing as an act of altruism isn't good enough. And that's precisely what these transgender activists are doing. All this will do is turn women off from campaigning.

I Wish my Name Were Donald Trump Jr.
Remember how Trump Jr. said he wishes his name were Hunter Biden (the son of Joe Biden) so he could use his name to make millions of dollars? Well, I wish my name was Donald Trump Jr. Then I'd be able to tell it as it is about transgenderism without the fear of a serious backlash.

When Trump Jr. wrote a best-selling book with a chapter on transgenderism, nobody seemed particularly outraged. Although there was one article that called Trump Jr. a TERF (262). Given the RF in TERF stands for radical feminist, this makes no sense. Trump Jr. is not a radical feminist (or any other kind of feminist for that matter). He is a conservative who is criticizing transgenderism from the conservative view on gender. What's interesting is that there is no phrase that is the equivalent of TERF for conservatives. Even though there are more trans-sceptical conservatives than there are gender critical feminists.

So why is it that women who speak out against transgenderism are demonized so much more than men who say similar things? There are two reasons. The first is plain old misogyny. The second is that trans-identified people seem to find being excluded from the category of womanhood more hurtful than anything any men do or say about transgenderism. The truth is transgenderism is only concerned with women's perception of trans-identified people. Men aren't required to accept trans-identified people. Only women are. Trans-identified males seem more hurt at being told they are not real women by women than they do by being told the same thing by men. You could argue that trans-identified males are understandably upset by being rejected by the people who should be their sisters. But what about trans-identified females? Trans-identified females are still seen as women and are happy to be considered as such. The website *Everyday Feminism* covers issues relating to trans-identified females and publishes articles written by them, such as an article on transmen and periods (263), an article on pregnancy in transmen (264) and a video on transmen and masculinity (265). It's far less common to hear people complain about trans-identified females being excluded from male spaces, or even for anyone to say "trans men are men". So are transmen not men after all? Why else would transmen's issues be covered on a feminist website? Because only women have to accept trans-identified people as women, a man saying "you are not a real woman" is a bigger problem for trans-identified people -both males and females- than having a woman say the same thing. If anything proves that transgenderism is really about keeping women down, it's the way that men who speak out about transgenderism are treated compared to women who say the same things.

The way that transgenderism has taken over political campaigning has serious implications for the rest of us. Traditional left-wing issues, like poverty and lack of access to healthcare, are being overlooked. World issues aren't on the agenda anymore either. As one woman fights for the right to have her vulva turned into a penis, another woman somewhere in the world is fighting not to be a victim of female genital mutilation. While a student fights to be called 'ze' at university, another bright young person misses out completely on the chance to go to university because of the costs and social pressure from their family. As a trans-identified male fights for lesbians to have sex with her even though she has a penis, a person in Saudi Arabia is sentenced to death for being gay. When you look at it this way, it's hard to believe that so much time is spent fighting for transgender rights, and not on more deserving issues.

8. Trans Inclusionary, Woman Exclusionary- Taking Over Women's Spaces and Rights

Women's services and spaces are increasingly being taken over by transgender people. As the *Guardian* journalist Suzanne Moore points out, it's only ever women's rights that are threatened by transgenderism. Men's spaces and rights hardly ever have to be compromised (266).

Trans-Identified Males in Women's Jobs
It's time for us women to recognize our cis privilege and let men who identify as women or non-binary into our spaces. Forget the millions of years of being oppressed by men; men who identify as women (or non-binary) need our help!

Trans-identified males are increasingly taking jobs and other roles reserved for women. In the UK, the Labour Party's Rochester and Strood branch women's officer, Lily Madigan is a trans-identified male (267). Madigan is also the woman's officer for Labour Students (268). There are many reasons having a trans-identified male in these roles is a problem. Firstly, women are under-represented in politics, so Madigan is taking the position that a woman should have been doing. In addition, Madigan won't have the same experiences as a woman. Because she is not biologically female, she won't menstruate, she can't get pregnant, and she won't be using women's health services (such as cervical and breast cancer screenings). She can't represent the local constituents or students who do experience these issues in the same way that a woman can. She also won't have experienced female socialization when growing up. By having a trans-identified male being the woman's officer, the Labour Rochester and Strood branch and Labour Students are letting down their female members. But this isn't the only time when Labour have let trans-identified males be counted as women. Labour has also said that anyone who self-identifies as a woman is allowed to be on all-woman shortlists to be candidates for MPs or local councillors (269).

It's not just in politics where women are being forced aside by trans-identified people. It's happening in business too. Philip Bunce, the director of Credit Suisse, who is a cross-dresser, was listed in the Financial Times Top 100 Businesswomen 2018 (270). A woman was pushed off the list to accommodate Bunce. Qualms about capitalism aside, women should not be pushed aside for men. As with politics, women are underrepresented in business. The aim of the list is to inspire women into going into business, but the chance to showcase a woman was taken by a man. It seems like a trivial thing, but it's part of a bigger trend of women being overshadowed by trans-identified males. Another time when this happened was when Caitlyn Jenner won *Glamor Magazine's* Woman of the Year award (271). Admittedly, women don't need much encouragement to get involved with celebrity culture, but it's still another time when a woman has lost out on an award because of a trans-identified male.

Why are trans-identified males in women's positions such a problem? After all, trans-identified people face prejudice, so why not let them be counted as women? The trouble is, women have their own issues to contend with, that trans-identified males don't face. The first way that women are disadvantaged is through reproduction. If a woman has a baby, she will need time away from work. She might have to go on maternity leave early in the pregnancy if there are health risks to her or the baby. The birth itself can be physically demanding, and a mother needs time to recover, especially if there were complications or she needed a caesarean. She may need several months or even a year for maternity leave. A man will have more time to work his way up the career ladder, so a woman will lose out on the opportunity for promotions. This will put her at a disadvantage at work, especially if she has multiple children and needs time off with each of them.

Additionally, women's socialisation also puts women at a disadvantage. Girls are taught to be meek and submissive. Henderson describes how girls are taught to be 'good', meaning compliant and eager to please adults (272). While this is great in childhood, the problem is, this doesn't work well in adulthood. It results in women who lack assertiveness. In addition, a girl who demonstrates strong leadership will often be referred to as 'bossy'. Adults around her will often say "Don't be so bossy" or "she's such a bossy boots". On the other hand, a parent or teacher will often describe a girl as "nice and quiet" if she is very shy, effectively praising her for lacking confidence. This makes it more difficult for women to stand up for themselves and to get into leadership roles as adults. And those two reasons are why we have positive discrimination for women; it helps women to overcome both the social and biological disadvantages that come from being a woman.

Trans-Identified Males in Woman's Spaces

More and more often, trans-identified males are using women's spaces and services.

Healthcare

Women's health services are starting to turn into transgender health services. Planned Parenthood, a US government-funded healthcare organization that originally specialized in providing birth control**Error! Bookmark not defined.**, is now providing cross-sex hormones for transgender people in 17 US states (273). This has nothing to do with contraception, so there is no reason for the organization to be providing this service. Doing this takes time and resources away from people in need of birth control- an issue which disproportionately affects women.

In the UK, trans-identified women are being placed in women's wards in NHS hospitals. In one case, a woman with Bipolar Disorder was placed in a women's psychiatric ward with a trans-identified male. At the time, she was suffering from a delusional belief that all men were trying to kill her, and she was greatly distressed by being in the same room as the trans-identified male. She reported her concerns to staff, but nothing was done. However, staff did record the incident in her notes, which she says made her feel like a "transphobic bigot" (274).

Transgender healthcare staff are also an issue. In today's woke climate, transgender women are real women, so when a woman wants to see a female healthcare worker, having a trans-identified male see to her is fine. In one case in the UK, a woman went to her doctor's surgery to have a cervical smear test. A member of staff with a male appearance entered the room to do the test. The patient had asked for a woman to do the test and told the member of staff this. The member of staff replied that they were transgender and identified as female. Understandably, the patient was not satisfied with this and refused to have the test performed by the trans-identified male (275).

Toilet Wars
Trans-identified people are increasingly demanding the right to use their preferred gender toilets. Transgender rights activist claim that this has no impact on women's safety. Paris Lees (276), a trans-identified male and transgender rights activist, describes concerns around transgender people using their preferred toilet as "imagined fears". Given that there have been multiple cases where women and girls have been sexually assaulted in toilets by trans-identified males or males pretending to be female, people are right to be concerned. There was an incident where a trans-identified male in Scotland sexually assaulted a 10-year-old girl in a supermarket toilet, and took pictures of a different girl at another supermarket while she was using the toilet (277). While in the US state of Virginia, a man in drag filmed multiple women in a toilet in a shopping centre. And in California, another man dressed as a woman was found guilty of secretly filming women in a department store's toilets (278).

As well as this, to satisfy transgender people, gender-neutral toilets - also known as all-gender toilets- are replacing men's and women's toilets in many buildings. These aren't the single-occupancy toilets you often find in small cafes and restaurants where there isn't enough space for separate men's and women's toilets. They are toilets with multiple cubicles for use by both men and women. Sometimes, only the woman's toilet is used as a gender-neutral toilet. In a branch of KFC in the UK, the women's toilet was changed to a gender-neutral toilet while the men's toilet remained exclusively for men (279). As with other toilets, trans-identified people claim that these toilets pose no danger to women (276). This is not true; there have been multiple cases where women using gender-neutral toilets have been attacked by men. A school in Wisconsin closed its gender-neutral toilets after a female student was sexually assaulted by a male student (280). And at the University of Toronto, two male students filmed female students while showering in a gender-neutral bathroom (278). Aside from the risk of attack, some people also feel insecure about using a gender-neutral toilet, especially children. A Scottish mother reported that her daughter and her friends felt uncomfortable using the gender-neutral toilets at her school, where most of the toilets had been made gender-neutral (281). This discomfort is understandable. Girls and boys both need privacy in the toilet, especially during puberty, where many children are coming to terms with changes in their bodies.

Changing Rooms
A similar trend is also occurring in changing rooms in clothing shops and leisure centres, with people being allowed to use the changing room that matches their gender identity. According to feminist campaigner Jean Hachette, the British retailer Marks and Spencer allowed a man to try on bras in the women's changing room, while a 15-year-old girl was waiting with her mother to have a bra fitting. When Marks and Spencer was challenged over this, they said that they are an inclusive retailer and that customers are permitted to use whichever changing room they prefer (282). Another large retailer, John Lewis, have also said that customers are free to use whichever changing room they feel most comfortable using (283).

But some retailers are going even further. Many retailers are converting their existing changing rooms into gender-neutral facilities. UK clothes shop, Topshop made their changing rooms gender-neutral after Travis Alabanza, a 'trans feminine' person, was not allowed to try on clothing in a woman's changing room (284). Photographs of Alabanza show that they have a relatively masculine appearance- it would be unlikely that at first glance, a person would know Alabanza's gender identity. And Topshop aren't the only retailer making their changing rooms gender-neutral. Primark, another UK clothing retailer, have built gender-neutral changing rooms instead of sex-segregated changing rooms in two of their shops (285).

This is a worrying trend that puts women at risk. Research has found that most sexual assaults at public swimming pools take place in unisex changing rooms (286). It's not difficult to imagine this will happen in other unisex changing rooms. Even if transgender people are no more likely to sexually assault women than other women, non-transgender men in changing rooms still pose a risk to women.

Prison
In many countries, trans-identified males who have been given a custodial sentence are now being placed in women's prisons. While this validates their gender identity, it puts women prisoners at risk.

There are multiple cases where trans-identified prisoners in women's prisons have committed sexual violence against other prisoners. For instance, in the UK, Karen White, a trans-identified male with a history of sex offences who still had a penis, sexually assaulted two women prisoners while she was held in New Hall Prison in Wakefield, West Yorkshire (287). In the USA, there was a case where a trans-identified male prisoner was accused of raping an inmate in an Illinois women's prison. The alleged victim says she was later coerced into retracting her complaint when she reported the rape (288). These cases clearly illustrate that putting trans-identified males in women's prison puts women in danger. The safety of women prisoners needs to be put ahead of the feelings of trans-identified people.

Shelters
Organizations for abused women are also being forced into allowing trans-identified males to use their services. Vancouver Rape Relief, a women's refuge, was defunded by the city because it does not allow trans-identified males to stay (289). Vancouver Rape Relief has a good reason for this policy. There have been men who've claimed to be transgender to gain access to women's-only shelters and attacked women. Christopher Hambrook, from Quebec, sexually assaulted two women while staying in two separate shelters. He posed as a transgender woman named Jessica to gain entry to the shelters. He had a long history of committing sexual assaults and had been in prison before for this (290). Imagine how terrible it must feel to have fled domestic abuse or have been made homeless, then to have been sexually assaulted in the place you went to for safety. This is yet another example of women's safety being compromised for transgender people.

Education
Women's colleges and universities are also letting trans-identified male students join. In the USA, Mount Holyoke College now allows any student who identifies as female or non-binary to join, along with any student who was born female who now identifies as male (291). Spelman College, Mills College and many other women's colleges also now admit trans-identified males. While in the UK, Murray Edwards College, a woman's-only constituent college at the University of Cambridge, has changed their admission policies so that any student who identifies as female can be admitted. In the past, only students who had either been born female or had a gender change certificate could join the college (292).

Sport
An extension of the denial of the existence of biological males is the inclusion of trans-identified males in women's sport. Fox Fallon, Rachel Mckinnon (also known as Veronica Ivy), Hannah Mouncey, Laurel Hubbard are all just some of the many athletes are trans-identified males and have participated in professional competitions

against women, often winning (293). In some cases, trans-identified athletes can even be a danger to other competitors. Fallon, an American trans-identified male Mixed Martial Arts (MMA) fighter, competes against female opponents. On one occasion, she broke her opponent's skull during a fight (294). As someone who is biologically male, Fallon is much stronger than any female opponent, and so can do much more damage.

It's not just professional athletics that's being taken over by trans-identified males. At the Connecticut's girl's high school track meet, two trans-identified male sprinters competed in one race. They came in first and second place (295). The *Schools in Transition* guidelines also recommends that trans-identified students compete as their preferred gender, claiming sex variations in sporting ability are a myth (166).

In all these cases, a woman has lost the chance to compete. Athletes work hard to get to competing at national and international level, but women athletes are now losing out to trans-identified males. Furthermore, trans-identified males have an unfair advantage over women. Sporting organizations claim that after a trans-identified male athlete's testosterone has fallen below a certain threshold, their performance is not advantaged by their sex (296). But the current testosterone limit of 10 nmol/L for trans-identified athletes is much higher than the average testosterone levels of 0.1 to 3.08 nmol/L for women elite athletes. In testimony from the International Association for Athletics Federations, two endocrinologists testified that it was impossible for a healthy woman to have a testosterone level of 10 nmol/L (73). So, trans-identified male athletes still have much higher testosterone levels than most female athletes. As well, studies have found that testosterone suppression in trans-identified athletes does not significantly reduce muscle strength, even after it has been used for many years (297). This shows that the male physical advantage cannot be eliminated simply by reducing testosterone levels.

In addition, men have other advantages besides testosterone. Men have a more efficient respiratory system than women; even new-born baby boys have bigger lungs than new-born baby girls (298). Furthermore, men also naturally carry approximately 10% less body fat than women (299). Men also have longer legs, which helps them to run faster. Conversely, women's wider hips make them slower runners because the quadriceps have to curve around the hips, making the muscles less efficient than men's muscles (300). All of these things put trans-identified males at an advantage over females, most of which cannot be fixed by reducing testosterone levels.

There are also many other aspects of the female body that impede athletic performance. Breasts interfere with many forms of exercise. They add extra weight, which is a disadvantage in many sports. In some sports such as golf and archery, breasts physically get in the way of the movements required for these sports (301). Breasts also bounce during exercise, which after a while can be painful. They chafe and they can cause back and neck pain (302). But transwomen don't have this issue. If you look at the cyclist Veronica Ivy, you'll notice she has virtually no breasts. Her breasts appear to be smaller than a typical A-cup bra size. It is rare to see an adult woman with such small breasts. Thus, her performance is not affected by this.

In addition, women also have to deal with menstruation. Periods can be rough. Many women have physical symptoms such as period pain, nausea and diarrhoea. Furthermore, as many as one in 10 women develop iron deficiency Anaemia because of the blood loss from menstruation (303). Anaemia causes symptoms such as fatigue and malaise. For an athlete who regularly pushes their body to the limit and needs to be in perfect physical condition, losing blood every month is going to be detrimental to her performance. As well, pads and tampons can cause chafing. While this isn't a huge issue, during a competition, athletes need everything to be perfect. Even the smallest thing can cost them victory.

Another issue that trans-identified males don't have to deal with is pregnancy and childbirth. Pregnancy and giving birth can hinder a woman's progress in sports. Women athletes who have a baby would have to have time away from training toward the end of the pregnancy and after the baby is born to recover from the birth. If they didn't, they could harm the baby or themselves. But while they're not training, their bodies would get out of condition, so they would need to train back up to the level they were at before they gave birth. All of these things mean women are at a disadvantage compared to men.

So how big is the advantage that men have over women? A website called Boys vs Women (304) compares the performance of women at the 2016 Olympics with high-school aged boy's performances in track and field and swimming events (the 2016 High School Boys New Balance Nationals Outdoor Finalists for track and field events and the 2016 High School Boys Speedo Junior National Championships Finalists for swimming). Bear in mind that this compares the best boys in the USA with the best women in the world. Out of the 87 events compared, the boys would have won 81 medals and women won just six. In many cases, no women performed better than any boys. Presumably, if women's and men's performances were compared, the women would not have won any medals at all. It just goes to show how much of an advantage male athletes have over female athletes.

Surprisingly, even Donald Trump Jr. (who isn't generally a big advocate for women's rights) has joined the condemnation of trans-identified males participating in women's sport. Trump Jr. (305) points out there aren't any high-profile trans-identified female athletes fighting to compete as men, presumably because they would not have a realistic chance of winning. Since Trump's book was published, the closest any trans-identified female has come to competing in the Olympics was Chris Mosier, a trans-identified female racewalker who was selected for Team USA and participated in a trial to compete in the Olympics. However, he did not finish the race due to an injury (306). It's funny how being born male does not put trans-identified males at an advantage over women because they have low testosterone, but trans-identified females can't reach the same level of fitness and strength as men, even though they take testosterone. There are also no trans-identified males fighting to take part in sports where women have an advantage. Take gymnastics for instance. The best gymnasts are usually short, slim women who are very graceful and agile. Why are there no trans-identified males fighting to be gymnasts? Because trans-identified males are generally taller and less agile than women, so they are unlikely to win in competitions.

Another argument that transgender rights activists make is that the chance for trans-identified males to participate in sports is more important than fairness in sport. According to Jonathan Liew (307), chief sports writer for *The Independent*, it doesn't matter that women would be pushed out of sport. He said:

> *"Let's say the floodgates do open. Let's say transgender athletes pour into women's sport, and let's say, despite the flimsy and poorly-understood relationship between testosterone and elite performance, they dominate everything they touch. They sweep up Grand Slam tennis titles and cycling world championships. They monopolise the Olympics. They fill our football and cricket and netball teams. Why would that be bad? Really? Imagine the power of a trans child or teenager seeing a trans athlete on the top step of the Olympic podium. In a way, it would be inspiring."*

But what about women? For girls seeing that there is yet another area of life where they have no chance of succeeding is not inspirational. When a girl sees all the women's sports competitions being won by trans-identified males, she will know she has no chance of being able to compete in elite level sport because she was born female. Sports is already dominated by men and many women don't compete in sport because it is perceived as masculine. We don't need to have even more discouragement from participating in sports.

Another argument that Liew makes is that sport isn't fair anyway, so it doesn't matter if trans-identified athletes have an advantage (307). It's true that all athletes will have natural advantages over other athletes and a truly level playing field is impossible to achieve. But the sports authorities try their best to make it fair. Elite athletes are carefully monitored to ensure fair competition. They are tested regularly for banned drugs and other forms of doping, with strict penalties for failing to comply with the rules (308). Even taking many common medicines is not allowed in elite sporting competitions in case it gives an unfair advantage (309). It's puzzling why the advantages that being transgender poses are overlooked.

Furthermore, other Olympic events have strict eligibility criteria. To compete in the Special Olympics, competitors need an IQ of less than 75 (310). Deaflympians need a hearing loss of at least 55db in their better ear (311). For every Paralympics event, athletes undergo testing to determine the extent of their disability, and only compete with athletes with a similar level of impairment (312). Would it be fair if we started letting people who didn't fit the criteria to take part in these events? Would it be 'inspirational' to see a person with no intellectual disability win medals in the Special Olympics? Or someone with no hearing impairment participating in the Deaflympics? Or someone with no disability win gold in the Paralympics? It's the same when a trans-identified male wins in a women's sports competition. To compete in woman's sports, a person should meet the criteria for being a woman.

It might make transgender people feel good to be able to compete as their preferred gender, but it's shutting out women who'll never have the same athletic abilities as someone born male. This is why there are male and female sports in the first place. Yet again, woman's rights are being sacrificed for trans-identified people.

Letting trans-identified people into women's spaces is damaging for women as it puts them in danger of attack when their spaces are compromised. It will make women less safe in public. And when we feel less safe in public, we will lose out on the chance to participate in so many activities. Trans-identified males using women's services are also taking opportunities away from women, including the chance to participate in sports competitions, to benefit from positive discrimination programs or to access birth control- something that has radically improved women's lives. It might not seem like a big issue, but it's yet another area where women's rights are being eroded. It is yet another example of transgender people's needs being put ahead of women's needs.

9. Erasing Women

The category of women is gradually being abolished because it is not 'inclusive' enough. This goes beyond the denial of the existence of biological sex. It is the specific erasure of the *female* sex. Talking about women, or their sex organs and reproductive functions is apparently too upsetting for transgender people to hear about. So, we can't talk about it anymore.

Don't Say Woman!
Woman is a bad word. It excludes trans-identified and non-binary people. You mustn't say it anymore. But a range of alternative phrases are coming into use that are inclusive of trans-identified and non-binary people. 'Uterus havers', 'vagina owners', 'menstruators' and 'people with a vagina' are all some of the many alternative words for women. And people are going to great lengths to avoid saying the W-word. Williams describes a number of situations where the word 'woman' has been avoided in order to be inclusive of transgender people. These include using the term 'humans with uteruses' at the Edinburgh Science Festival (313). Planned Parenthood have also referred to women as 'menstruators' in their campaign literature (314). In another case, the UK's Green Party youth wing put out a Tweet inviting "non-men" to join their women's Facebook group (315). Displaying the dictionary definition of women isn't acceptable either. Sefton Council in Merseyside, England, placed flags with the dictionary definition of women up on two town halls for International Women's Day. However, transgender rights activists complained that the flags were transphobic, and so they were taken down and the council issued an apology (316).

This line of reasoning has spread into health campaigns too. Cancer Research UK used the term "everyone with a cervix" instead of 'women' in a campaign to promote cervical cancer screening. They state that this was done to include trans-identified males (317). However, Cancer Research still refers to men in their literature on prostate and testicular cancers (318,319). It would appear that only the word 'women' needs to be erased for the sake of cancer prevention. The trouble is, the term "people with a cervix" could be confusing to some women. It's easy to take for granted that all women would know what their cervix is, but there may be some women who are not aware. For instance, women with learning disabilities, poor literacy or education or who don't speak English as their first language may not understand what the term "people with a cervix" means. Therefore, some vulnerable women may end up missing out on having screening because they don't realize that they have a cervix.

The spelling of the word 'woman' is also offensive. Womxn (pronounced 'wo-minx') is a new spelling of woman, which is intended to include trans-identified males. This spelling was used by the Wellcome Collection library and museum in London in an advertisement for an event to promote women's art and literature (320). It was also used by the University of Leicester for International Women's week (313). And by Oxfam (321). How using this spelling is beneficial to women (or even trans-identified males) is a mystery. Also, why isn't man now spelt mxn to include trans-identified females?

Instead of saying natal sex or biological sex, you should say 'assigned male/female at birth' (AMAB or AFAB). As if a midwife or doctor has arbitrarily decided the child's sex. Of course, babies are not assigned a sex at birth; they are assigned a sex at conception when either a sperm with an X chromosome or a Y chromosome fertilizes the egg. The baby's sex can be identified on the ultrasound before it is born, so sex isn't assigned at birth anyway, but observed at birth (28).

Why does it matter if people use other words for women? Shouldn't we aim to be inclusive? The trouble is, these alternative phrases give the wrongful impression that women are a minority group. For instance, feminist author Caroline Criado-Perez rightfully pointed out that the term "non-men" implies that men are the default sex (315). We are used to seeing men as the default sex because men are vastly overrepresented in so many fields. When we see a group of people (for example, cabinet ministers, the cast of a film, the board of a company), we are used to seeing less than 50% of them being women. With a minority group such as people from ethnic minorities, lesbian, gay and bisexual people or disabled people, we know these groups are only a small segment of society. We wouldn't expect to see 50% of cabinet ministers being from an ethnic minority background or 50% of a large company board being visibly disabled, because less than 50% of the general population fall into these categories (this doesn't mean that these groups are frequently underrepresented. Of course they are). Yet with women, we should be used to seeing 50% of a group being women. Because 50% of the population are women. If we are used to thinking of women as a minority, it hides how badly underrepresented women are in many fields.

Additionally, the word 'man' is not a problem. So why is the word 'woman' such an enormous issue? Also, what about trans-identified females? Nobody is talking about making manhood more inclusive or broadening the definition of 'man' to include trans-identified females. This is just about women. Which is why Cancer Research never talks about "people with prostates" or "people with testicles" in their literature. Nor do people and organizations call men "ejaculators" (after all, transwomen ejaculate too!). Science events aren't referring to men as "humans with penises" either. It is only the category of womanhood that is too exclusive.

That's Cissexist!
Another way that women are erased is through the concept of cissexism. Cissexism is the assumption that a person's gender identity matches their biological sex (260). It's very easy to be cissexist without realizing. To avoid cissexism, you shouldn't impose a gender identity on a child. Asking a pregnant woman "is it a boy or a girl?" is cissexist, as the child could be trans-identified. According

to Ferguson, "Since genitals do not determine gender, you actually won't know your child's gender identity until they're able to tell you". Ferguson also claims teaching the biology of reproduction in schools is cissexist because it teaches that sex is binary (260). Of course, the reason that schools teach that biological sex is binary is because it is. There is also a Twitter feed devoted to highlighting cissexism. For instance, having only male and female tick boxes on a form is cissexist. Not having gender-neutral toilets is also cissexist. Not including the title 'Mx.' on forms is also -you guessed it- cissexist (322).

A problem with this is that concerns about cissexism can be used to conceal women's oppression. For instance, in data collection, having more than man/woman options on a form is problematic. It can hide women's oppression by not showing how many women are represented. An example of where this has occurred is when Wikipedia conducted a survey into the gender ratio of their users. 90% of Wikipedia's editors are male. From this it could be deduced that 10% of editors are female. The actual survey shows that there were three options to choose from: male, female and transgender. Only nine percent of editors were women and one percent were transgender (323). Although this is only a one percent difference, the inclusion of a third option may be distorting the true figures and giving the appearance that there are fewer male editors and more female editors than there truly is. We don't know what the birth sex of the people who ticked the transgender box were, or even what gender they identify as. Therefore, we don't know how many men and women actually edit Wikipedia. This is just one example. How many other surveys or statistical data will have this problem? Especially if third gender options become more commonplace. Thus, allowing people to self-identify as neither male nor female may hide how badly underrepresented women are in certain fields.

As well, although eradicating cissexism is outwardly about removing the gender binary, in practice it is helping to stigmatize the female sex and replace concerns about sexism with concerns about *cis*sexism. Jeffreys (35) argues that transgender rights activists use the concept of cissexism to make feminists feel guilty for not including transgender people in their activism, which results in feminists either being silenced or feeling pressured into supporting transgenderism.

Trigger Warning: Menstruation

Women's bodily functions are also problematic. In recent years, women have been more openly talking about their periods. This has been fantastic for women's rights, as it has raised awareness of many issues that were previously never spoken of, including period poverty and sales tax on sanitary items. Talking more openly about periods also reduces the stigma around menstruation, making women feel more at ease. In addition, by talking about periods, women will have a better idea of what is and isn't normal, enabling them to find out if they have a condition such as Polycystic Ovary Syndrome (PCOS) or Endometriosis.

But transgender activists say we must stop talking about periods so freely as it's upsetting for transgender people. Burns (324), a trans-identified male, says "Many trans women yearn for their own fertility, and being told that we're not real women because of our lack of menstruation is one of the most hurtful, personal attacks you can wage on us". Indeed, it might make transgender people sad that they are not biologically the sex they identify as. That doesn't make it untrue. Also, the author of this piece has fathered two children, so infertility and childlessness aren't an issue for her. Some people go even further than this. Blogger Casey O'Brien (325) warns that hearing about periods can be "triggering" for transgender people and recommends using content warnings (also known as trigger warnings) before discussing menstruation online. She also says it's wrong to define the category of woman based on menstruation, because this excludes transgender people (325).

Yes, there are women who don't menstruate. For instance, menopausal women, women with some health conditions such as

PCOS and women who have had a hysterectomy. However, it is rare for a woman to never experience menstruation in their life. Nonetheless, women who don't menstruate are still women. There are many other aspects of womanhood that women who have never menstruated will experience, that a trans-identified male will not, including female socialization, the shorter physical stature and the lower physical strength. Even simple things, such as urination, female adolescence and sex, involve experiences which are unique to women. There is also a difference between finding out you're infertile or losing your fertility involuntarily (for instance, needing a hysterectomy due to cancer) than choosing to have medications and medical procedures that make you infertile.

As well, a woman who did not menstruate would still hear other women discussing menstruation. Yet these women do not seem to have quite as many emotional difficulties with discussing menstruation as trans-identified males do. It seems that trans-identified males are real women sometimes, and should be treated exactly like other women, and delicate little lambs at other times, who need their friends to tip-toe around them to avoid upsetting them.

Men have Periods too!
Transmen, being biologically female, often have periods in the early stages of hormone treatment. Transgender rights activists have taken this to mean that periods are not an exclusively female phenomenon. In 2019, social media influencer, Milly Bhaskara posted a picture on Instagram of her 4-year-old son (who is not transgender) holding a sign saying: "Some men have periods too. If I can get that, so can you". Bhaskara placed the caption: "If a 4 year old can grasp it I'm sure most of us can have a crack at unlearning transphobic/misinformed norms and open our minds... ya think?" on the post (326). The post was widely praised for teaching transgender inclusivity. But this is misguided. Firstly, like most four-year-olds, Bhaskara's son probably doesn't really understand what a period is. He almost certainly cannot read the sign he is holding. The boy is

being used as a pawn in a culture war. Moreover, it's not that people are "close-minded" by saying only women have periods. Only women *do* have periods. Nobody who is biologically male ever menstruates. Women who identify as men have periods, but you can't change biology; they are still female.

But it doesn't stop there. Menstrual products are now being marketed to transmen. To satisfy trans-identified females, the Venus sign has been removed from the Always sanitary towels packaging (327). In addition, Thinx, who make padded underwear for menstruation, also have a line of boxer-short style products for trans-identified females. This was launched after the company received negative feedback from the transgender community for failing to include transmen in their branding (328,329).

Period tracking apps are also having to become inclusive of trans-identified females. The menstrual app *Clue* started to use the term 'fem@le' in the app, which it said was to be inclusive of "people with cycles" (330). Although, according to transgender rights activists, period tracking apps don't go far enough in including transgender people. Transgender people have criticized the branding of other apps, particularly the use of pink and purple colourings. Cass Clemmer, an artist and trans-identified female said: "it just serves as another reminder that my period is something the world sees as inherently feminine". The problem is, menstruation is inherently feminine. But colours aren't. The idea that a certain colour represents a certain gender is a prime example of how gender is a social construct. It only matters to trans-identified females because they make it matter to them.

...So Do Transwomen
It's not just transmen who have periods. Transwomen have them too! According to transgender activists, many trans-identified males experience bloodless periods. Riedel (331) describes multiple trans-identified males who claim to have many symptoms that may accompany a period on a cyclic basis, but without the bleeding.

These symptoms include cramps, diarrhoea nausea, fatigue, migraines and mood swings (331). The only trouble is, what they're claiming isn't actually possible. Many menstrual symptoms are caused by the period itself. The cramps, nausea and diarrhoea are caused by contractions in the uterus that happen during menstruation. The uterus contracts to remove the lining that builds up during the rest of the cycle. Hormones called prostaglandins build up in the uterus lining, which trigger menstruation and cause the other symptoms associated with periods (332). Trans-identified males don't have a uterus, therefore they can't have a period. Furthermore, Bauer (333) points out that many women don't experience any symptoms during their period, demonstrating that these aren't a defining characteristic of menstruation. Also, she states that the most likely cause of the symptoms that trans-identified males experience, is side effects from the cross-sex hormones they take. While these can be cyclical if the hormone injections are given every month, they are not the same as a menstrual period.

Furthermore, many of the symptoms which these trans-identified males are attributing to menstruation are vague. Take fatigue for example. Fatigue is a subjective concept; many people don't feel as energetic as they'd like to be, and different people mean different things by fatigue. As well, other symptoms affect many people regardless of whether they are menstruating. For example, migraines can be brought on by menstruation, but they can be caused by many other things too, such as tiredness and stress. More worryingly, many of these symptoms could be caused by a different condition altogether. For instance, if someone is regularly having severe abdominal pains, diarrhoea, nausea and fatigue, these can be symptoms of a gastrointestinal disorder, such as Inflammatory Bowel Disease or Celiac Disease, or other disorders, including kidney disease, Diabetes and many others. If a trans-identified male regularly attributes their symptoms to their 'period', then they might not seek the medical help they need to find the actual cause of their symptoms. Which is why the myth of the bloodless period is dangerous.

Abolishing Motherhood

Transgender activists are fighting against the concept of motherhood. Only women can give birth. But because having a baby is something that is uniquely and innately female, transgender rights activists must make it 'inclusive' by pretending that men can have babies too. Like with the word 'woman', many organisations are now using new language to refer to mothers and pregnant women.

When talking about women being prosecuted for having an abortion (or in some cases, having a miscarriage) Planned Parenthood has started using the term "people criminalized for their pregnancy outcomes" (314). What about if you're talking about a pregnant woman? In that case, you should say 'pregnant person' instead of pregnant woman, because men and non-binary people can get pregnant too (334). In addition, there are claims that the new Irish abortion law will exclude trans-identified males and non-binary people, because the legislation uses the term 'pregnant woman' instead of pregnant person (335). (Of course, this is nonsense).

Not Breastfeeding, Chestfeeding

The word "chestfeeding" has started to replace the word 'breastfeeding'. This word is intended to make trans-identified females who are breastfeeding feel more comfortable (336). Trans-identified females might not like to acknowledge that they have breasts, but coining a new word to avoid saying 'breasts' doesn't change that fact. Also, if people start to routinely avoid saying the word 'breast', this is stigmatizing breasts and breastfeeding. This is a problem because making breastfeeding a bigger taboo will stop women from breastfeeding. There have been great strides in making women feel comfortable with breastfeeding in public, which in turn has led to more women breastfeeding their babies. We know that babies who are breastfed grow up to be healthier than formula-fed babies, so it would be incredibly sad if this progress stalled.

Of course, breastfeeding isn't just for biological women anymore. Now, trans-identified males can breastfeed too. In 2018, a study was done on inducing lactation in a trans-identified male. Using several drugs, she was able to produce enough milk to breastfeed her adopted baby for six weeks (337). But the participant in this study wasn't the first trans-identified male to breastfeed. Burns gives accounts of other trans-identified males who have induced lactation (338). In most cases, these people used domperidone to stimulate lactation. Domperidone is an anti-nausea drug that has been banned in USA because it may cause cardiac arrest and sudden death (339). In the UK, where domperidone isn't banned, taking this drug while breastfeeding is not recommended as small amounts of the drug pass into the breastmilk (340). This practice could therefore put both the parent and the baby's health in danger. While breastmilk is better than formula milk in most circumstances, until the risks of domperidone in breastmilk are fully understood, nobody should be using this drug to induce lactation.

Parent 1 Instead of Mother
The very word 'mother' is too much for some trans-identified people to cope with. In the UK, Freddie McConnel, a *Guardian* journalist and trans-identified female, is fighting for the right to not be classed as the mother of his child. He has taken two different human rights cases about this- one where he fought to be listed as the father, and another where he argued that the terms 'mother' and 'father' on birth certificates should be replaced with 'parent 1' and 'parent 2' (341). He has lost both of these cases so far, but he has said he intends to take it to the Supreme Court (342). McConnel also fought to have his name kept hidden by the court to protect his privacy. Given that he starred in a fly-on-the-wall documentary about the pregnancy, which was released at the same time as the court case was underway, the court did not believe the injunction was necessary (343). Apart from his gender identity, McConnel is a mother in every sense of the word; the child was conceived using a sperm donor with McConnel's eggs, grew in his uterus and he gave birth to the child. Nothing can ever change those facts.

'His'story- Transgendering Historical Women

It's not just women in the present day who are being erased. Many people are now claiming that various female historical figures were transgender men. For instance, Joan of Arc is now said to be a transgender man because she regularly dressed in men's clothing (344,345). Queen Kristina of Sweden is also now said to be a transgender man (345). Furthermore, Historic England have also been transgendering numerous women for their LGBT heritage project, including soldiers Hannah Snell and Mary Ann Talbot (346).

The evidence for these women being transgender is weak. In the case of Joan of Arc, she never claimed to be a man. In fact, she emphasized her femininity by referring to herself as Joan the Maid (347). Admittedly, Joan of Arc probably did have either a psychiatric or neurological disorder that caused her to have the visions that she regularly experienced, which might have caused her to behave in unusual ways, including cross-dressing. But that doesn't mean she was transgender.

Furthermore, claiming women who dressed or acted like men ignores the reason why these women would cross-dress. Historically, many high-profile women pretended to be male because of oppression. In the past, the idea of women doing many things was outrageous. Thus, women were often forced to conceal their gender if they were to be in the public eye. Howell (348) points out that this was often done for purely practical purposes, rather than because these women felt discomfort with their gender identity.

In many cases, women weren't allowed to do certain activities at all. For instance, Hannah Snell, who fought in the army as a soldier and a sailor in the 18th century, had to pretend to be a man because women weren't allowed to serve at the time. Once she had left the army, she didn't hide that she was a woman. In fact, she embraced her gender; she opened a pub named the Female Warrior, presumably as a reference to her military past (346).

Even women who didn't cross-dress often had to adopt other measures to pretend to be male. For example, many women authors published under men's names. Charlotte Bronte published under the name 'Currer Bell' and Mary Anne Evans used the penname 'George Elliot'. Even in the late 1990s, women were pressured to hide their gender. JK Rowling was told by her publisher to use her initials instead of her name to hide her gender, which they said was to make her books more marketable to boys (349).

While it would make transgender people feel good to have more transgender historical figures, it is a problem for women. There aren't many women historical figures, so it's a shame to see any of them be retrospectively turned into men. This is depriving women and girls of inspirational figures to look up to, which in turn limits their aspirations. Also, bear in mind that male historical figures aren't being retrospectively found to be transwomen. There were male historical figures who might be described as transgender in modern terms- although none of them were as well-known as the female figures who are now being said to be transgender men.

Ultimately, we pretend that women don't exist to make transgender people happy. This isn't progress. It's misogyny. We are returning to a time when women weren't acknowledged. Also, by making the word 'women' taboo, this stigmatizes women. Williams makes the point that women are being dehumanized when they cannot be named (313). If women start to feel that being female is something shameful, it will damage the mental wellbeing of women as individuals and it will also set back women's rights. Not being able to talk about being a woman stops women speaking out. After all, if we can't talk about being a woman, how can we organize and fight for our rights? When women feel able to talk about our issues, we can find solutions. For example, the tampon tax has only been abolished in many countries because women were prepared to talk openly about their periods and the cost of sanitary products. Male politicians and policy makers would have almost certainly been unaware that this was an issue, but because women were able to come together and campaign, they were able to highlight this issue. In addition, female erasure can be used as a tactic for disguising women's oppression. There's a saying: "if you don't see sex, you don't see sexism". When women are placed into some broad 'non-man' category, which includes people who are biologically male, women's oppression can easily be overlooked.

10. Not Allowed to Speak Out

Transgenderism is threatening free speech. You are not allowed to question the transgender narrative anymore. When a person does question transgenderism, they are immediately demonized and called 'transphobic' or a 'TERF'. That person is then silenced as a punishment for upsetting trans-identified people. As a result, you can be ostracized, lose your job, banned from social media or no-platformed. It's very easy to find yourself on the wrong side of this- even simply not being sufficiently inclusive of transgender people can be enough to ire the transgenderists.

"You're Fired!": Transgenderism and Employment

Many people have lost their jobs because of their opinions on transgenderism. In the UK, Maya Forstarter, a tax consultant for a think-tank, did not have her employment contract renewed because she had Tweeted that a man could not become a woman. She was Tweeting outside of work, in a personal capacity, so it had no bearing on her work. She took her employer to an employment tribunal, arguing that she was discriminated against on the grounds of religion or belief (another one of the protected characteristics listed in the Equality Act). An employment tribunal ruled that her belief was "not worthy of respect in a democratic society", meaning that she (or anyone else who expresses similar sentiments) are not protected under the Equality Act and that her employer was allowed to not renew her contract (350). This ruling is deeply troubling. That a person cannot change sex is not an opinion. It is not even remotely controversial. It is a scientific fact. It is chilling to think that a scientific fact is deemed to be "not worthy of respect". This goes to show how the transgender dogma is so deeply ingrained in society.

In another case, a schoolteacher was disciplined for saying "well done girls", to a group of children that included a trans-identified female student. Joshua Sutcliffe, who is a Christian, said that although he did not believe that people could change gender, the comment was an innocent mistake and he tried to be respectful of pupils. The child's family also complained that Sutcliffe referred to the child by his name rather than he/him pronouns, and claimed their child was repeatedly being given unfair detentions- which was later found to be untrue by the school's investigation (351). Sutcliffe was forced to attend a disciplinary hearing and eventually resigned (352).

Lynsey McCarthy-Calvert was forced to resign from her position as spokesperson for an organization representing doulas, for saying only women can have babies in a Facebook post. In the post, she also complained about Cancer Research's use of the term "cervix owner" and about gender inequality more generally. Doula UK found that her comments breeched their equality and diversity regulations and said that she would be suspended if she did not delete the Facebook post. She refused to delete the post and decided to leave the organization (353).

Louise Moody, an academic researcher, lost her job after she made a joke on Twitter about Lily Madigan coming out as a lesbian. Madigan then contacted Moody's employer, the University of York and encouraged them to sack Moody over the joke. In her complaint, Madigan wrongly implied that she was a student of the University of York (Madigan mentioned she was a student, but not that she is at a different university). Soon after, Moody- who herself is a lesbian- found her temporary job was then withdrawn, leaving her unemployed (254).

It's not just in the UK where this is happening. Peter Vlaming, a teacher from Virginia, was sacked for refusing to use a trans-identified female student's preferred pronouns because he felt it was against his religious beliefs. However, Vlaming had made other adjustments for the student. Vlaming taught French and allowed all the students to be referred to by a French nickname. When the student came out as transgender, he let all the students in the class choose a new name so that the transgender student could choose a male name. He also avoided referring to the student by female pronouns, except on one occasion, when he apologized afterwards. Vlaming is now suing the school district (354).

Kenneth Zucker, a Canadian psychiatrist, ran a clinic for people with Gender Dysphoria, that included treating children. In 2015, he was dismissed and then his clinic was closed, ostensibly because he was practicing 'conversion therapy' (28). Although Zucker often prescribed sex-change treatments for adults, he felt that with children who wanted to change sex, it was better to offer psychological therapies, which often resulted in the Gender Dysphoria abating. This goes against the transgender narrative of being 'born in the wrong body', so transgender people were not happy. As a result, an external review of the clinic was conducted (28). Anderson reports that this included some remarks suggesting that the reviewers had a poor understanding of psychiatric care, including a comment about concerns that it was "harmful or improper to help patients in a mental-health clinic understand why they are the way they are" (28). As this is the mainstay of psychiatric care in general, it is worrying that this was given as a reason for closing the clinic. The real reason the clinic closed appears to be because its practices went against the transgender ideology.

"You're Banned!" Censorship on Social Media

Big tech is also complicit with transgenderism. Twitter bans users who refer to trans-identified people by their original name or gender (355). However, posting "I punch TERFS" or "die cis scum" are absolutely fine (given that there are thousands of posts that consist of these words, which have never been removed by Twitter). Furthermore, the blogging site host, WordPress has also closed gender critical sites. For instance, the feminist blog, GenderTrender was taken down (356). Facebook has also banned gender critical feminists. Feminist activist Posie Parker was banned from Facebook because of her views on transgenderism (357).

Social media users themselves also shadow-ban gender critical people. There are block lists for social media, which automatically block the social media accounts of 'transphobic' people. One well-known list is Terfblocker,, which lists over 13,000 accounts belonging to 'TERFs' (358). While nobody is obliged to look at anyone's social media pages, it's not good for people to behave in this way. It shuts down healthy debate and dialogue between communities, ultimately worsening conflicts.

"Get out of My Pub!"

Physical locations are also censoring trans-sceptical views. A woman in Macclesfield, who was wearing a t-shirt with the dictionary definition of woman, was thrown out of a pub for transphobia after another customer complained. The man who complained, who is not known to be transgender, reportedly cried after seeing the t-shirt. He tweeted that seeing the t-shirt was "disgusting and I'm so upset by it" (359). Another woman was thrown out of a gay nightclub in Glasgow for wearing a t-shirt with the LGB Alliance logo on it. A transgender customer had complained that the t-shirt was transphobic because the acronym omits the 'T' from LGBT, and so the woman was asked to turn her t-shirt inside out by the bouncer. She refused and was made to leave (360).

Trans-Exclusionary Arts

Feminist arts have also been targeted for failing to include transgender people. Nina Edge was targeted by a group of artists called The White Pube, who tried to have her sacked from her job as a lecturer at Liverpool John Moore's University because of her trans-sceptical views. Fortunately, the university have stood by her and have not terminated her employment. Other artists have also been attacked because of their opinions. The TERFs Out of Art campaign group have targeted many feminist artists, including conceptual artist Rachel Ara, who was disinvited from speaking at Oxford Brookes University because she had expressed gender critical views on social media (361).

Performance arts have also been censored because they are not sufficiently inclusive of transgender people. Mount Holyoke College stopped their annual performance of *The Vagina Monologues* because it reduces the concept of womanhood down to the ownership of a vagina, which excludes trans-identified males (362). In an email sent to all students, Erin Murphy, the representative of the school's theatre board said "At its core, the show offers an extremely narrow perspective on what it means to be a woman" (363). What's chilling about this is that the performance wasn't censored because it was anti-transgender; it was censored because it wasn't specifically pro-transgender. The same could be said of so many works of arts. That would mean practically any artwork or performance could be censored for not supporting transgenderism.

Cancel Culture

If you displease transgender rights activists online, you might find yourself being 'cancelled'. When a person is cancelled, they are boycotted. Their social media accounts are blocked on a large scale, and often public engagements and sponsorship deals are cancelled too (364). Admittedly, it's extremely rare for a celebrity's career to die out completely as a result of being cancelled, but it does highlight how easily upset the woke crowd are. One high-profile victim of cancel culture is the author JK Rowling. Rowling tweeted in support of Maya Forstarter, which resulted in widespread condemnation from transgender activists. Many fans said they felt 'betrayed' by Rowling. One transgender person even said that Rowling's support of Forstarter made them cry. Even worse, the transgender rights group, Human Rights Campaign demanded an apology from Rowling (365). The way the woke crowd behave is terrifying. They are always waiting to pounce on anyone who doesn't completely conform to their prescribed set of beliefs. The problem is that nobody is perfect, and nobody ever agrees with everyone all the time. Cancel culture holds people to unrealistically high standards. You must believe in what woke people believe, and even the smallest deviation is not allowed.

Suppression of Research

Universities have traditionally been bastions of free speech, but now even they are censoring people who question the transgender dogma. Academic research with findings that do not support the tenants of transgenderism is increasingly being hidden away.

In 2017, *Hypatia*, a feminist academic journal, published an article by philosopher Rebecca Tuvel, which argued transracialism (where someone identifies as a member of a different race) was valid, and that transracial people should be allowed to live as their preferred race. In this article, the author made comparisons with transracialism and the acceptance of transgenderism. Although the author was sympathetic to transgender people, transgender rights activists said that equating transracialism with transgenderism was transphobic. As a result, the paper got taken down (366). In this instance, because it was a theoretical paper, there couldn't have been said to be a methodological issue- transgender activists simply didn't like Tuvel's line of reasoning. Case also describes how in response to the paper, an anonymous trans-identified male graduate student wrote an open letter with a list of demands, amongst them, that transphobic papers aren't published anymore and that conferences no-platform transphobic speakers and papers (366). There is no good academic reason to do this- it would simply be to avoid upsetting transgender people.

But this isn't the only time a paper has been redacted because it upset the transgender community. Littman's paper on Rapid-Onset Gender Dysphoria in young people (49) caused a lot of upset amongst the transgender community, who claimed the study was transphobic. Because of this, it was retracted and removed from Brown University's, news distribution (367).

In the media, non-scientists were criticizing the study's design, complaining the sample was biased. Tannehill (368) described the paper as "junk science" because it did not have a representative sample. This criticism is unwarranted. This paper did not claim to have a representative sample. It is intended to describe ROGD, and so focuses on parents of people with ROGD. Many studies do this. It is perfectly normal for a study that uses interviews, focus groups or other forms of qualitative research to have a non-representative sample. This type of research is done when a representative sample would not be useful. For example, if a market research team were looking at people's views on a new product, they wouldn't include a sample of people who had never tried the new product. And a piece of medical research describing a rare genetic disorder wouldn't include a sample of people who didn't have the disorder. Doing this simply wouldn't yield any relevant information. There are times when a representative sample is needed; if it were a study on the prevalence of ROGD within the trans-identified community, not having a representative sample would be a problem. To establish the validity of ROGD, more research that includes a more representative sample will need to be done in the future. Doing other research to build on an earlier study is a completely normal part of science. It doesn't mean Littman has done anything wrong. Therefore, there were no serious methodological issues with the paper.

Also, why is selection bias never an issue when the results of a study are favourable to transgender people? There are undoubtably many papers with a similar methodology that are favourable to transgenderism. And just as there are people who want to talk about their negative perceptions of transgenderism and Gender Dysphoria, there are also many people who support transgenderism and will participate in studies to show that view. But oddly, study design is only a concern when the results portray transgenderism negatively.

Fortunately, the paper was later republished, albeit with amendments stating that the study was an observational study and that the findings were the parent's perception. The study's conclusion was also changed to reflect the supposed limitations of the parent's reports (369). Given that the peer reviewers had thought the article was acceptable (which is far from a given- many papers are rejected, and even when a paper is accepted, usually revisions are required) the paper was changed purely because of pressure from activists rather than because of any methodological failings.

But that wasn't the last time a paper was retracted because of the reaction of the transgender community. In 2019, Stephen Gliske (370) wrote a paper proposing a new theory of Gender Dysphoria in *eNeuro*, a neurology journal. Gliske's paper suggested that Gender Dysphoria might not be caused by a person's brain gender being mismatched to the person's body, but from a person having an issue with how they sense their gender (371). Like Littman's paper, it attracted criticism from the transgender community, who launched a petition to have it removed. As a result, the paper was first 'corrected,' with a section on the medical implications of the findings being removed. Then, the paper was re-reviewed by a group of academics who specialized in Gender Dysphoria. As a result of the review, the paper was retracted. A synthesis of the reviews was published, showing that many of the criticisms are not related to the scientific aspects of the paper. For example, there is a lengthy section about the author's use of language, which alleges that Gliske is disrespectful towards transgender people (372). It comes across that the reviewer's motivations in removing the paper were ideological. In response to the situation, Gliske says that the paper offered a new theory, not conclusive proof that that theory was true. Additionally, he makes the point that no theory of Gender Dysphoria has ever been proven (372). It wasn't that there was a methodological problem with the paper but that it was upsetting to transgender people. In an article on the Gliske affair, the blog *Retraction Watch* said: "we see this sort of thing not infrequently. 'Wait, all of those people are angry at us. We'd better retract this paper and blame the author for slipping one by us.'"(373). This is not a good reason to retract a paper.

Some universities won't even allow controversial studies to be conducted in the first place. In the UK, Bath Spa University denied ethical approval on a postgraduate research project looking at trans-identified people who returned to living as their original gender. The university said the study was "potentially politically incorrect" and could attract controversy. James Caspian -the student who wished to do the study- is a psychotherapist who specializes in working with trans-identified people. He works for a charity supporting trans-identified people (374). He is not a 'TERF' or doing the research with the intention of upsetting trans-identified people. It appears he is actually very supportive of trans-identified people and simply wanted to look into an under-researched area.

Suppressing research into transgenderism is very dangerous. Research may prevent any harms of transgenderism by identifying them and finding ways to avert these dangers. Even if the research does not find any harms that arise from transgenderism, it should still be done to prove that transgenderism isn't harmful. Because something is controversial, it doesn't mean it shouldn't be researched. Jussim points out that throughout history, many academics have said controversial things that have later turned out to be true. For instance, Galileo was convicted of heresy for saying that the planets revolved around the sun rather than the Earth. Although this went against Christian beliefs, Galileo's observations were later proven to be correct (375). Cases like this underline the importance of academic freedom.

No Platforming
No platforming of controversial speakers has gone on for many years, but recently, it has gotten worse. Many speakers have not been allowed to give talks at universities because of their views on transgenderism, even when the event the speaker was invited to was not about transgenderism. There are numerous examples of speakers who have not been allowed to speak. Germaine Greer was no-platformed from speaking at the University of Cardiff. Transgender activists claim that her speaking would endanger trans-identified people, and that the safety of trans-identified people is more important than free speech (376).

At Oxford University, a talk given by historian Selina Todd was cancelled. Again, the talk was not on transgenderism, but because

Todd has links with Woman's Place UK, and has spoken in favour of retaining single-sex spaces, she was not allowed to speak (377). Todd now has been given police protection because of the number of threats she receives from transgender rights activists (378). Todd wasn't just no-platformed at Oxford University. When she was invited to talk at the University of Kent, an open letter saying her mere presence would imply that "trans identity is up for discussion" and that hosting her would be upsetting for transgender students. The letter also said that allowing Todd to speak at the event would make it appear that the university supported Todd's views (379). As well as this, the letter states that Todd's views are harmful, claiming that her views promote hate crimes against transgender people. The reason she is problematic in the eyes of the university is that "Her views refuse to acknowledge that trans women ARE women, and that trans women's rights ARE women's rights" (380). These aren't facts about transgender people. They are opinions. Williams points out that the letter implies that free speech and academic freedom is merely an excuse for anti-transgender bigotry (379). The letter itself displays a shocking lack of critical thinking. Whoever wrote this letter doesn't grasp the difference between fact and opinion, or that one person's opinion may contradict another's opinion. This doesn't bode well for universities, where learning to think critically is one of the key aims of the university experience.

More chillingly, some speakers who are supporters of transgenderism have been no-platformed for simply supporting free speech. Veteran gay rights activist Peter Tatchell was no-platformed by Canterbury Christ University for signing an open letter condemning no-platforming (381). The student union's LGBT representative said that by signing the letter, Tatchell was condoning violence against trans-identified people. Given that Tatchell has supported transgender rights for many years, it is a huge leap in logic to say that supporting free speech means Tatchell is transphobic. But that's how pervasive transgenderism is- even criticising anything that relates to transgenderism, however remotely, is transphobic.

A panel held by the Centre for Crime and Justice Studies at the Open University campus was also cancelled because the organization had recommended that transgender people be held in the prison for their biological sex rather than their gender identity. Transgender rights activists said that this recommendation was "state-sanctioned murder" because it could lead to transgender people committing suicide. What makes this frightening is that the event itself was not actually about transgender people in prison specifically, but about penal reform in general (382).

Other organizations are also censoring any talks about transgenderism. The NSPCC- a large UK children's charity- cancelled a talk on trans-identified children because of accusations of transphobia. It was part of a series called "Dare to Debate", which featured discussions on controversial child protection issues. The NSPCC said the debate would look at how to support trans-identified children (383), but this still wasn't acceptable for transgender activists.

"My Identity is not for Debate"

"My identity isn't for debate" is a well-known rallying cry of trans-identified people fighting free speech. In one case Owl Fisher (384), a trans-identified male, criticized a Channel 4 program discussing trans-identified people's rights. She says she should not have to share a platform with people who question transgenderism. She references the high rates of suicide and mental health problems in trans-identified people as a reason not to debate transgenderism. The message is clear: debating transgenderism is killing trans-identified people.

This sets a frightening precedent. What else will be not up for debate? Bear in mind that people debate identities all the time. For instance, Brexit was partly about a conflict between British identity and European identity. Doctors debate the validity of certain diagnoses and the cut-off between disabled and non-disabled. Immigration debates are often related to national identity and ethnic identity. The Scottish Nationalist Party is campaigning for Scottish independence- an issue relating to Scottish identity. People debate religious identity and who is and is not a member of a certain religion. There are hundreds of aspects of a person's identity that get debated. Identity isn't sacrosanct. Also, most ideas about gender identity come from academics questioning the concept of gender identity. If philosopher Judith Butler had been forbidden from examining the validity of gender, there would be no people claiming to be gender non-binary today.

It's not just debating transgenderism which is killing transgender people. Fighting for women's rights is too. Moore's article in *The Guardian* on women's right to organize and protect their rights (266) was attacked by transgender rights activists. Hannah Daisy, a high-profile social media influencer and artist, posted an illustration of a woman holding a copy of the *Guardian* with Moore's article on display, while tearing it up, with the caption "transphobic articles like this endanger trans people's lives" (385). Apparently, simply advocating free speech can kill trans-identified people.

The truth is, gender critical feminists aren't killing transgender people. There has not been a single reported case of a transgender person being killed by a feminist anywhere in the world. Murders of transgender people -like with most murders- are committed predominantly by men. Admittedly, some murders are motivated by the hatred of transgender people, but many others are unrelated to the victim's gender identity. Even when murders are motivated by a hatred of transgender people, it's unlikely that the murderer was spurred on by an article on woman's rights, a speaker at a university or a book on feminist theory. Of course, sexism is at the root of the targeting of feminists. There is a longstanding idea that women have to regulate men's emotions. As if men can't help but be violent when all these women have got him riled up. This is patronising toward men and puts an unfair burden on women. This is why women are blamed for violence towards transgender people, even when it is perpetrated by men.

Looking at the issue more broadly, free speech exists for people to say controversial things. Even if that's hurtful. Everyone who restricts free speech thinks they have the moral high ground. Whether it be restrictions on criticizing the government or anti-blasphemy laws, there is always a 'good reason' for banning that speech. Transgenderism is no different. There is no reason why questioning transgenderism should be exempt from free speech. Transgenderism is an important issue and a failure to question it could seriously endanger many people. Furthermore, sometimes people have to question orthodoxy. It's what got us to where we are now- a democratic society where public officials are held to account, where there are scientific advancements that were contrary to religious teachings and where women have rights.

11. Hope?

Are we beginning to see the end of transgenderism? There are some promising signs that the tide is turning, and the transgender craze is starting to come to an end.

Will COVID-19 Put Things into Context?

For much of the world, the Coronavirus pandemic is probably the most serious thing that has happened for many years. At its peak, thousands of people were dying from Coronavirus every day. The lockdown measures have disrupted life like never before and shook everyone to the core. However, there is one tiny slither of hope from this; Coronavirus has put so many things into perspective. Issues that used to feel huge have now been completely forgotten. Murphy points out that compared to thousands of people dying a day, transgender rights now look incredibly trivial (386). Will left-wing activists now realize that there are more important issues than transgenderism?

As well, because of COVID-19, 'vital' sex change treatments aren't going ahead. Sex reassignment surgeries have been cancelled because they are non-essential (387,388). As well, some transgender people can't get their cross-sex hormones because they can't get to the hospital for their injections (389). After all this, what if we see how little transgender people have been affected by the supposedly 'life-threatening' delays to their surgeries or not being able to have cross-sex hormones?

There is also a sexed aspect of the Coronavirus Pandemic; more men die of Coronavirus than women (390). Given that men have weaker immune systems than women (391), this isn't surprising. No statistics exist for 'non-binary' people affected by Coronavirus- after all, your immune system doesn't know what your gender identity is. Nor is there such a thing as a 'non-binary' immune system. Maybe now, even the most ardent transgenderists will be forced to admit that biological sex does exist after all.

More generally, people might realize there is more to life than their gender identity. Once the pandemic is over, life will have changed forever. So many of us will have lost friends and family to COVID-19. And there are so many things that we can't take for granted anymore -the shop will always have food and toiletries, we can always to outside, or that medical science will always have an answer to disease- all things that COVID-19 has shown not to be true. When you look at it this way, things like having your non-binary gender validated by being called 'xe' or being included in abortion campaigns aren't going to seem so important. Perhaps those who have kindly humoured transgenderism will now run out of patience. As well, transgenderism is no longer in the news anywhere as much as it used to be, having been replaced by far more pressing matters. As a result, people won't think about transgenderism so much and interest will fall away. Of course, we cannot guarantee that transgenderism will end after the COVID-19 pandemic is over. But it certainly is possible. After all, nothing quite like this has ever occurred in recent memory.

History Repeating Itself?
Another thing to remember is that similar medico-legal fads have happened before and gone away. In the 1980s and 1990s, there was the recovered memory scandal, where people claimed to have repressed memories of severe child abuse. There was a theory that many adults with mental illnesses had been abused as children and repressed the memories. Counsellors began to encourage their patients to explore repressed trauma as a cause of their present-day issues, leading to people 'recovering' memories of abuse. Books such as *Michelle Remembers* (an autobiography of a woman who claims she was abused by a Satanic cult as a child) and *The Courage to Heal* (a self-help book that claims to help people recognize the signs that they have repressed memories of child abuse, and how to cope with learning this) spread this idea.

The reality was that therapists were unintentionally planting false memories in the patient's head by suggesting that the person had been abused. In some cases, therapists explicitly told patients that their symptoms showed they had been abused as children. The therapy to recover memories was actually encouraging people to imagine that they had been abused as children. Methods such as hypnosis and guided imagery were used to help the person 'remember' their abuse (392). Some people's memories were very fragmented, but those with more detailed recollections often described incidents that were very surreal and featured practices such as cannibalism and ritual animal sacrifices (393). According to Paul McHugh, the psychiatrist who closed Johns Hopkins Gender Dysphoria clinic, and who also gave testimony in a high-profile court case about the unreliability of recovered memories (394) like with transgenderism, you were either with victims or against them; questioning what they said was not acceptable (80). People who did question the validity of recovered memories were often accused of being paedophiles or perpetrators of satanic ritual abuse themselves.

There were other similarities too. As with transgenderism, people who felt they might have repressed memories of abuse were encouraged not to question themselves. Today's transgender people say, "If you think you're non-binary, you are non-binary" or "anyone who says they are transgender is transgender". The rallying cries of the Satanic ritual abuse survivor's movement was "If you think you were abused, you were abused" and "anyone who says they were abused, was abused".

Furthermore, both transgenderism and the abuse survivor's movement involved people re-writing their personal histories (in the case of transgender people, saying they had always felt discomfort with their biological sex, even when reports from parents contradict this, while people with recovered memories recalled serious child abuse when they had previously claimed to have had a happy childhood). In both movements, there were also vocal proponents who upheld the narrative, either telling the public to listen to people claiming to be abuse victims or to transgender people's proclaimed gender identities. Finally, any logical inconsistencies in what people claim are glossed over- whether it be that an adult was secretly abused by strangers in their bedroom without showing any signs or their family noticing that people were in the bedroom, or that a person is both born in the wrong body and actively choosing to defy the gender binary.

Although the recovered memory craze came to an end, it still had a huge negative impact on many people. Because of recovered memories, people were falsely convicted of child abuse and sent to prison. Brown University maintains a large list of cases where people were convicted on the basis of recovered memories, which include many cases where memories of childhood abuse have been recovered by a therapist (395). Even when no criminal charges were brought, families were still torn apart. The journalist Meredith Maran stopped talking to her father after recovering memories of being sexually abused by him (396). She started to believe she had been abused after researching incest and recovered memories for her articles. She then began to spend more time around incest survivors, and even began a romantic relationship with a woman who claimed she had been a victim of Satanic Ritual Abuse. Many years later, she began to doubt her recovered memories. After her partner's stories of childhood abuse became increasingly farfetched, Maran left her. At this point, she realized her memories were not real and decided to rekindle her relationship with her father. Sadly, he had developed Alzheimer's Disease. The time she could have spent with her father had been lost forever because of recovered memories.

The recovered memories craze also had a devastating impact on the mental health of the patients themselves. Contrary to the claim that by reliving the memories, they would be somehow released and the patient's mental health would improve, many patients suffered serious trauma after 'learning' that they were abused. For instance, one young woman with mental health problems killed herself after 'discovering' that as a child, a group of Satan worshipers would go into her bedroom every night and take her away to abuse her (397). According to Tallmadge, the young woman -who was her niece- was never doubted by the many healthcare professionals involved in her care, despite the unlikeliness of her claims (for instance, that strangers were managing to enter her room regularly without anyone else in the house noticing). This did not help her mental health, and she apparently came to the conclusion that the only way to free herself of the mental torment she was experiencing was to end her life (397).

Fortunately, because people questioned the narratives pushed by activists, even when they were demonized, the recovered memory craze faded. Admittedly, things will never be the same for many people affected by the recovered memory craze. And sadly, once the transgender craze is over, people will still be left with physical and mental scars. But at least no more people will be harmed. Based on the length of time that the recovered memory craze lasted for, McHugh, expects that the transgenderism craze will last between ten to 15 years after it started (80). The good news is that if McHugh, is correct, we can expect to see the end of the transgender craze within a few years. Of course, it will take many people to stand up and be prepared to be accused of transphobia before this craze fades, but McHugh, shows it can be done.

Fightback on Self-Identification
Another promising sign that the transgender craze is coming to an end is that governments are starting to grasp the importance of biological sex in legal documentation. The UK government has indefinitely paused their plans to allow people to legally change their gender without having medical treatments for Gender Dysphoria (398). For a while, the Scottish government was planning to go ahead with self-identification after the UK government paused their plans, but they too have put their plans on hold (399). New Zealand has also paused their plans for a similar system (400). As well as this, the UK's Court of Appeal has rejected a legal case where campaigner

Jamie Windust was fighting for non-binary gender markers on passports (401). Some territories have gone even further. The US state of Idaho has banned trans-identified people from changing sex on legal documents completely (402). A similar law has passed in Hungary, and as a result, previous legal sex changes have been reversed and everyone's legal documents have gone back to showing their biological sex (403,404).

Keeping Children Safe
Another victory for trans-sceptical people is that healthcare providers are finally starting to question the wisdom of letting children undergo gender transition.

The UK government has announced a ban on children under 18 having sex change surgeries. Prior to this, children could have the surgery if their parents gave consent (405). In addition, a judge has given permission for a judicial review into the NHS's child Gender Dysphoria services (406). The case involves two women: Kira Bell, a woman who began transitioning to male as a child and has returned to her original gender and 'Mum A', a mother of a 15-year-old girl with Autism who is on a waiting list for treatment for Gender Dysphoria (407).

In an interview in *The Daily Mail*, Bell says she transitioned because she believed becoming a boy would cure her Depression (408). Bell claims nobody at the clinic challenged this belief. At the age of 16, after just three one-hour appointments, she was allowed to start puberty blockers. A year later, she started receiving testosterone injections. Her care was then transferred to an adult Gender Dysphoria clinic and she had her breasts removed. She also changed her name and received a Gender Recognition Certificate, making her male in the eyes of the law. However, at the age of 22, Bell decided that she no longer wanted to be a man. She has stopped having testosterone injections and she is looking to have her Gender Recognition Certificate annulled. But the effects of the testosterone injections may be irreversible; Bell still has a male appearance and grows facial hair. She also reports that she is often perceived as male by strangers. Bell told *The Daily Mail* that her motivation in bringing the case is so that nobody else will have to go through what she has gone through. While what Bell has suffered is incredibly sad, it is good that she is helping to prevent other children from going through the same thing, by taking legal action. Bell's case also serves as a sombre warning for anyone who thinks they can simply stop taking hormones and return to their original gender.

The other person in the case, Mum A, whose daughter wishes to transition to a boy, argues that the combination of her child's young age, Autism and mental health problems mean she cannot understand the risks of taking puberty blockers (409). Mum A also says that her daughter's communication difficulties mean that she is not able to accurately explain her feelings, so she may not be able to convey what she wants to happen to her (407). As well, Mum A says that at 15 years of age, her daughter cannot understand the long-term implications of her choices. Mum A is also concerned about the lack of evidence on the long-term effects of puberty blockers, and feels that not having this information makes it impossible for her daughter to make an informed decision about her care (410).

Independently of the judicial review, NHS England is also conducting its own review of the use of puberty blockers and cross-sex hormones for trans-identified children (407). The review will examine the evidence on the safety of using these drugs in children (411). While there are no guarantees that this review will stop doctors prescribing these medicines, it is good to see the NHS has recognized the possible dangers of giving puberty blockers and cross-sex hormones to children.

The USA is also making progress on this issue- in some cases, going much further than the UK has. A law has passed in Alabama which forbids doctors from giving children under the age of 19 puberty blockers or cross-sex hormones (412). In South Dakota, a bill to restrict child sex transition, including the use of puberty blockers is also currently going through the state legislature (413). If the bill passes, doctors could be imprisoned if they give puberty blockers or cross-sex hormones to children under the age of 16. Furthermore, Georgia, (414) Colorado, Florida, Illinois, Oklahoma, Missouri and New Hampshire have all had bills proposed in their state legislatures to ban child gender transitions (415).

Other countries are also starting to rethink their policies on child sex changes. In Sweden, a law which would have made it easier for children to change sex has been put on hold after a psychiatrist published a high-profile article on the issue (24). Dr Christopher Gillberg, who wrote the article, described allowing children to change gender as "a big experiment" and warned that it could later turn into a huge scandal (416). The law would have reduced the age a child can change sex medically from 18 to 15, allowed children to change their legal sex from the age of 12 and removed the requirement for parents to give their consent for the child to change sex (24).

Saving Women's Sports
People are also starting to see the unfairness of allowing trans-identified males to compete in women's sports. As a result, several US states are beginning to take action to protect women's sports. The Arizona state legislature has banned trans-identified athletes from competing in girl's school sports competitions. All students will have to compete as the sex they were born as, and they can undergo sex chromosome testing if their sex is disputed (417). Similar bills are also going through the state legislatures in Idaho (418), Alabama (419), Tennessee (420) and Ohio (421).

People are also starting to take legal action against having to compete with trans-identified athletes. In Connecticut, the families of the girls who were forced to compete against trans-identified students in the state's high-school athletics competition are now suing over the potential loss of titles and college scholarships (422). The US Justice Department has become involved in this case, and have said that trans-identified males should not be allowed to compete in girls' sports events (423).

Sport authorities have also begun to take action against trans-identified athletes competing in women's sports. USA Powerlifting has banned all trans-identified males from participating in women's powerlifting competitions after JayCee Cooper, a trans-identified male, won the women's powerlifting state championship in Minnesota (424).

Furthermore, people are starting to protest the inclusion of transwomen in women's sports. A website called Savewomenssports.com has been set up to campaign on the issue of trans-identified athletes competing in women's sports (425). That this issue is gaining increased recognition is a positive step. The more people protest, the sooner this will come to an end.

Protecting Women's Spaces
The dangers of abolishing women's spaces are also starting to be understood. In the UK, ministers from the Department for Communities and Local Government have said that women have the legal right to single-sex toilets, and that public venues have legal duty to make places feel safe for women (426). More recently, the women's minister, Baroness Berridge has called for trans-identified males to be banned from women's toilets. She points out that the Equality Act allows for transgender people to be excluded from single-sex spaces if there is a legitimate reason for doing so (427). Furthermore, MP Jackie Doyle-Price, who was a former health minister, has called for the Equality Act to be amended to give greater legal protection for single-sex spaces (428). There may also be more protections introduced in the future. The equalities minister, Liz Truss, has said that the upcoming reforms to the Gender Recognition Act will prioritize the protection of single-sex spaces (429).

There is also action to protect other types of female-only spaces. In the UK, the Crown Prosecution Service have withdrawn their guidance on anti-transgender hate crime in schools. The guidance- which said that not letting transgender children use their preferred toilet and changing rooms at school was a hate crime- was withdrawn after a legal challenge from a 14-year-old girl (430). These rules also restricted expressing opposition to transgenderism. According to the girl's lawyers, if she had told another student she wouldn't date a transgender person or she had campaigned against transgender rights at school, she could have been breaking the law (431).

In addition, there is a judicial review taking place of Oxfordshire County Council's guidelines for transgender children in schools, on the grounds that this endangers other children. One of the recommendations is that trans-identified children use the toilets and changing rooms of the gender they identify as and stay in rooms with other children of their identified gender on residential trips. The parents bringing the case argue that this is putting the rights of trans-identified children above the rights of other children (432). A High Court judge has said that this case can be heard in full, and the hearing will go ahead later in 2020 (433,434).

Hospitals are also beginning to realize the importance of women's spaces. NHS Glasgow and Clyde Trust is reviewing its guidelines for dealing with female patients who show discomfort at being placed on a ward with trans-identified male patients. In the past, patients who complained about trans-identified males on the ward were to be chastised by staff and told that the patient is female. This practice is now being reviewed (435). Although this doesn't seem like a big win for trans-sceptical people, -after all, this policy should never have been put in place- all progress towards accepting biological sex is good progress, no matter how small it is.

In the USA, steps have also been taken to protect women's spaces. The Obama bathroom law, which gave school students the legal right to use the bathroom of their choice, was repealed by the Trump government shortly after he came to power (436), protecting the privacy and safety of female students. Additionally, the Department of Education have confirmed that they no longer investigate complaints about students not being allowed to use the toilets or other single sex facilities that of their gender identity (437). Furthermore, the US government is currently considering reversing the Equal Access rule. The Equal Access rule means that women's homeless shelters can only receive federal funding if they accept trans-identified male residents (438). Additionally, the government has also said that prisoners should be placed in a prison for people of their biological gender and should only be accommodated in a prison on the basis of their gender identity in exceptional circumstances (438).

Protection of Free Speech
Governments and legal systems are starting to take action to protect the right to criticize transgenderism. Partly in response to the no-platforming of gender critical speakers at universities, Gavin Williamson, the UK's secretary of state for education, has warned universities to protect free speech, or else they may be forced by law to do this (439). Since he said this, the UK government has begun preparing a bill to protect free speech at universities, which would fine student unions for no-platforming controversial speakers (440). While this measure is extreme (arguably, too extreme) it is good to see that the government recognizes the seriousness of the issue and the importance of free speech and academic freedom at universities.

The judicial system is also starting to protect freedom of expression in relation to transgenderism. Harry Miller, a former police officer and small business owner, made several Tweets about transgenderism, including one which said: "I was assigned mammal at birth, but my orientation is fish. Don't mis-species me". The police interviewed Miller about this on the phone and then visited his place of work to speak to him. They also recorded his Tweets as a transphobic non-crime hate incident. Fortunately, Miller challenged this at the High Court, who ruled that the Tweets did not break the law and that the investigation was disproportionate. The judge said "I find the combination of the police visiting the claimant's place of work, and their subsequent statements in relation to the possibility of prosecution, were a disproportionate interference with the claimant's right to freedom of expression because of their potential chilling effect" (441).

Progress in Healthcare
Finally, governments are now waking up to the issues around transgenderism in healthcare. In the US Affordable Care Act, Trump has removed the requirement for insurers to fund sex changes and other treatments for transsexual people, such as cross-sex hormones (442). This will benefit everyone because they don't have to pay for medically unnecessary sex change procedures and hormones through their insurance. This saving could hypothetically be passed on to the customer by reducing insurance premiums. In addition, the Department of Health and Human Services has revised their anti-discrimination policies from under the Obama administration, and gender identity is no longer included in protections from sex discrimination (438). Furthermore, the Trump administration has also allowed healthcare workers to refuse to perform sex-reassignment related treatments if they have moral or religious objections to this (443). This was blocked by a federal judge several months before this book was published, but it may be appealed in the future (437).

We can only hope that this progress continues. But that will require the work of the many people who do not support rampant transgenderism to ensure this. Even small victories are important. But we cannot be complacent. Transgenderism is still hurting many people. We must continue to fight.

12. Conclusion

'You are a slow learner, Winston,' said O'Brien gently.

'How can I help it?' he blubbered. "How can I help seeing what is in front of my eyes? Two and two are four.'

'Sometimes, Winston. Sometimes they are five. Sometimes they are three. Sometimes they are all of them at once. You must try harder. It is not easy to become sane.' (1)

Transgender dogma is permeating every aspect of society. Clever and otherwise logical people have begun to deny the most basic of biological facts; that there is no such thing as sex. Or that humans can change their sex. Or that it is possible for a person to be 'born in the wrong body'. Transgenderism has changed people's perceptions of reality in a way that wouldn't have previously been thought possible. That an ideology can have such a powerful impact on people is chilling. But it's not just the existence of biological sex that is in question. So many other things have been distorted too.

Moral lines have been blurred. Misguided left-wingers have allowed trans-identified people to behave in totally unacceptable ways in their race to be the most 'woke'. Violence against so-called 'TERFs' is now tolerated, while the mildest of insults- or even innocent mistakes- must now be punished with the full force of the law. Feelings are being placed ahead of facts. The way transgender people feel is being put ahead of anyone else's needs, and more importantly, ahead of scientific facts about sex differences. If women are upset about, say, being beaten in a sports competition by a trans-identified male, that's not okay. Instead, she must embrace the new reality where a woman competing with someone who is biologically male is completely fair. Free speech is also being jettisoned in favour of 'safe speech'. After all, what could matter more than a transgender person's feelings?

Statistics have been misused. We have been led to believe that transgender people are in immense danger, both from harm from others, and from suicide. We hear figures that are shocking but are in fact completely baseless. We have also been told that sex change procedures are wonderfully successful in preventing suicides. So much so that they are the only option for treating Gender Dysphoria and that they save healthcare systems money. These spurious statistics have helped gain public sympathy for transgenderism. But none of these things are correct. The whole transgender ideology is built on statistics that are either widely inaccurate, or in some cases, completely false. Poor quality studies are regularly used to justify transgenderism, but nobody is allowed to question it.

Science has been abused. We have been convinced that a toddler can be aware of their gender identity, that a nine-year-old is mature enough to make the decision to take powerful medication to stop puberty and that a 16-year-old can decide to take hormones that will cause irreversible changes to their body. Any evidence (or even simple common sense) that tells us that children are not able to know what they want or understand what a huge impact their choices will have on their body is completely overlooked. We know that children's brains are not developed enough to make good decisions, and that children do not have the insight to fully grasp the implications of changing sex. Yet healthcare practitioners will happily go along with a child's whims.

And the laws and society at large are increasingly forcing us to accept this. Given that the existence of biological sexes is now "not worthy of respect in a democratic society", and the dictionary definition of woman is deemed transphobic, we are reaching a stage where it is impossible for a person to speak out against transgenderism without facing serious repercussions. This has reached to all areas of society, even in many domains which previously championed freedom of expression, such as academia and the arts.

Many people are being hurt by transgenderism. Women's rights, spaces and services are being systematically destroyed. Men are being allowed to identify their way into women's spaces and services. The concerns of trans-identified males and 'non-binary' people are replacing women's rights. We are losing our right to safe spaces. Our birth control clinics are being transformed into gender identity clinics. Language is being changed to try and erase our existence. History is being re-written. And trans-identified males are increasingly taking over women's representation.

Worst of all, women can't talk about their oppression in case it upsets transgender people. Just as we were getting the confidence to talk publicly about issues such as menstruation, we are silenced by transgender people. In the past we were silenced by men who felt repulsed by menstruation. Now, we are silenced by trans-identified males, who claim to find menstruation triggering because it reminds them that they're not real women. (Although in practice, trans-identified males are most likely having the same objections that men had to discussing menstruation all along).

As a result, we are losing our ability to campaign for our rights. The word 'women' is gradually turning into a dirty word. When we campaign, we cannot talk about our reproductive abilities or our genitals, because that would be 'trans-exclusionary'. The problem is, who else will fight for these rights? Women need to be safe. We need sex-specific healthcare and we need access to birth control. What will happen to those things if women cannot campaign for them anymore because we have to include transgender people in our activism?

LGB rights are also being pushed back by transgenderism. It's difficult to understand why transgender activists can feel so entitled as to demand that lesbians have sex with them. After all, nobody chooses their sexual orientation (or as transgender rights activists call it, genital preferences). And it's not a lesbian's job to validate trans-identified male's perception that they are real women by having sex with them. It's as if transgender rights activists think that if these women tried hard enough, they would be able to become straight (as in attracted to members of the male sex, even if they identify as women) and enjoy having heterosexual sex. This is nothing but homophobia.

The invention of non-binary genders has also hurt women. By claiming to be neither male nor female, people who identify as non-binary reinforce gender roles. These gender roles hurt women much more than they hurt men. The traditional place for a woman is in the home, being subservient to her husband. While the man goes out, earns money and makes a success of himself. Feminists have spent many years fighting these gender roles, but non-binary people enforce the notion that these roles are natural, and by extension, that women's oppression is natural. It is also splitting feminism. Concerns about cis privilege have taken over from concerns about male privilege, and many feminists are now more focused on fighting cissexism rather than sexism. Also, what role do 'non-binary' women have in feminism? A woman who says she is biologically female but on the other hand, she says she is not a woman has put herself in a difficult position. How is this helpful for anyone? She might feel liberated, but she has left her sisters behind.

We often forget how hard our ancestors fought for women's rights. Or how these rights are so fragile. Women matter. Women's spaces matter. Woman's organizations matter. Women's rights matter. We must not sacrifice our rights for trans-identified people. Yet measures to help women gain equality are also endangered by transgenderism. Every time a trans-identified male takes a woman's place in a sports competition, a woman's award or a job reserved for a woman, an actual woman loses out. All this does is make women even less equal to men.

However, the biggest victims of transgenderism are transgender people themselves. Transsexualism is a mental illness that causes a delusion. In an attempt to validate that delusion, millions of people around the world have been mutilated. They have been left infertile- even banked eggs or sperm don't guarantee a baby. They have been given hormones that may shorten their lives. And they have been told that if they don't transition, they will become suicidal. We will never know how many transgender people have died of suicide because of social contagion. But what we do know is every one of those deaths is a tragedy. What is especially worrying is that there are well-tested therapies that can help with Gender Dysphoria that don't involve drastic surgery and other irreversible medical interventions. Yet these can no longer be used without doctors being accused of practicing 'conversion therapy'.

The growing number of people returning to their original gender also shows the damage that transgenderism can do. Many people will have to live with the effects of transitioning for the rest of their lives. They will never recover their fertility, or their female voice, or their original genitalia. The emotional impact of this must also be enormous, both on the person themselves and their family and friends. Sadly, some things can't be undone. Which is what makes the current fad for changing sex, and medical professional's rush to validate people's gender identity so dangerous.

The plight of transgender children is particularly tragic. Many children will not know what they have lost in terms of fertility and their genital function until it is too late. As a society, we accept that children need protection. There are so many things that they are too young to understand. But by letting a child change sex, we have failed to provide that protection. Families who have disagreed with letting their child change sex and have had their child taken into care as a result have also been torn apart. We will not know the full consequences of this for many years. We also don't know what impact transgenderism will have on a child's mental health when they grow up. But we do know that many transgender children don't grow up to be transgender adults. What will happen to those who started their medical transition in childhood? How will these children cope with romantic relationships if their sexual development has been stunted by puberty blockers? How will their infertility affect their mental health when they're desperate to have a child of their own? And nothing will ever bring someone's childhood back. These children's lives could easily be ruined forever.

So how can we end transgenderism? The left and the right will have to work together to solve this. If we don't, all that will happen is that women's rights, the right to free speech and all the other rights that transgenderism is threatening will continue to be eroded. Whenever someone is arrested, prosecuted or censored for saying something 'transphobic' -even if they're on the opposite side of the political spectrum- remember that it could be you next. When it comes to fighting transgenderism, anyone who agrees that a man cannot turn into a woman can work together. Facts are facts, wherever you lie on the political spectrum.

If you're a man, think of the women in your life. Mothers, sisters, wives, girlfriends, daughters, nieces, grandmothers, friends, granddaughters. They are all being put at risk by transgenderism. If you're a woman, don't feel pressured into accepting transgenderism. Trans-identified males are not our sisters. We do not need to let them into our spaces. Or let them use our services. We certainly shouldn't let ourselves be coerced into having sex with them. We do not need to be 'nice' (as women are so often socialized to do); we need to be strong and we need to stand up for our rights.

But how do we fight? Retaliation is not the answer. An eye for an eye leaves the whole world blind. It may feel good, but it rarely solves the problem. But there are lots of things that we can do. Firstly, get people to support the cause; tell other people about the impact of transgenderism. Tell people the truth about the "transgender people are incredibly vulnerable" myth. Show them the data that prove that trans-identified people are no more likely to be murdered than the general population. Tell them about the cases where women have been attacked or spied on in gender-neutral toilets, or when women in female-only spaces have been attacked by trans-identified males. Point out that the winner in the woman's sports event they're watching on television is actually a trans-identified male. Tell them that you can be arrested and fined for saying that a trans-identified male is biologically male. Tell people about how words like 'pregnant person' and 'people with a cervix' are being used in healthcare. Spread the word.

The second thing you can do is to support gender critical feminism. Sign petitions that support women's causes. Join organizations that promote gender critical feminism, such as Woman's Place UK, LGB Alliance, Fair Play for Women and the Woman's Human Rights Campaign. If you can, donate to them or volunteer for them too. Supporting individual activists is also important. If a gender critical feminist is facing a legal battle because of her views, consider donating money towards their legal fees. Or if you are involved in the legal profession yourself, you could take on the case, either pro-bono or for a reduced fee. You can also help with the psychological toll of campaigning by providing emotional support for other campaigners, either online or in real life. That way, we can help make it safe for people to speak out against transgenderism.

Political campaigning will also help. Campaign on any gender-related issue, big or small. Object to your child's school having a gender-neutral toilet. Write to your MP about the infringement of free speech. Tell your state senator about how transgender people in sports means your daughter has no chance of winning anymore. Write to local counsellors, MPs, mayors, senators, representatives or your country's equivalents whenever women's rights are being hit. Attend demonstrations and marches if you can. Also, think carefully about voting for a candidate or party who puts transgender rights above women's rights. If a party doesn't serve the interests of 50% of the population, should you really vote for them? On the other hand, if voting for a pro-transgender party is better than any alternative candidates, or not voting for them could lead to a worse party getting in power, then on balance, voting for a pro-transgender party might be the best option.

When it comes to private companies, hit them where it hurts- in the pocket. Boycott companies who have gender-neutral toilets or changing rooms and write to tell them why. Stop using social media sites that ban people for 'misgendering' trans-identified people. Companies won't listen unless it's affecting their profit margins. So vote with your feet and make them take notice. It's not just private companies you have to watch out for. Avoid donating to not-for-profits who support transgenderism. Even organizations whose main cause isn't transgenderism might be promoting transgenderism, so think carefully before you donate to a charity.

What about pro-transgenderism in the media? If you're in the UK, contact either the BBC Trust (for programs on the BBC) or OFCOM (for programs on any other television channel or radio station) and make a complaint, if you see a program that has a pro-transgender bias, could promote self-harm or suicide in transgender people or contains factual inaccuracies about transgenderism. For newspaper and magazine articles, complain to IPSO. If you live in another country, complain to your local media regulator if you have one. If there is no media regulator who has the power to deal with media bias or inaccurate information, try complaining to the television station, radio station or publisher. As well, think about boycotting channels, stations and publications that repeatedly show pro-transgender content. Admittedly, this is difficult and on balance, if the media outlet in question has good coverage on other issues, you might be as well to continue using them. Another idea is to praise content that questions the transgender narrative. You could write to a media outlet and tell them how pleased you are to see someone examining transgenderism critically rather than going along with what transgender activists say. These measures might not have a big impact alone, but if we all join together, media companies will start to take notice.

If you have anything to do with university, fight for free speech on campus. If you're a student or an academic, protest no-platforming. Explain the importance of listening to perspectives you disagree with to others. If you're a lecturer, support others who are being no-platformed and protest against conferences and other events being cancelled because of transgenderism. Also, protest against, and consider boycotting journals that retract trans-sceptical research. Fight against your university if they try and stop or suppress research into transgenderism. Remind people that many modern ideas and views were once controversial. Discussing transgenderism doesn't make someone a bigot. Nor does researching transgenderism.

How can we stop children being indoctrinated by transgenderism? If you're a parent, the best solution is to prepare your child to deal with transgenderism. You can't shield them away from hearing about transgenderism anymore, but you can propaganda-proof your children by talking about sex, gender and transgenderism at home from an early age. At one time, the idea of talking to a four-year-old about transgenderism would have seemed preposterous. Nowadays, a four-year-old could easily encounter trans-identified classmates or be 'educated' about transgenderism by their teacher at nursery or school. Tell them before they find out from someone else. Teach them what makes a boy a boy and what makes a girl a girl. Explain that this can never change and that a boy will grow into a man and a girl will grow into a woman. Whey they are old enough, make sure your child is getting the facts about puberty and reproduction. Both boys and girls should know about each other's reproductive systems. Just because your child's school does sex education does not mean your child is learning the truth, because schools are starting to have more 'trans-inclusive' education that teaches biological inaccuracies. As well as this, teach them to think critically in general. Talk about sources of information and if they're good sources or bad sources. Teach them the difference between fact and opinion. Explain to them what bias is too. If they know how to think for themselves, they are much less likely to fall for what other people tell them about transgenderism.

What if your child comes out as transgender or non-binary? Remember that you don't have to go along with everything your child says. Good families don't give each other automatic validation. They question each other. They feel able to raise disagreements. They are able to calmly consider other people's opinions. That's true of gender identity and all kinds of other things. It's not healthy to agree all the time on everything. Ultimately, hearing other people's opinions helps us make better decisions and see other perspectives on a certain issue. It's not hate or abuse to disagree with someone. If your child is used to listening to your opinion in a calm manner, they might be more receptive to you disagreeing with letting them change gender. Of course, it's up to your family to consider how exactly to deal with this specific situation.

What about pro-transgender people? Dealing with the 'right-on' woke types is tricky. The solution is to persuade, not argue. Have you ever heard the story of the Sun and the Wind? You can't force people into agreeing with you- they will just dig their heels in. Instead, pick your battles wisely. A person is more likely to feel able to listen to someone who has previously been calm and patient than they are to someone they've fought with in the past. If the time is right, listen and gently show you disagree. Phrases like "I'm not really sure about that" or "I see where you're coming from but..." can be useful. If you think they might be receptive to it, explain how transgenderism affects you personally. For instance, "as a woman, I'm really worried about sharing a public toilet with men in case I get attacked" or "I don't think it's right that you could be prosecuted for saying that sex is real because if that happens, what could you be prosecuted for next?" Carefully pointing out contradictions in the transgender ideology might also be helpful. Also, showing why a person's behaviours are unreasonable could work, but only if the person is prepared to listen. For example, when a person talks about the cotton ceiling, try saying "how would you like it if a gay man insisted you have sex with him? Why would this be okay?" However, remember that many transgender rights activists are deeply delusional and arguing with them would be fruitless. On the other hand, there are many young, impressionable people who have been caught up in transgenderism. Work on helping those people to realize the truth. Remember that people can -and do- change.

And most importantly, don't let transgender rights activists wear you down. Don't fall for their emotional blackmail. You are not responsible for transgender people's emotional wellbeing. Don't let them make you feel guilty. It can be tough. Having the support of other gender critical people will help you to cope with transgender rights activists. Remember that transgender rights activists only win when people let them. They can't carry on forever. Keep fighting and the tide will turn!

Too much is at stake for us not to fight. If it carries on, transgenderism will have a devastating effect on society. The biggest casualty will be women's rights. When we can't protest about sex-based issues, the rights afforded to us are threatened. Politics is still heavily male-dominated, so women have to fight for their issues to be recognized. How can we fight for our rights when we're not allowed to even say the word 'woman' or talk about our periods or our pregnancies? It's not hard to imagine that in this climate, women's rights will fall by the wayside. When women are deprived of safe spaces, it limits what we can do in life. Think about this; if a woman doesn't feel comfortable using gender-neutral public toilets, and there are no single-sex toilets available, she won't be able to spend much time away from her home. If she can't get changed at the swimming pool or gym without the fear of sexual abuse, she will stop using these facilities. If women fleeing domestic abuse don't feel safe in shelters, they will have no choice but to remain in an abusive relationship. And as for women's sports, will we see starting lines filled with burley, flat-chested 'women', with whom a biological woman has no realistic chance of competing with? Or worse, how many more women will suffer serious injuries because of trans-identified males in contact sports? Eventually, all the rights women fought hard for will be lost and women's status as the lesser sex will become even more firmly cemented.

LGB rights will also be lost. If transgender rights activists continue to say that genital preferences are transphobic, people will return to believing that being gay or a lesbian is a choice. This will provide fuel for religious groups who say that being gay or lesbian is sinful.
After all, if someone is choosing to prefer homosexual sex to heterosexual sex, then they can change their 'sinful' sexuality. As a result, the general public's sympathy toward LGB people may decline and homophobic discrimination could increase.

For transgender people, there will also be serious implications. More people will be left with irreversible damage to their bodies. Sadly, their mental health will be unlikely to improve as the result of trying to change sex. Furthermore, trans-identified children will grow into adults who regret their childhood sex change. Many will be unable to have children without fertility treatments- and even then, it's far from guaranteed. Ultimately, they will be left with irreparable physical and mental scars.

What will become of the 'they-bys'? Or the other non-binary children? For a small child, it must be so confusing to be the only child in your class at school who doesn't have a gender. For any child, being the 'odd one out' is difficult. It would invite bullying and feelings of isolation. As well, gender has a big impact on the way children socialize with each other. For better or for worse, gendered social groups are a big component of many children's lives. If a child is told they are neither a boy nor a girl, would they be accepted as part of these gendered social groups? If they are not accepted, how will that affect them mentally?

This will also have a big impact on healthcare. With the growing number of desisters, and evidence that many children's Gender Dysphoria will desist in adulthood, it won't be long until the lawsuits for wrongful sex transition start. After all, the very people who doctors aimed to help have been harmed by their treatment. The problem is that health services will bear the costs of compensation for people who were wrongly allowed to transition. It won't just be the compensation and other legal costs they'll have to pay. They'll also have to pay for sex change reversal surgeries, life-long hormone replacement therapy, fertility treatments and psychiatric care. Ultimately, this burden will be passed on to the taxpayer or health insurance customers; we will all have to pay for this.

Transgenderism will also have a big impact on children. For all children- transgender or not- the ridiculous woke education on gender will leave children confused about sex and puberty. Boys will be expecting their periods and girls will not know that they -and only they- can get pregnant. Worryingly, this could cause unintentional pregnancies if a couple don't understand how pregnancy happens and how it can be prevented.

Legally, there will also be alarming consequences if transgenderism carries on the way it currently is. The law will compel people to accept transgenderism. In terms of freedom of expression, more people will find themselves being prosecuted, sued or sacked for failing to accept transgenderism. Even the most trivial of remarks may result in a legal penalty. Governments and social media will keep restricting our speech. In the penal system, transgender people will continue to be prioritized over other offenders and be treated more leniently. We will live in a climate of fear. Mistakenly misgendering a person or accidentally using their old name will attract serious consequences, while transgender people will get away with all sorts of crimes.

As a result of the diminishment of academic freedoms, academics won't be able to research the serious issues with transgenderism. What if sex changes aren't so brilliant? Or letting children transition isn't the best idea? Because universities aren't allowing these topics to be researched, we will never know the answers to these questions.

Furthermore, what 'politically incorrect' research will be not allowed to happen next? After all, so many pieces of research are controversial, and many academics say controversial things. Even things that are intended to be sympathetic to transgenderism can be construed to be hateful. Where will it end if universities keep restricting research? It could easily spread to other areas of the academy.

And what about other oppressed people? Not everyone is a middle-class, social media wokester who can shout about their personal issues. As transgenderism commands a disproportionate amount of people's time, how many other people's issues have been ignored? We no longer care about people who don't tend to be on social media, like the impoverished and the elderly. Their concerns have been drowned out by transgenderism. So we don't know what kind of help they need anymore. Because we don't know what they need, we can't fix it. Also, the concerns of transgender people have been put ahead of everyone else's needs. Can an elderly person who can't see very well cope with a huge list of genders on a form? Can a woman who has Dyslexia and can't read well understand the word 'menstruator' in a leaflet from her doctor? Does the woman who has only just arrived in this country know that she is a 'person with a cervix' who should be having regular cervical smears?

Democracy will also be damaged. Freedom of expression is a keystone of a democracy. Without it, democracy doesn't function. But what is to stop the current limitations on freedom of speech extending into other areas? With transgenderism, the legal framework has been put in place for allowing greater restrictions on freedom of expression. As left-wingers, we cannot assume that because the current policies are in favour of 'our side', that will always be the case. What if suddenly, we find we are no longer allowed to say things in favour of abortion? Or birth control? What if we are no longer allowed to talk about gay and lesbian issues? By putting the legal frameworks in place for restricting freedom of expression, these things could happen. We could find ourselves in a position where it is illegal to criticize the government or where we are forced to practice a certain religious belief. Given that we are living in a world where even stating the most simple of biological facts is deemed unacceptable, it is alarming to think what views could be criminalized next. We've all heard the saying: "the path to hell is paved with good intentions". Well-meaning ideas can easily turn into a serious problem in the future. At the moment, most limits on free speech are about avoiding upsetting transgender people. Yet the rush to be kind and validate transgender people's gender identities could later be turned into something far more sinister.

And in the end, we will all be like Winston Smith at the end of 1984. We will all be unable to say what we truly think without the threat of arrest and imprisonment. We will all be unable to think for ourselves. We will all be unable to question what the government says. We will all be unable to tell what is true and what is not true. We will all think that a man can turn into a woman and a woman can turn into a man. We will all think that biological sex does not exist. We will all be unable to see what is before our eyes. We will all believe that $2+2=5$.

References

1. Orwell G. Nineteen Eighty-Four. Penguin Classics; 1949.

2. Greer G. The Whole Woman. London: Black Swan; 2007. 464 p.

3. Office for National Statistics. Gender Pay Gap in the UK [Internet]. Office for National Statistics. 2019 [cited 2020 Mar 9]. Available from: https://www.ons.gov.uk/employmentandlabourmarket/peoplei nwork/earningsandworkinghours/bulletins/genderpaygapinthe uk/2019

4. Gabrielsen P. Why Males Pack a Powerful Punch [Internet]. Phys.org. 2020 [cited 2020 Feb 12]. Available from: https://phys.org/news/2020-02-males-powerful.html

5. Office for National Statistics. Sexual Offences in England and Wales [Internet]. Office for National Statistics. 2017 [cited 2020 Mar 9]. Available from: https://www.ons.gov.uk/peoplepopulationandcommunity/crim eandjustice/articles/sexualoffencesinenglandandwales/yearendi ngmarch2017

6. UN Women. Facts and Figures: Ending Violence Against Women [Internet]. UN Women. 2019 [cited 2020 Mar 9]. Available from: https://www.unwomen.org/en/what-we-do/ending-violence-against-women/facts-and-figures

7. BBC News. Women Are Most Likely to Be Killed by Partner or Ex. BBC News [Internet]. 2020 Feb 20 [cited 2020 Mar 9]; Available from: https://www.bbc.com/news/newsbeat-51572665

8. World Health Organisation. Understanding and Addressing Violence Against Women [Internet]. World Health Organisation. 2012 [cited 2020 Mar 9]. Available from:

https://apps.who.int/iris/bitstream/handle/10665/77421/WHO_RHR_12.38_eng.pdf;sequence=1

9. Flores AR, Herman JL, Gates GJ, Brown TNT. How Many Adults Identify as Transgender in the United States? [Internet]. Los Angeles: The Williams Institute; 2016 Jun p. 13. Available from: https://williamsinstitute.law.ucla.edu/wp-content/uploads/How-Many-Adults-Identify-as-Transgender-in-the-United-States.pdf

10. Government Equalities Office. Trans people in the UK. Gov.uk. 2018.

11. Miller M. The Real-Life Danish Girl: The Story of 1920s Transgender Artist Lili Elbe [Internet]. PEOPLE.com. 2015 [cited 2020 Mar 15]. Available from: https://people.com/movies/the-real-life-danish-girl-the-story-of-1920s-transgender-artist-lili-elbe/

12. Hadjimatheou C. Christine Jorgensen: 60 Years of Sex Change Ops. BBC News [Internet]. 2012 Nov 30 [cited 2020 Mar 15]; Available from: https://www.bbc.com/news/magazine-20544095

13. Historic England. Transsexual Pioneers [Internet]. Historic England. [cited 2020 Mar 15]. Available from: http://historicengland.org.uk/research/inclusive-heritage/lgbtq-heritage-project/trans-and-gender-crossing-histories/transsexual-pioneers/

14. Pace E. Harry Benjamin Dies at 101; Specialist in Transsexualism. The New York Times [Internet]. 1986 Aug 27 [cited 2020 Mar 5]; Available from: https://www.nytimes.com/1986/08/27/obituaries/harry-benjamin-dies-at-101-specialist-in-transsexualism.html

15. Whittle S. A Brief History of Transgender Issues. The Guardian [Internet]. 2010 Jun 2 [cited 2020 Mar 15]; Available from:

https://www.theguardian.com/lifeandstyle/2010/jun/02/brief-history-transgender-issues

16. Pacheco K. Johns Hopkins Hospital Reaffirms Its Commitment to Transgender Community [Internet]. Baltimore Magazine. 2019 [cited 2020 Mar 15]. Available from: https://www.baltimoremagazine.com/section/health/johns-hopkins-gender-identity-clinic-transgender-surgery

17. Gilbert S. Homophobia and the Modern Trans Movement [Internet]. Quillette. 2019 [cited 2020 Mar 3]. Available from: https://quillette.com/2019/01/31/homophobia-and-the-modern-trans-movement/

18. North West Lancashire Health Authority v A, D and G [Internet]. Clair McNab. 1999 [cited 2020 Mar 3]. Available from: http://www.pfc.org.uk/caselaw/Appeals%20Court%20judgment%20in%20the%20case%20of%20North%20West%20Lancashire%20Health%20Authority%20v%20A,%20D%20and%20G.pdf

19. Van Kück v. Germany [Internet]. 2003 [cited 2020 Mar 23]. Available from: https://hudoc.echr.coe.int/eng#{%22itemid%22:[%22001-61142%22]}

20. American Medical Association. Issue Brief: Health Insurance Coverage for Gender-Affirming Care of Transgender Patients [Internet]. American Medical Association. 2019. Available from: https://www.ama-assn.org/system/files/2019-03/transgender-coverage-issue-brief.pdf

21. Lyons K. Gender Identity Clinic Services Under Strain as Referral Rates Soar. The Guardian [Internet]. 2016 Jul 10 [cited 2020 Mar 8]; Available from: https://www.theguardian.com/society/2016/jul/10/transgender-clinic-waiting-times-patient-numbers-soar-gender-identity-services

22. Rayner G. Minister Orders Inquiry into 4,000 Per Cent Rise in Children Wanting to Change Sex. The Telegraph [Internet]. 2018 Sep 16 [cited 2020 Mar 8]; Available from: https://www.telegraph.co.uk/politics/2018/09/16/minister-orders-inquiry-4000-per-cent-rise-children-wanting/

23. Nutt AE. Transgender Surgeries Are on the Rise, Says First Study of Its Kind [Internet]. Washington Post. 2018 [cited 2020 Mar 23]. Available from: https://www.washingtonpost.com/news/to-your-health/wp/2018/02/28/transgender-surgeries-are-on-the-rise-says-first-study-of-its-kind/

24. Orange R. Teenage Transgender Row Splits Sweden as Dysphoria Diagnoses Soar by 1,500%. The Observer [Internet]. 2020 Feb 22 [cited 2020 Mar 15]; Available from: https://www.theguardian.com/society/2020/feb/22/ssweden-teenage-transgender-row-dysphoria-diagnoses-soar

25. Drescher J. Gender Diagnoses and ICD-11. Psychiatrics News [Internet]. 2016 Aug 15 [cited 2020 Mar 6]; Available from: https://psychnews.psychiatryonline.org/doi/abs/10.1176/appi.pn.2016.8a15

26. Jacques J. 10 Great Transgender Films [Internet]. British Film Institute. 2019 [cited 2020 Apr 28]. Available from: https://www.bfi.org.uk/news-opinion/news-bfi/lists/10-great-transgender-films

27. Reuters/Nielsen. 'Pregnant Man' Documentary in the Works. Reuters [Internet]. 2008 Jul 11 [cited 2020 Apr 27]; Available from: https://www.reuters.com/article/us-beatie-idUSL107413020080711

28. Anderson RT. When Harry Became Sally: Responding to the Transgender Moment. New York: Encounter Books; 2018.

29. Lees P. My Transsexual Summer: A New View of Gender. The Guardian [Internet]. 2011 Nov 7 [cited 2020 Apr 28]; Available from:

https://www.theguardian.com/world/2011/nov/07/my-transsexual-summer-channel-4

30. Wollaston S. Transformation Street Review – Three Eloquent Case Studies Discuss Changing Gender. The Guardian [Internet]. 2018 Jan 12 [cited 2020 Apr 28]; Available from: https://www.theguardian.com/tv-and-radio/2018/jan/12/transformation-street-review-three-eloquent-case-studies-discuss-changing-gender

31. Haimson OL, Dame-Griff A, Capello E, Richter Z. Tumblr was a Trans Technology: The Meaning, Importance, History, and Future of Trans Technologies. Feminist Media Studies. 2019 Oct 18;0(0):1–17.

32. Pariser E. The Filter Bubble: What the Internet Is Hiding From You. London: Penguin; 2012. 304 p.

33. Shivaram AT Elizabeth Kneebone, and Ranjitha. Signs of Digital Distress: Mapping Broadband Availability and Subscription in American Neighborhoods [Internet]. Brookings. 2017 [cited 2020 Feb 21]. Available from: https://www.brookings.edu/research/signs-of-digital-distress-mapping-broadband-availability/

34. Anderson M, Kumar M. Digital Divide Persists Even as Lower-Income Americans Make Gains in Tech Adoption [Internet]. Pew Research Center. 2019 [cited 2020 Apr 3]. Available from: https://www.pewresearch.org/fact-tank/2019/05/07/digital-divide-persists-even-as-lower-income-americans-make-gains-in-tech-adoption/

35. Jeffreys S. Gender Hurts. Abingdon: Routledge; 2014.

36. American Psychiatric Association. Gender Dysphoria [Internet]. 2013 [cited 2020 Dec 5]. Available from: https://www.psychiatry.org/File%20Library/Psychiatrists/Practice/DSM/APA_DSM-5-Gender-Dysphoria.pdf

37. Berry S. Dr. Quentin Van Meter: Transgenderism Invented in 1950s University Lab [Internet]. Breitbart. 2018 [cited 2020 May 14]. Available from: https://www.breitbart.com/politics/2018/10/24/dr-quentin-van-meter-transgenderism-invented-1950s-johns-hopkins-lab/

38. Australian Associated Press. US Professor, Who Says Being Transgender is a 'Delusion', to Speak at WA University [Internet]. The Guardian. 2018 [cited 2020 May 14]. Available from: http://www.theguardian.com/australia-news/2018/aug/15/us-professor-who-says-being-transgender-is-a-delusion-to-speak-at-wa-university

39. Corradi RB. Psychiatry Professor: 'Transgenderism' Is Mass Hysteria Similar To 1980s-Era Junk Science [Internet]. The Federalist. 2016 [cited 2020 Mar 3]. Available from: https://thefederalist.com/2016/11/17/psychiatry-professor-transgenderism-mass-hysteria-similar-1980s-era-junk-science/

40. Meybodi AM, Hajebi A, Jolfaei AG. The Frequency of Personality Disorders in Patients with Gender Identity Disorder. Medical Journal of the Islamic Republic of Iran. 2014 Sep 10;28:90.

41. Anzani A, De Panfilis C, Scandurra C, Prunas A. Personality Disorders and Personality Profiles in a Sample of Transgender Individuals Requesting Gender-Affirming Treatments. International Journal of Environmental Research and Public Health [Internet]. 2020 Mar [cited 2020 May 18];17(5). Available from: https://www.ncbi.nlm.nih.gov/pmc/articles/PMC7084367/

42. Veague HB, Collins CE. Personality Disorders [Internet]. Infobase Publishing; 2007. 127 p. Available from: https://books.google.co.uk/books?id=EGZZgqcIkm0C&pg=PA62&dq=personality+disorder+cause&hl=en&sa=X&ved=0ahUKEwiZ3JWnt7TpAhUzTxUIHe5PDdQQuwUILjAA#v=onepage&q=personality%20disorder%20cause&f=false

43. Rajkumar RP. Gender Identity Disorder and Schizophrenia: Neurodevelopmental Disorders with Common Causal Mechanisms? [Internet]. Vol. 2014, Schizophrenia Research and Treatment. Hindawi; 2014 [cited 2020 May 17]. p. e463757. Available from: https://www.hindawi.com/journals/schizort/2014/463757/

44. Davey GCL. Is Anxiety a Delusion? [Internet]. Psychology Today. 2015 [cited 2020 May 11]. Available from: https://www.psychologytoday.com/blog/why-we-worry/201510/is-anxiety-delusion

45. Perry L. What Is Autogynephilia? An Interview with Dr Ray Blanchard [Internet]. Quillette. 2019 [cited 2020 Mar 30]. Available from: https://quillette.com/2019/11/06/what-is-autogynephilia-an-interview-with-dr-ray-blanchard/

46. Bailey JM, Triea K. What Many Transgender Activists Don't Want You to Know: and Why You Should Know it Anyway. Perspectives in Biology and Medicine. 2007 Oct 16;50(4):521–34.

47. Dreger A. Galileo's Middle Finger: Heretics, Activists, and One Scholar's Search for Justice. Penguin Books; 2015. 354 p.

48. Hartley E. Why do so Many Teenage Girls Want to Change Gender? [Internet]. 2020 [cited 2020 Apr 1]. Available from: https://www.prospectmagazine.co.uk/magazine/tavistock-transgender-transition-teenage-girls-female-to-male

49. Littman L. Correction: Parent Reports of Adolescents and Young Adults Perceived to Show Signs of a Rapid Onset of Gender Dysphoria. PLOS ONE. 2019 Mar 19;14(3):e0214157.

50. Reynolds M. Gender Identity Issues for Brighton High School's 76 Pupils [Internet]. Express.co.uk. 2018 [cited 2020 Mar 11]. Available from: https://www.express.co.uk/news/uk/1051523/Gender-identity-Brighton-school-gender-fluid-education-transgender

51. Grant J. Trans Family Trolled After Revealing Daughter, 5, Born a Boy Wants to be Girl [Internet]. Daily Record. 2019 [cited 2020 Mar 11]. Available from: https://www.dailyrecord.co.uk/news/scottish-news/scots-trans-family-abused-trolls-13852091

52. Veissière SP. Why Is Transgender Identity on the Rise Among Teens? [Internet]. Psychology Today. 2018 [cited 2020 Mar 30]. Available from: https://www.psychologytoday.com/blog/culture-mind-and-brain/201811/why-is-transgender-identity-the-rise-among-teens

53. Jones K. Wachowski Sisters: Second 'Matrix' Director Comes Out as Transgender [Internet]. Breitbart. 2016 [cited 2020 Mar 26]. Available from: https://www.breitbart.com/entertainment/2016/03/08/wachowski-sisters-second-matrix-director-comes-transgender/

54. Haney S. An Entire Family of Four- Man, Woman, Son and Daughter- is Transgender [Internet]. Mail Online. 2017 [cited 2020 Mar 11]. Available from: http://www.dailymail.co.uk/news/article-5185209/An-entire-family-four-transgender.html

55. Lewis R. Is Transgender Identity Inherited? [Internet]. Plos DNA Science Blog. 2017 [cited 2020 Mar 30]. Available from: http://blogs.plos.org/dnascience/?p=6589

56. Diamond M. Transsexuality Among Twins: Identity Concordance, Transition, Rearing, and Orientation. International Journal of Transgenderism. 2013 Jan 1;14(1):24–38.

57. Sullivan PF, Kendler KS, Neale MC. Schizophrenia as a Complex Trait: Evidence from a Meta-analysis of Twin Studies. Archives of General Psychiatry. 2003 Dec 1;60(12):1187–92.

58. Dunn EC, Brown RC, Dai Y, Rosand J, Nugent NR, Amstadter AB, et al. Genetic Determinants of Depression: Recent Findings and Future Directions. Harvard Review of Psychiatry. 2015;23(1):1–18.

59. Levey DF, Gelernter J, Polimanti R, Zhou H, Cheng Z, Aslan M, et al. Reproducible Genetic Risk Loci for Anxiety: Results From ~200,000 Participants in the Million Veteran Program. AJP. 2020 Jan 7;177(3):223–32.

60. Kerner B. Genetics of Bipolar Disorder. The Application of Clinical Genetics. 2014 Feb 12;7:33–42.

61. Pinheiro AP, Root T, Bulik CM. The Genetics of Anorexia Nervosa: Current Findings and Future Perspectives. International Journal of Child and Adolescent Health. 2009;2(2):153–64.

62. Bodkin H. Transgender Brain Scans Promised as Study Shows Structural Differences in People with Gender Dysphoria. The Telegraph [Internet]. 2018 May 22 [cited 2020 May 14]; Available from: https://www.telegraph.co.uk/news/2018/05/22/transgender-brain-scans-promised-study-shows-structural-differences/

63. Khorashad BS, Khazai B, Talaei A, Acar F, Hudson AR, Borji N, et al. Improving Reliability in Clinical Neuroimaging: A Study in Transgender Persons. bioRxiv. 2019 Dec 2;861864.

64. Eliot L. Neurosexism: The Myth that Men and Women have Different Brains. Nature. 2019 Feb 27;566(7745):453–4.

65. Joel D, Berman Z, Tavor I, Wexler N, Gaber O, Stein Y, et al. Sex Beyond the Genitalia: The Human Brain Mosaic. Proceedings of the National Academy of Sciences. 2015 Dec 15;112(50):15468–73.

66. Eliot L. Girl Brain, Boy Brain? [Internet]. Scientific American. 2009 [cited 2020 Mar 29]. Available from:

https://www.scientificamerican.com/article/girl-brain-boy-brain/

67. Jabr F. Cache Cab: Taxi Drivers' Brains Grow to Navigate London's Streets [Internet]. Scientific American. 2011 [cited 2020 May 15]. Available from: https://www.scientificamerican.com/article/london-taxi-memory/

68. Cell Press. Political Views are Reflected in Brain Structure [Internet]. ScienceDaily. 2011 [cited 2020 May 15]. Available from: https://www.sciencedaily.com/releases/2011/04/110407121337.htm

69. Sun SD. Stop Using Phony Science to Justify Transphobia [Internet]. Scientific American Blog Network. 2019 [cited 2020 Mar 4]. Available from: https://blogs.scientificamerican.com/voices/stop-using-phony-science-to-justify-transphobia/

70. Genetics Home Reference. Swyer syndrome [Internet]. Genetics Home Reference. 2020 [cited 2020 May 17]. Available from: https://ghr.nlm.nih.gov/condition/swyer-syndrome

71. Genetics Home Reference. Campomelic Dysplasia [Internet]. Genetics Home Reference. 2020 [cited 2020 May 17]. Available from: https://ghr.nlm.nih.gov/condition/campomelic-dysplasia

72. Genetics Home Reference. 46, XX Testicular Disorder of Sex Development [Internet]. Genetics Home Reference. 2020 [cited 2020 May 17]. Available from: https://ghr.nlm.nih.gov/condition/46xx-testicular-disorder-of-sex-development

73. Carr G. Here's What The 2018 Olympic Gender Regulations Look Like [Internet]. Daily Caller. 2017 [cited 2020 Mar 9].

Available from: https://dailycaller.com/2017/07/03/heres-what-the-2018-olympic-gender-regulations-look-like/

74. Holland K, Cruickshank H. Signs and Symptoms of High Estrogen: Diagnosis, Treatment, and More [Internet]. Healthline. 2018 [cited 2020 Apr 28]. Available from: https://www.healthline.com/health/high-estrogen

75. Hilton E. Project Nettie [Internet]. Project Nettie. [cited 2020 Apr 12]. Available from: https://projectnettie.wordpress.com/

76. Younger R. Britain has Reached a 'Point of Crisis' Over Transgender Services, Support Group Says [Internet]. ITV News. 2015 [cited 2020 Mar 10]. Available from: https://www.itv.com/news/2015-10-29/transgender/

77. Parry H. How Much Transgender Soldiers REALLY Cost the US Military [Internet]. Mail Online. 2017 [cited 2020 Mar 10]. Available from: http://www.dailymail.co.uk/~/article-4735902/index.html

78. Go JJ. Should Gender Reassignment Surgery be Publicly Funded? Journal of Bioethical Inquiry. 2018;15(4):527–34.

79. Coleman E, Bockting W, Botzer M, Cohen-Kettenis P, DeCuypere G, Feldman J, et al. Standards of Care for the Health of Transsexual, Transgender, and Gender-Nonconforming People [Internet]. Seventh. World Professional Association for Transgender Health; 2012 [cited 2020 Apr 23]. Available from: https://wpath.org/media/cms/Documents/SOC%20v7/Standards%20of%20Care_V7%20Full%20Book_English.pdf

80. Payne D. Casualties of a Social, Psychological, and Medical Fad: The Dangers of Transgender Ideology in Medicine [Internet]. Public Discourse. 2018 [cited 2020 Apr 3]. Available from: https://www.thepublicdiscourse.com/2018/01/20810/

81. Batty D. Sex Changes are not Effective, Say Researchers [Internet]. the Guardian. 2004 [cited 2020 May 12]. Available from: http://www.theguardian.com/society/2004/jul/30/health.mentalhealth

82. Aggressive Research Intelligence Facility. Gender Reassignment [Internet]. Public Health. 2004. Available from: https://www.birmingham.ac.uk/Documents/college-mds/haps/projects/ARIF/completed-requests.pdf

83. Dhejne C, Lichtenstein P, Boman M, Johansson ALV, Långström N, Landén M. Long-Term Follow-Up of Transsexual Persons Undergoing Sex Reassignment Surgery: Cohort Study in Sweden. PLOS ONE. 2011 Feb 22;6(2):e16885.

84. Schreiber K. Why Transgender People Experience More Mental Health Issues [Internet]. Psychology Today. 2016 [cited 2020 Mar 11]. Available from: https://www.psychologytoday.com/blog/the-truth-about-exercise-addiction/201612/why-transgender-people-experience-more-mental-health

85. Schumacher H. Why More Men than Women Die by Suicide [Internet]. BBC Future. 2019 [cited 2020 Mar 11]. Available from: https://www.bbc.com/future/article/20190313-why-more-men-kill-themselves-than-women

86. Payne D. Transgender Suicide Rate Isn't Due to Discrimination [Internet]. The Federalist. 2016 [cited 2020 Mar 31]. Available from: https://thefederalist.com/2016/07/07/evidence-the-transgender-suicide-rate-isnt-due-to-discrimination/

87. Brådvik L. Suicide Risk and Mental Disorders. International Journal of Environmental Research and Public Health [Internet]. 2018 Sep [cited 2020 Apr 1];15(9). Available from: https://www.ncbi.nlm.nih.gov/pmc/articles/PMC6165520/

88. Devitt P. 13 Reasons Why and Suicide Contagion [Internet]. Scientific American. 2017 [cited 2020 Mar 16]. Available from: https://www.scientificamerican.com/article/13-reasons-why-and-suicide-contagion1/

89. Chalk C. Validating Suicide in Response to Transgender Skepticism is Irresponsible [Internet]. The Federalist. 2020 [cited 2020 Mar 16]. Available from: https://thefederalist.com/2020/03/05/validating-suicide-in-response-to-transgender-skepticism-is-horrifically-irresponsible/

90. Ditum S. If you Believe Trans Lives Matter, don't Share Leelah Alcorn's Suicide Note on Social Media [Internet]. New Statesman. 2015 [cited 2020 Apr 25]. Available from: https://www.newstatesman.com/sarah-ditum/2015/01/if-you-believe-trans-lives-matter-dont-share-leelah-alcorns-suicide-note-social

91. Moore E, Wisniewski A, Dobs A. Endocrine Treatment of Transsexual People: A Review of Treatment Regimens, Outcomes, and Adverse Effects. The Journal of Clinical Endocrinology & Metabolism. 2003 Aug 1;88(8):3467–73.

92. NHS. Cosmetic Procedures - Breast Reduction (Female) [Internet]. nhs.uk. 2019 [cited 2020 May 15]. Available from: https://www.nhs.uk/conditions/cosmetic-procedures/breast-reduction-female/

93. Toro R. How Gender Reassignment Surgery Works (Infographic) [Internet]. livescience.com. 2013 [cited 2020 Mar 29]. Available from: https://www.livescience.com/39170-how-gender-reassignment-surgery-works-infographic.html

94. Garcia MM. Men's Health and Transgender Surgery: A Urologist's Perspective. Translational Andrology and Urology. 2016 Apr;5(2):225–7.

95. Melloni C, Melloni G, Rossi M, Rolle L, Carmisciano M, Timpano M, et al. Lower Urinary Tract Symptoms in Male-to-

Female Transsexuals: Short Terms Results and Proposal of a New Questionnaire. Plastic and Reconstructive Surgery Global Open [Internet]. 2016 Mar 18 [cited 2020 Mar 2];4(3). Available from: https://www.ncbi.nlm.nih.gov/pmc/articles/PMC4874299/

96. Salgado CJ, Nugent A, Kuhn J, Janette M, Bahna H. Primary Sigmoid Vaginoplasty in Transwomen: Technique and Outcomes [Internet]. Vol. 2018, BioMed Research International. Hindawi; 2018 [cited 2020 May 13]. p. e4907208. Available from: https://www.hindawi.com/journals/bmri/2018/4907208/

97. Horbach SER, Bouman M-B, Smit JM, Özer M, Buncamper ME, Mullender MG. Outcome of Vaginoplasty in Male-to-Female Transgenders: A Systematic Review of Surgical Techniques. The Journal of Sexual Medicine. 2015 Jun;12(6):1499–512.

98. Parkins K. Meet the Gender Reassignment Surgeons: 'Demand is Going Through the Roof'. The Guardian [Internet]. 2016 Jul 10 [cited 2020 Mar 24]; Available from: https://www.theguardian.com/society/2016/jul/10/meet-the-gender-reassignment-surgeons-demand-is-going-through-the-roof

99. Rashid M, Tamimy MS. Phalloplasty: The Dream and the Reality. Indian Journal of Plastic Surgery. 2013;46(2):283–93.

100. Center for Devices and Radiological Health. Questions and Answers about Breast Implant-Associated Anaplastic Large Cell Lymphoma (BIA-ALCL) [Internet]. FDA. FDA; 2019 [cited 2020 May 12]. Available from: https://www.fda.gov/medical-devices/breast-implants/questions-and-answers-about-breast-implant-associated-anaplastic-large-cell-lymphoma-bia-alcl

101. Center for Devices and Radiological Health. Risks and Complications of Breast Implants [Internet]. FDA. FDA; 2019 [cited 2020 May 13]. Available from:

https://www.fda.gov/medical-devices/breast-implants/risks-and-complications-breast-implants

102. Bellinga RJ, Capitán L, Simon D, Tenório T. Technical and Clinical Considerations for Facial Feminization Surgery with Rhinoplasty and Related Procedures. JAMA Facial Plastic Surgery. 2017 May;19(3):175–81.

103. Södersten M, Nygren U, Hertegård S, Dhejne C. Interdisciplinary Program in Sweden Related to Transgender Voice. Perspectives on Voice and Voice Disorders. 2015 Jul;25(2):87–97.

104. Jacques J. 'Vocal Restraint is Constantly Demanded of Women' [Internet]. the Guardian. 2010 [cited 2020 May 16]. Available from: http://www.theguardian.com/lifeandstyle/2010/nov/16/transgender

105. Human Fertilisation and Embryology Authority. What is IVF? The Process, Risks, Success Rates and More. [Internet]. Human Fertilisation and Embryology Authority. [cited 2020 Apr 23]. Available from: https://www.hfea.gov.uk/treatments/explore-all-treatments/in-vitro-fertilisation-ivf/

106. Praderio C. There's a Dark Side to Egg Freezing that no one is Talking About [Internet]. Insider. 2017 [cited 2020 Apr 16]. Available from: https://www.insider.com/egg-freezing-failure-risks-2017-3

107. Weaver J, Edwards E. Malfunction at Egg Freezing Facility Affects Hundreds of Patients [Internet]. NBC News. 2018 [cited 2020 Apr 15]. Available from: https://www.nbcnews.com/health/womens-health/malfunction-egg-freezing-facility-affects-hundreds-patients-n855016

108. Lopez G. The Debate About Transgender Children and 'Detransitioning' is Really About Transphobia [Internet]. Vox. 2016 [cited 2020 Mar 5]. Available from:

https://www.vox.com/2016/8/9/12404246/transgender-children-detransitioning-transphobia

109. Shute J. Sex Change Regret: Gender Reversal Surgery is on the Rise, so Why Aren't We Talking About it? The Telegraph [Internet]. 2017 Oct 1 [cited 2020 Mar 11]; Available from: https://www.telegraph.co.uk/health-fitness/body/gender-reversal-surgery-rise-arent-talking/

110. O'Neil T. Ex-Transgender Network Set Up for 'Hundreds' of Detransitioners in UK [Internet]. News and Politics. 2019 [cited 2020 Apr 12]. Available from: https://pjmedia.com/trending/ex-transgender-network-set-up-for-hundreds-of-detransitioners-in-uk/

111. Akbar J. Reverse Transsexual Walt Heyer says Becoming Woman was a Mistake [Internet]. Mail Online. 2015 [cited 2020 Mar 5]. Available from: https://www.dailymail.co.uk/news/article-2921528/The-man-s-TWO-sex-changes-Incredible-story-Walt-Laura-REVERSED-operation-believes-surgeons-quick-operate.html

112. Heyer W. I Was a Transgender Woman [Internet]. Public Discourse. 2015 [cited 2020 Mar 22]. Available from: https://www.thepublicdiscourse.com/2015/04/14688/

113. McFadden J. 'Transition Caused More Problems than it Solved'. The Guardian [Internet]. 2017 Sep 16 [cited 2020 Mar 22]; Available from: https://www.theguardian.com/lifeandstyle/2017/sep/16/transition-caused-more-problems-than-it-solved

114. Proctor LP and L. From She to He - and Back to She Again. BBC News [Internet]. 2020 Mar 10 [cited 2020 Mar 10]; Available from: https://www.bbc.com/news/stories-51806011

115. Petter O. Gender Reversal Surgery is More In-demand than Ever Before [Internet]. The Independent. 2017 [cited 2020 Mar 22]. Available from: http://www.independent.co.uk/life-

style/gender-reversal-surgery-demand-rise-assignment-men-women-trans-a7980416.html

116. Vincent J. Facebook Introduces More Than 70 New Gender Options to UK [Internet]. The Independent. 2014 [cited 2020 Mar 9]. Available from: http://www.independent.co.uk/life-style/gadgets-and-tech/facebook-introduces-more-than-70-new-gender-options-to-the-uk-we-want-to-reflect-society-9567261.html

117. Virtual Space Amino. Here are 63 Genders of the Hundreds of Genders [Internet]. aminoapps.com. [cited 2020 Mar 9]. Available from: https://aminoapps.com/c/virtual-space/page/blog/here-are-63-genders-of-the-hundreds-of-genders/J1Id_uPD0bGDNakkXVJa4YoNL2ZNlN

118. Thienenkamp M. Gender: Is 'The Guardian' Wrong? Is Everyone Non-Binary? [Internet]. ComicsVerse. 2017 [cited 2020 Mar 8]. Available from: https://comicsverse.com/gender-guardian-non-binary/

119. Young S. This is What it Means to be Non-Binary [Internet]. The Independent. 2019 [cited 2020 Mar 5]. Available from: https://www.independent.co.uk/life-style/non-binary-meaning-gender-definition-genderqueer-sam-smith-a8829261.html

120. Bulman M. HSBC is Now Offering 10 Gender-Neutral Titles for Trans Customers [Internet]. The Independent. 2017 [cited 2020 Apr 23]. Available from: http://www.independent.co.uk/news/uk/home-news/hsbc-bank-transgender-customers-neutral-titles-mx-ind-mre-a7659686.html

121. Ask a Non-Binary. Ask a Non-Binary [Internet]. Tumblr. 2014 [cited 2020 Mar 8]. Available from: https://askanonbinary.tumblr.com/post/74544202338/list-of-pronouns

122. Goldberg M. What Is a Woman? [Internet]. The New Yorker. 2014 [cited 2020 Apr 29]. Available from: https://www.newyorker.com/magazine/2014/08/04/woman-2

123. Sherman N. Should your Email Say if You're He, She or They? BBC News [Internet]. 2020 Feb 19 [cited 2020 Mar 5]; Available from: https://www.bbc.com/news/business-51331571

124. Busby E. Edinburgh University Students to be Given Gender Pronoun Badges During Freshers Week [Internet]. The Independent. 2018 [cited 2020 Mar 11]. Available from: https://www.independent.co.uk/news/education/education-news/edinburgh-university-gender-pronoun-badges-transgender-students-freshers-welcome-week-a8511136.html

125. Forsyth L. University Hands out 'Pronoun' Badges to Students to Avoid 'Misgendering' [Internet]. The Mirror. 2018 [cited 2020 Apr 20]. Available from: https://www.mirror.co.uk/news/uk-news/university-hands-out-pronoun-badges-13362943

126. Retta M. Work Sucks, Especially When People Get Your Pronouns Wrong [Internet]. Vice. 2019 [cited 2020 Apr 14]. Available from: https://www.vice.com/en_us/article/kzmy39/pronouns-at-work-trans-nonbinary

127. Williams ACS and JA. Why We Should All Use They/Them Pronouns [Internet]. Scientific American Blog Network. 2019 [cited 2020 Mar 5]. Available from: https://blogs.scientificamerican.com/voices/why-we-should-all-use-they-them-pronouns/

128. Ahmed M, Hanna A, Keyes O, Stevens NL. Actually, We Should Not All Use They/Them Pronouns [Internet]. Scientific American Blog Network. 2019 [cited 2020 Mar 5]. Available from: https://blogs.scientificamerican.com/voices/actually-we-should-not-all-use-they-them-pronouns/

129. Kerr B. Pronouns are Rohypnol [Internet]. Fair Play for Women. 2019 [cited 2020 Mar 11]. Available from: https://fairplayforwomen.com/pronouns/

130. Finch SD. Help! I Think I Might Be Non-Binary, But How Can I Know? [Internet]. Everyday Feminism. 2015 [cited 2020 Mar 5]. Available from: https://everydayfeminism.com/2015/07/am-i-non-binary/

131. Maglaty J. When Did Girls Start Wearing Pink? [Internet]. Smithsonian Magazine. 2011 [cited 2020 Apr 17]. Available from: https://www.smithsonianmag.com/arts-culture/when-did-girls-start-wearing-pink-1370097/

132. Pinsker J. Why Some Parents Turn Boys' Names into Girls' Names [Internet]. The Atlantic. 2018 [cited 2020 Apr 23]. Available from: https://www.theatlantic.com/family/archive/2018/09/girls-names-for-baby-boys/569962/

133. Boseley S. Children are Straitjacketed into Gender Roles in Early Adolescence, Says Study. The Guardian [Internet]. 2017 Sep 20 [cited 2020 Mar 10]; Available from: https://www.theguardian.com/society/2017/sep/20/children-are-straitjacketed-into-gender-roles-in-early-adolescence-says-study

134. Oksman O. Are Gendered Toys Harming Childhood Development? The Guardian [Internet]. 2016 May 28 [cited 2020 Mar 10]; Available from: https://www.theguardian.com/lifeandstyle/2016/may/28/toys-kids-girls-boys-childhood-development-gender-research

135. Talusan M. This Is What Gender-Nonbinary People Look Like [Internet]. them. 2017 [cited 2020 Apr 29]. Available from: https://www.them.us/story/this-is-what-gender-nonbinary-people-look-like

136. Hilleary C. Native American Two-Spirits Look to Reclaim Lost Heritage [Internet]. Voice of America. 2018 [cited 2020

Mar 8]. Available from: https://www.voanews.com/usa/native-american-two-spirits-look-reclaim-lost-heritage

137. Williams WL. The 'Two-Spirit' People of Indigenous North Americans. The Guardian [Internet]. 2010 Oct 11 [cited 2020 Mar 20]; Available from: https://www.theguardian.com/music/2010/oct/11/two-spirit-people-north-america

138. Trently D. 10 Examples of Nonbinary Genders Throughout History [Internet]. Listverse. 2015 [cited 2020 Mar 20]. Available from: https://listverse.com/2015/10/21/10-examples-of-nonbinary-genders-throughout-history/

139. Driskill Q-L. Doubleweaving Two-Spirit Critiques: Building Alliances between Native and Queer Studies. GLQ: A Journal of Lesbian and Gay Studies. 2010 Jan 1;16(1–2):69–92.

140. Jackman J. Jason Mraz Slammed for Appropriation After Coming Out as Two Spirit [Internet]. PinkNews. 2018 [cited 2020 Mar 8]. Available from: https://www.pinknews.co.uk/2018/07/23/jason-mraz-slammed-appropriation-coming-out-two-spirit/

141. Tobia J. Do You Know What It Means to Be Genderqueer? [Internet]. them. 2018 [cited 2020 Mar 20]. Available from: https://www.them.us/story/inqueery-genderqueer

142. Madden E. How Tumblr Created Space for Nonbinary Communities to Thrive [Internet]. Nylon. 2020 [cited 2020 Mar 28]. Available from: https://nylon.com/nonbinary-communities-on-tumblr

143. Shupe J. I Was America's First 'Nonbinary' Person. It Was All a Sham. [Internet]. The Daily Signal. 2019 [cited 2020 Mar 3]. Available from: https://www.dailysignal.com/2019/03/10/i-was-americas-first-non-binary-person-it-was-all-a-sham/

144. Finch SD. 130+ Examples of Cis Privilege in All Areas of Life for You to Reflect on and Address [Internet]. Everyday Feminism. 2016 [cited 2020 Mar 10]. Available from: https://everydayfeminism.com/2016/02/130-examples-cis-privilege/

145. Bell L. Trigger Warnings: Sex, Lies and Social Justice Utopia on Tumblr. Networking Knowledge: Journal of the MeCCSA Postgraduate Network [Internet]. 2013 Aug 8 [cited 2020 Feb 3];6(1). Available from: http://www.ojs.meccsa.org.uk/index.php/netknow/article/view/296

146. Bergner D. The Struggles of Rejecting the Gender Binary. The New York Times [Internet]. 2019 Jun 4 [cited 2020 Mar 24]; Available from: https://www.nytimes.com/2019/06/04/magazine/gender-nonbinary.html

147. O'Donnell E. Please Stop Calling Non-Binary People 'Special Snowflakes' [Internet]. Her Campus. 2017 [cited 2020 Mar 23]. Available from: https://www.hercampus.com/school/sfu/please-stop-calling-non-binary-people-special-snowflakes

148. Rea S. Why I Won't be Referred to as a 'Non-Male' by the Green Party [Internet]. The Independent. 2016 [cited 2020 Apr 15]. Available from: http://www.independent.co.uk/voices/i-wont-be-referred-to-as-non-male-by-the-green-party-women-have-suffered-prejudice-because-of-their-a6967926.html

149. Russell N. Allowing a Three-Year-Old to be Transgender is Insane [Internet]. Washington Examiner. 2017 [cited 2020 Apr 29]. Available from: https://www.washingtonexaminer.com/allowing-a-three-year-old-to-be-transgender-is-insane

150. LoBue V. When do Children Develop their Gender Identity? [Internet]. The Conversation. 2019 [cited 2020 Mar 19].

Available from: http://theconversation.com/when-do-children-develop-their-gender-identity-56480

151. de Vries ALC, Noens ILJ, Cohen-Kettenis PT, van Berckelaer-Onnes IA, Doreleijers TA. Autism Spectrum Disorders in Gender Dysphoric Children and Adolescents. Journal of Autism and Developmental Disorders. 2010 Aug;40(8):930–6.

152. Allen V. Councils are Taking Children who Want to Change Gender into Care [Internet]. Mail Online. 2019 [cited 2020 Apr 19]. Available from: https://www.dailymail.co.uk/news/article-6797093/Councils-taking-children-want-change-gender-care.html

153. Zucker KJ, Wood H, Singh D, Bradley SJ. A Developmental, Biopsychosocial Model for the Treatment of Children with Gender Identity Disorder. Journal of Homosexuality. 2012 Mar;59(3):369–97.

154. Cretella M. I'm a Pediatrician. How Transgender Ideology Has Infiltrated My Field and Produced Large-Scale Child Abuse. [Internet]. The Daily Signal. 2017 [cited 2020 Mar 2]. Available from: https://www.dailysignal.com/2017/07/03/im-pediatrician-transgender-ideology-infiltrated-field-produced-large-scale-child-abuse/

155. Manning S. Revealed: 800 Children as Young as 10 Given Puberty-Blockers [Internet]. Mail Online. 2017 [cited 2020 Apr 29]. Available from: http://www.dailymail.co.uk/~/article-4743036/index.html

156. Boghani P. When Transgender Kids Transition, Medical Risks are Both Known and Unknown [Internet]. FRONTLINE. 2015 [cited 2020 Apr 29]. Available from: https://www.pbs.org/wgbh/frontline/article/when-transgender-kids-transition-medical-risks-are-both-known-and-unknown/

157. Jewett C. Lupron, Used to Halt Puberty in Children, may Cause Lasting Health Problems [Internet]. STAT. 2017 [cited

2020 Mar 10]. Available from: https://www.statnews.com/2017/02/02/lupron-puberty-children-health-problems/

158. Scutti S. Transgender Youth: Are Puberty-Blocking Drugs an Appropriate Medical Intervention? [Internet]. Medical Daily. 2013 [cited 2020 Mar 10]. Available from: https://www.medicaldaily.com/transgender-youth-are-puberty-blocking-drugs-appropriate-medical-intervention-247082

159. Nodin N, Peel E, Tyler A, Rivers I. The RaRE Research Report [Internet]. London: PACE; 2015 [cited 2020 Feb 23]. Available from: http://www.queerfutures.co.uk/wp-content/uploads/2015/04/RARE_Research_Report_PACE_2015.pdf

160. Dilsaver SC. Suicide Attempts and Completions in Patients with Bipolar Disorder [Internet]. Psychiatric Times. 2007 [cited 2020 Apr 1]. Available from: https://www.psychiatrictimes.com/suicide-attempts-and-completions-patients-bipolar-disorder

161. Fuller-Thomson E, Hollister B. Schizophrenia and Suicide Attempts: Findings from a Representative Community-Based Canadian Sample. Schizophrenia Research and Treatment [Internet]. 2016 [cited 2020 Apr 1];2016. Available from: https://www.ncbi.nlm.nih.gov/pmc/articles/PMC4764754/

162. Young T. The Tricky Business of Gender Identity [Internet]. Standpoint. 2019 [cited 2020 Feb 23]. Available from: https://standpointmag.co.uk/issues/february-2019/features-february-2019-toby-young-tricky-business-gender-identity/

163. Transgender Trend. A Scientist Reviews Transgender Suicide Stats [Internet]. Transgender Trend. 2016 [cited 2020 Feb 23]. Available from: https://www.transgendertrend.com/a-scientist-reviews-transgender-suicide-stats/

164. Donnelly L. Children's Transgender Clinic Hit by 35 Resignations in Three Years as Psychologists Warn of Gender

Dysphoria 'Over-Diagnoses'. The Telegraph [Internet]. 2019 Dec 12 [cited 2020 Mar 4]; Available from: https://www.telegraph.co.uk/news/2019/12/12/childrens-transgender-clinic-hit-35-resignations-three-years/

165. Horton H. Boys Can Have Periods Too, Children to Be Taught in Latest Victory for Transgender Campaigners. The Telegraph [Internet]. 2018 Dec 16 [cited 2020 Feb 19]; Available from: https://www.telegraph.co.uk/news/2018/12/16/boys-can-have-periods-schoolchildren-taught-latest-victory-transgender/

166. Orr A, Baum J, Brown J, Gill E, Kahn E, Salem A. Schools in Transition. A Guide for Supporting Transgender Students in K-12 Schools [Internet]. Koninklijke Brill NV; [cited 2020 Apr 19]. Available from: https://primarysources.brillonline.com/browse/human-rights-documents-online/schools-in-transition-a-guide-for-supporting-transgender-students-in-k12-schools;hrdhrd99702015013

167. Driscoll B. Transgender Teddy Teaches Kids That Everyone's Story Deserves to Be Told [Internet]. HuffPost UK. 2016 [cited 2020 Mar 10]. Available from: https://www.huffingtonpost.co.uk/entry/introducing-teddy-jessica-walton_uk_57517a26e4b04a0827f18926

168. Diversity Picture Books for KS1 [Internet]. Findel Education. [cited 2020 Feb 3]. Available from: https://www.findel-education.co.uk/product/curricular/english/reading/diversity-picture-books-for-ks1/he1775781

169. Gillette S. Jonathan Van Ness Writes Kids' Book About Gender Nonbinary Guinea Pig to 'Celebrate' Differences [Internet]. PEOPLE.com. 2020 [cited 2020 Apr 6]. Available from: https://people.com/parents/jonathan-van-ness-childrens-book-peanut-goes-for-the-gold/

170. HarperCollins Australia. Peanut Goes for the Gold [Internet]. HarperCollins Australia. [cited 2020 Apr 6]. Available from:

https://www.harpercollins.com.au/9780062941008/peanut-goes-for-the-gold

171. Weale S. Book Explaining Gender Diversity to Primary School Children Sparks Furore. The Guardian [Internet]. 2017 Jan 2 [cited 2020 Apr 17]; Available from: https://www.theguardian.com/society/2017/jan/02/book-explaining-gender-diversity-to-primary-school-children-sparks-furore

172. O'Hara ME. Meet Sam, the Trans Doll Helping Kids to Transition. The Daily Beast [Internet]. 2017 Jul 12 [cited 2020 Mar 13]; Available from: https://www.thedailybeast.com/meet-sam-the-trans-doll-helping-kids-to-transition

173. Goldberg AB, Adriano J. 'I'm a Girl' -- Understanding Transgender Children [Internet]. ABC News. 2007 [cited 2020 Mar 5]. Available from: https://abcnews.go.com/2020/story?id=3088298&page=1

174. Jennings J. Jazz Jennings: When I First Knew I Was Transgender [Internet]. Time. 2016 [cited 2020 Mar 5]. Available from: https://time.com/4350574/jazz-jennings-transgender/

175. Miller K, Nied J. Jazz Jennings Just Posted A Hospital Photo After Her 3rd Gender Confirmation Surgery [Internet]. Women's Health. 2020 [cited 2020 Mar 19]. Available from: https://www.womenshealthmag.com/health/a23828566/jazz-jennings-gender-confirmation-surgery-complication/

176. Muldowney K, Torres I, Valiente A. Transgender Teen and 'I Am Jazz' Star Jazz Jennings on Sharing the Final Steps of her Transition Journey: Her Gender Confirmation Surgery [Internet]. ABC News. 2018 [cited 2020 Mar 19]. Available from: https://abcnews.go.com/Health/transgender-teen-jazz-star-jazz-jennings-sharing-final/story?id=58513271

177. Lubitz R. Jazz Jennings is Bringing Trans Representation to the Shaving Aisle [Internet]. Refinery29. 2019 [cited 2020 Mar 19]. Available from: https://www.refinery29.com/en-us/2019/03/226907/jazz-jennings-transgender-gillette-venus-campaign

178. Mulkerrins J. Transgender Jazz Jennings Knew she was a Girl Born in a Boy's Body [Internet]. Mail Online. 2015 [cited 2020 Mar 19]. Available from: https://www.dailymail.co.uk/home/you/article-3184776/Transgender-Jazz-Jennings-knew-girl-born-boy-s-body.html

179. Fortin J. Transgender Doll Based on Jazz Jennings to Debut in New York. The New York Times [Internet]. 2017 Feb 17 [cited 2020 Mar 19]; Available from: https://www.nytimes.com/2017/02/17/business/transgender-doll-jazz-jennings.html

180. Muhammad N. Meet the Theyby Babies: Kids Raised Without Gender [Internet]. Advocate. 2018 [cited 2020 Apr 7]. Available from: https://www.advocate.com/youth/2018/11/25/meet-theyby-babies-kids-raised-without-gender

181. Ritschel C. This Couple is Raising their Child as a Gender-Neutral 'They-By' [Internet]. The Independent. 2018 [cited 2020 Mar 19]. Available from: https://www.independent.co.uk/life-style/health-and-families/theyby-gender-neutral-child-parents-raise-couple-kyl-myers-zoomer-a8286876.html

182. Myers K. Raising Zoomer (@raisingzoomer) • Instagram photos and videos [Internet]. 2019 [cited 2020 Apr 7]. Available from: https://www.instagram.com/raisingzoomer/

183. Myers K. Navigating Sex, Gender, & Formal Documents [Internet]. Raising Zoomer. 2018 [cited 2020 Apr 7]. Available from: http://www.raisingzoomer.com/article/documents

184. Tracey J. I'm Not a Boy or a Girl. I'm Both. [Internet]. iPM. BBC Radio 4; 2016 [cited 2020 Mar 14]. Available from: https://www.bbc.co.uk/programmes/b07v37fb

185. BBC News. 'I'm a Non-Binary 10-Year-Old'. BBC News [Internet]. 2016 Sep 18 [cited 2020 Feb 23]; Available from: https://www.bbc.com/news/magazine-37383914

186. Wente M. Transgender Kids: Have we Gone Too Far? The Globe and Mail [Internet]. 2018 Nov 5 [cited 2020 Mar 19]; Available from: https://www.theglobeandmail.com/opinion/transgender-kids-have-we-gone-too-far/article16897043/

187. Lewis H. The Boy Made to Live as a Girl — or the Girl Made to Live as a Boy? [Internet]. Medium. 2016 [cited 2020 Mar 14]. Available from: https://medium.com/@helenlewis/the-boy-made-to-live-as-a-girl-or-the-girl-made-to-live-as-a-boy-e76221bb50c

188. Farmer B. Boy, 7, is Taken Away from Mum who 'Forced him to Live his Whole Life as a Girl' [Internet]. The Mirror. 2016 [cited 2020 Mar 6]. Available from: http://www.mirror.co.uk/news/uk-news/seven-year-old-boy-who-9098500

189. Crane E. Judge Rules James Younger's Dad can Have Say in Transition [Internet]. Mail Online. 2019 [cited 2020 Mar 6]. Available from: https://www.dailymail.co.uk/news/article-7611057/Judge-rules-James-Youngers-dad-say-transition.html

190. Equality and Human Rights Commission. Gender Reassignment Discrimination [Internet]. Equality and Human Rights Commission. 2019 [cited 2020 Mar 3]. Available from: https://www.equalityhumanrights.com/en/advice-and-guidance/gender-reassignment-discrimination

191. Hasson P. Every Democratic 2020 Frontrunner Supports Bill Forcing Male Athletes into Girls' Sports [Internet]. Daily Caller. 2019 [cited 2020 Apr 10]. Available from:

https://dailycaller.com/2019/06/18/2020-democrats-transgender-athletes-equality-act/

192. National Geographic. The Legality of Gender Change [Internet]. National Geographic Magazine. 2016 [cited 2020 Mar 11]. Available from: https://www.nationalgeographic.com/magazine/2017/01/gender-identity-map-where-you-can-change-your-gender-on-legal-documents/

193. O'Neill B. The Orwellian Nightmare of Transgender Politics [Internet]. Spiked! 2017 [cited 2020 Mar 6]. Available from: https://www.spiked-online.com/2017/07/25/the-orwellian-nightmare-of-transgender-politics/

194. Faye S. A Brief History of the Gender Recognition Act [Internet]. Vice. 2018 [cited 2020 May 2]. Available from: https://www.vice.com/en_uk/article/negm4k/a-brief-history-of-the-gender-recognition-act

195. Lambda Legal. Changing Birth Certificate Sex Designations: State-By-State Guidelines [Internet]. Lambda Legal. 2018 [cited 2020 May 3]. Available from: https://www.lambdalegal.org/know-your-rights/article/trans-changing-birth-certificate-sex-designations

196. McDonald H. Ireland Passes Law Allowing Trans People to Choose their Legal Gender. The Guardian [Internet]. 2015 Jul 16 [cited 2020 May 1]; Available from: https://www.theguardian.com/world/2015/jul/16/ireland-transgender-law-gender-recognition-bill-passed

197. Reuters. Nonbinary? Intersex? 11 U.S. States Issuing Third Gender IDs. Reuters [Internet]. 2019 Jan 31 [cited 2020 Mar 28]; Available from: https://www.reuters.com/article/us-us-lgbt-lawmaking-idUSKCN1PP2N7

198. Parsons V. All the Places with Better Rights for Non-Binary People than the UK [Internet]. PinkNews. 2019 [cited 2020 Apr 30]. Available from:

https://www.pinknews.co.uk/2019/07/14/non-binary-rights-countries-better-than-uk/

199. Fair Play For Women. In Brief: Why is GRA Reform Bad for Women and why Should you Care? [Internet]. Fair Play For Women. 2019 [cited 2020 Apr 30]. Available from: https://fairplayforwomen.com/gra_basics/

200. Castricum S. Our Gender is not for Others to Decide. A Bill for Trans People to Self-Identify is a Good Start. The Guardian [Internet]. 2019 Jun 20 [cited 2020 May 4]; Available from: https://www.theguardian.com/world/2019/jun/20/our-gender-is-not-for-others-to-decide-a-bill-for-trans-people-to-self-identify-is-a-good-start

201. BBC News. New Hate Crime Laws put Forward. BBC News [Internet]. 2020 Apr 24 [cited 2020 Apr 30]; Available from: https://www.bbc.com/news/uk-scotland-scotland-politics-52411696

202. Kirkup J. Why are the Police Stopping a 74-Year-Old Tweeting about Transgenderism? [Internet]. The Spectator. 2019 [cited 2020 May 4]. Available from: https://www.spectator.co.uk/article/why-are-the-police-stopping-a-74-year-old-tweeting-about-transgenderism-5-february-2019

203. Potter T. Apology for Blogger whose Gender Comments led to Call from Police [Internet]. Ipswich Star. 2019 [cited 2020 May 4]. Available from: https://www.ipswichstar.co.uk/news/ipswich-humanist-stands-by-transgender-tweets-1-5879996

204. Slater T. This PC Policing has Got to Stop [Internet]. Spiked! 2019 [cited 2020 May 4]. Available from: https://www.spiked-online.com/2019/02/06/this-pc-policing-has-got-to-stop/

205. Halliday J. Graham Linehan Given Police Warning after Complaint by Transgender Activist. The Guardian [Internet].

2018 Oct 7 [cited 2020 Mar 3]; Available from: https://www.theguardian.com/culture/2018/oct/07/graham-linehan-police-warning-complaint-by-stephanie-hayden-transgender-activist-twitter

206. Beckford M. Mother, 38, is Arrested in Front of her Children and Locked in a Cell for Seven HOURS after Calling a Transgender Woman a Man on Twitter [Internet]. Mail Online. 2019 [cited 2020 Mar 2]. Available from: https://www.dailymail.co.uk/news/article-6687123/Mother-arrested-children-calling-transgender-woman-man.html

207. Wright J. Woman who Called Transgender Woman 'Pig in Wig' in Tweets is Convicted [Internet]. Mail Online. 2020 [cited 2020 Mar 3]. Available from: https://www.dailymail.co.uk/news/article-8004175/Mother-called-transgender-woman-pig-wig-convicted-sending-offensive-tweets.html

208. Evans M, Swerling G. Devout Catholic 'Who Used Wrong Pronoun to Describe Transgender Girl' to be Interviewed by Police. The Telegraph [Internet]. 2019 Mar 19 [cited 2020 Apr 14]; Available from: https://www.telegraph.co.uk/news/2019/03/19/devout-catholic-interviewed-police-trans-twitter-row/

209. Barlow E. Teen in Court after Asking if Transgender PCSO was 'Boy or Girl' [Internet]. Wales Online. 2020 [cited 2020 Mar 2]. Available from: https://www.walesonline.co.uk/news/wales-news/teen-prosecuted-after-asking-whether-17651755

210. The Crown Prosecution Service. Transphobic Hate Crime Results in Increased Sentence for Mold Teenager [Internet]. The Crown Prosecution Service. 2020 [cited 2020 Mar 2]. Available from: https://www.cps.gov.uk/cymruwales/news/transphobic-hate-crime-results-increased-sentence-mold-teenager

211. Kearns M. Thought Police Target Teen with Asperger's [Internet]. National Review. 2020 [cited 2020 Mar 2]. Available from: https://www.nationalreview.com/corner/thought-police-target-teen-with-aspergers/

212. Nichols C. Claims Mislead about California Forcing Jail Time for Using Wrong Transgender Pronoun [Internet]. Politifact. 2017 [cited 2020 Apr 19]. Available from: https://www.politifact.com/article/2017/sep/26/claims-mislead-about-california-bill-forcing-jail-/

213. Ffrench A. Oxford at WAR over Transphobic Stickers [Internet]. Oxford Mail. 2019 [cited 2020 Apr 14]. Available from: https://www.oxfordmail.co.uk/news/17960516.sticker-fight-transphobic-messages/

214. BBC News. Woman Billboard Removed after Trans Row. BBC News [Internet]. 2018 Sep 26 [cited 2020 Apr 24]; Available from: https://www.bbc.com/news/uk-45650462

215. The Telegraph. London's Knife Crime Epidemic Continues with Three Fatal Stabbings. The Telegraph [Internet]. 2019 Nov 24 [cited 2020 Apr 14]; Available from: https://www.telegraph.co.uk/news/2019/11/24/londons-knife-crime-epidemic-continues-three-fatal-stabbings/

216. Doyle A. Putting the Thoughtpolice on Trial [Internet]. Spiked! 2019 [cited 2020 May 4]. Available from: https://www.spiked-online.com/2019/11/22/putting-the-thoughtpolice-on-trial/

217. BBC News. Focus on Crime not Misogyny - Police Chief. BBC News [Internet]. 2018 Nov 1 [cited 2020 Apr 14]; Available from: https://www.bbc.com/news/uk-46053069

218. Stack L. European Court Strikes Down Required Sterilization for Transgender People. The New York Times [Internet]. 2017 Apr 12 [cited 2020 Mar 9]; Available from: https://www.nytimes.com/2017/04/12/world/europe/european-

court-strikes-down-required-sterilization-for-transgender-people.html

219. Ahlander J. Sweden to Offer Compensation for Transgender Sterilizations. Reuters [Internet]. 2017 Mar 27 [cited 2020 Apr 10]; Available from: https://www.reuters.com/article/us-sweden-transgender-sterilisation-idUSKBN16Y1XA

220. Amnesty International. LGBTI Rights and what Amnesty is Doing to Protect Them [Internet]. Amnesty International. [cited 2020 Mar 5]. Available from: https://www.amnesty.org/en/what-we-do/discrimination/lgbt-rights/

221. Glass J. Swedish Parliament Makes Historic Decision to Pay Forcibly Sterilised Trans People $25,000 [Internet]. PinkNews. 2018 [cited 2020 Mar 3]. Available from: https://www.pinknews.co.uk/2018/03/23/swedish-parliament-makes-historic-decision-to-pay-forcibly-sterilised-trans-people-25000/

222. Amato P. Fertility Options for Transgender Persons [Internet]. Transgender Care. 2016 [cited 2020 Mar 10]. Available from: https://transcare.ucsf.edu/guidelines/fertility

223. Doward J. NHS Sued for Failure to Help Transgender Patients with Fertility. The Observer [Internet]. 2018 Sep 22 [cited 2020 Mar 3]; Available from: https://www.theguardian.com/society/2018/sep/22/nhs-taken-to-court-over-fertility-services-for-transgender-patients

224. Barlow A. Hammer-Wielding Thief Spared Prison Because she is Transgender [Internet]. The Argus. 2020 [cited 2020 Mar 4]. Available from: https://www.theargus.co.uk/news/18264144.brighton-hammer-thief-spared-prison-trangender/

225. BBC News. Trump Signs New Transgender Military Ban. BBC News [Internet]. 2018 Mar 24 [cited 2020 Apr 9];

Available from: https://www.bbc.com/news/world-us-canada-43525549

226. Shupe J. I Was a Transgender Soldier. Gender Dysphoria Poses Real Problems for the Military. [Internet]. The Daily Signal. 2017 [cited 2020 Mar 23]. Available from: https://www.dailysignal.com/2017/08/07/transgender-soldier-gender-dysphoria-poses-real-problems-military/

227. Rodger J. Can Transgender People Serve in the British Army? [Internet]. Birmingham Mail. 2017 [cited 2020 Apr 24]. Available from: http://www.birminghammail.co.uk/news/uk-news/can-transgender-serve-british-army-13389045

228. Ministry of Defence. Medical - British Army Jobs [Internet]. [cited 2020 Apr 9]. Available from: https://apply.army.mod.uk/how-to-join/can-i-join/medical

229. Goodwin C. Cliff Goodwin on Twitter: 'Today I'm showing my support to #InternationalTransgenderDayofVisibility (TDOV) - an annual event dedicated to celebrating #transgender people & raising awareness of discrimination faced by this part of our community whilst also celebrating their contributions to society ▢. https://t.co/YXWQDLpoiM' / Twitter [Internet]. Twitter. 2020 [cited 2020 May 1]. Available from: https://twitter.com/cliff_goodwin/status/1244856499542900736

230. Brown K. One in Twelve [Internet]. On the Science of Changing Sex. 2013 [cited 2020 Apr 4]. Available from: https://sillyolme.wordpress.com/2013/08/27/one-in-twelve/

231. Lee G. FactCheck: How Many Trans People are Murdered in the UK? [Internet]. Channel 4 News. 2018 [cited 2020 Mar 14]. Available from: https://www.channel4.com/news/factcheck/factcheck-how-many-trans-people-murdered-uk

232. Reilly W. Are We in the Midst of a Transgender Murder Epidemic? [Internet]. Quillette. 2019 [cited 2020 Apr 8]. Available from: https://quillette.com/2019/12/07/are-we-in-the-midst-of-a-transgender-murder-epidemic/

233. Greene CF. I Crunched the Data. The Violence 'Epidemic' Against Transgender People is a Myth [Internet]. The Federalist. 2019 [cited 2020 Mar 16]. Available from: https://thefederalist.com/2019/11/04/the-left-is-lying-about-a-hatred-and-violence-epidemic-against-transgender-people/

234. Lewis H. What the Row Over Banning Germaine Greer Is Really About [Internet]. New Stateman. 2015 [cited 2020 Mar 14]. Available from: https://www.newstatesman.com/politics/feminism/2015/10/what-row-over-banning-germaine-greer-really-about

235. Powys Maurice E. Labour Manifesto Vows to put LGBT Rights 'at the Heart of Government' – but there's a Catch [Internet]. PinkNews. 2019 [cited 2020 Mar 11]. Available from: https://www.pinknews.co.uk/2019/11/21/labour-manifesto-lgbt-ambassador-foreign-office-general-election-prep-gender-recognition-act/

236. BBC News. Swinson Defends Stance on Transgender Rights. BBC News [Internet]. 2019 Dec 9 [cited 2020 Mar 11]; Available from: https://www.bbc.com/news/election-2019-50711195

237. Swinford S. Don't Allow Labour Become Trans 'Pressure Group', Pleads Tony Blair. 2020 Feb 20 [cited 2020 Feb 21]; Available from: https://www.thetimes.co.uk/article/dont-allow-labour-become-trans-pressure-group-pleads-tony-blair-f8qsj3jtl

238. Woman's Place UK. About [Internet]. Woman's Place UK. 2018 [cited 2020 Mar 6]. Available from: https://womansplaceuk.org/about/

239. Petter O. 'LGB Alliance' Group Faces Criticism for Being Transphobic [Internet]. The Independent. 2019 [cited 2020 Mar 9]. Available from: https://www.independent.co.uk/life-style/lgb-alliance-group-transphobic-alison-bailey-lesbian-gay-bisexual-a9169091.html

240. Weaver M. Labour Leadership Contenders Split Over Trans Group Pledge Card. The Guardian [Internet]. 2020 Feb 13 [cited 2020 Mar 4]; Available from: https://www.theguardian.com/politics/2020/feb/13/labour-leadership-contenders-split-over-trans-group-pledge-card

241. Serwotka M. The Drive to Expel Feminists from Labour is Creating a Hostile Environment for Women. Morning Star [Internet]. 2020 Feb 20 [cited 2020 Mar 6]; Available from: https://morningstaronline.co.uk/article/f/drive-expel-feminists-labour-creating-hostile-environment-women

242. Parker J. Expel 'Transphobic' Labour Members - Long-Bailey. BBC News [Internet]. 2020 Feb 12 [cited 2020 Mar 5]; Available from: https://www.bbc.com/news/uk-politics-51465800

243. Munro N. Joe Biden: 'Transgender Equality Is the Civil Rights Issue of Our Time' [Internet]. Breitbart. 2020 [cited 2020 Mar 23]. Available from: https://www.breitbart.com/politics/2020/01/26/joe-biden-transgender-equality-is-the-civil-rights-issue-of-our-time/

244. Morris K. Elizabeth Warren Applauds Transgender 9-Year-Old [Internet]. Breitbart. 2019 [cited 2020 Feb 27]. Available from: https://www.breitbart.com/politics/2019/10/10/elizabeth-warren-applauds-transgender-9-year-old-choose-education-secretary/

245. Warren E. Securing LGBTQ+ Rights and Equality [Internet]. ElizabethWarren.com. 2020 [cited 2020 Apr 8]. Available from: https://elizabethwarren.com/plans/lgbtq-equality

246. Starr P. Bloomberg: Transgender Rights Should Include Free Surgery, Hormones [Internet]. Breitbart. 2020 [cited 2020 Mar 22]. Available from: https://www.breitbart.com/politics/2020/01/29/bloomberg-transgender-rights-should-include-federally-funded-sex-surgery-housing-based-on-gender-identity/

247. Burrows T. Radical Transgender Group Says it is FINE to Punch Women [Internet]. Mail Online. 2017 [cited 2020 Feb 15]. Available from: http://www.dailymail.co.uk/~/article-4914582/index.html

248. Shaw D. Transgender Activists in Multiple Countries Call For, Launch Organized Violent Uprisings Against Women [Internet]. Women Are Human. 2020 [cited 2020 Mar 19]. Available from: https://www.womenarehuman.com/transgender-activists-in-multiple-countries-call-for-launch-organized-violent-uprisings-against-women/

249. Rhodes M. Co-Founder of Stonewall Calls for Calm [Internet]. Holyrood Website. 2019 [cited 2020 Mar 30]. Available from: https://www.holyrood.com/inside-politics/view,cofounder-of-stonewall-calls-for-calm_14648.htm

250. Moody L. A Note on Recent Events [Internet]. Medium. 2019 [cited 2020 Mar 31]. Available from: https://medium.com/@drlouisejmoody/a-note-on-recent-events-963266becdd5

251. Bannerman L. Trans Goldsmiths Lecturer Natacha Kennedy Behind Smear Campaign Against Academics. The Times [Internet]. 2018 Aug 9 [cited 2020 Mar 8]; Available from: https://www.thetimes.co.uk/article/trans-goldsmiths-lecturer-natacha-kennedy-behind-smear-campaign-against-academics-f2zqbl222

252. Awford J. Trans Woman who Sued Beauticians for Refusing to Wax her Scrotum Loses Lawsuit [Internet]. The Sun. 2019 [cited 2020 Apr 16]. Available from:

https://www.thesun.co.uk/news/10201139/jessica-yaniv-trans-loses-scrotum-wax-case/

253. Adams J. Transgender Activist Claims Information from Mumsnet was Misleading [Internet]. Mail Online. 2019 [cited 2020 Apr 24]. Available from: https://www.dailymail.co.uk/news/article-6912343/Transgender-activist-claims-information-given-Mumsnet-misleading.html

254. Moody L. University of York Abolished Research Associate Position to Silence Me [Internet]. Uncommon Ground. 2019 [cited 2020 Mar 21]. Available from: https://uncommongroundmedia.com/university-of-york-abolished-research-associate-position-to-silence-me/

255. Yardley M. The Cotton Ceiling [Internet]. Miranda Yardley. 2014 [cited 2020 Mar 6]. Available from: https://mirandayardley.com/en/the-cotton-ceiling/

256. Blair KL, Hoskin RA. Transgender Exclusion from the World of Dating: Patterns of Acceptance and Rejection of Hypothetical Trans Dating Partners as a Function of Sexual and Gender Identity. Journal of Social and Personal Relationships [Internet]. 2018 May 31 [cited 2020 Mar 2]; Available from: https://journals.sagepub.com/doi/10.1177/0265407518779139

257. Riley EA, Clemson L, Sitharthan G, Diamond M. Surviving a Gender-Variant Childhood: The Views of Transgender Adults on the Needs of Gender-Variant Children and Their Parents. Journal of Sex & Marital Therapy. 2013 May;39(3):241–63.

258. Solis M. How the Women's March's 'Genital-Based' Feminism Isolated the Transgender Community [Internet]. Mic. 2017 [cited 2020 Apr 11]. Available from: https://www.mic.com/articles/166273/how-the-women-s-march-s-genital-based-feminism-isolated-the-transgender-community

259. Curl J. Transgender 'Women' Are Oppressed Because Pussy Hats Are 'Genital-Based' [Internet]. The Daily Wire. 2017 [cited 2020 Apr 11]. Available from: https://www.dailywire.com/news/transgender-women-are-oppressed-because-pussy-hats-joseph-curl

260. Ferguson S. 3 Examples of Everyday Cissexism [Internet]. Everyday Feminism. 2014 [cited 2020 Mar 6]. Available from: https://everydayfeminism.com/2014/03/everyday-cissexism/

261. Trans Voices for Repeal. Trans Voices for Repeal Call on the Together for Yes Campaign to Formally Apologise to Trans People for the Exclusionary Campaign Ran [Internet]. Medium. 2018 [cited 2020 Apr 16]. Available from: https://medium.com/@transvoicesforrepeal/trans-voices-for-repeal-call-on-the-together-for-yes-campaign-to-formally-apologise-to-trans-people-84931f0fa85d

262. Merrow I. Don Jr. Spews Transphobia in Botched Attempt at Feminism [Internet]. Betches. 2019 [cited 2020 Feb 25]. Available from: https://betches.com/don-jr-spews-transphobia-in-botched-attempt-at-feminism/

263. Reading W. My Period and Me: A Trans Guy's Guide to Menstruation [Internet]. Everyday Feminism. 2014 [cited 2020 Mar 12]. Available from: https://everydayfeminism.com/2014/11/trans-guys-guide-menstruation/

264. Kellaway M. 4 Off-Putting Messages We Send to Trans Men Considering Pregnancy [Internet]. Everyday Feminism. 2015 [cited 2020 Mar 12]. Available from: https://everydayfeminism.com/2015/02/messages-trans-men-pregnancy/

265. Everyday Feminism. 3 Touching Journeys Through Trans Masculinity [Internet]. Everyday Feminism. 2015 [cited 2020 Mar 12]. Available from: https://everydayfeminism.com/2015/11/journeys-trans-masculinity/

266. Moore S. Women Must Have the Right to Organise. We Will Not be Silenced. The Guardian [Internet]. 2020 Mar 2 [cited 2020 Mar 3]; Available from: https://www.theguardian.com/society/commentisfree/2020/mar/02/women-must-have-the-right-to-organise-we-will-not-be-silenced

267. Whelan E. Lily Madigan is not a Woman [Internet]. Spiked! 2017 [cited 2020 Feb 24]. Available from: https://www.spiked-online.com/2017/11/22/lily-madigan-is-not-a-woman/

268. Labour Students. Labour Students National Committee 2019/2020 [Internet]. Labour Students. [cited 2020 May 18]. Available from: https://labourstudents.org.uk/your-national-committee/

269. Waugh P. Labour Confirms Trans Women Eligible for All-Women Shortlists [Internet]. HuffPost UK. 2018 [cited 2020 Mar 14]. Available from: https://www.huffingtonpost.co.uk/entry/labour-confirms-self-identifying-trans-women-eligible-for-all-women-shortlists-and-womens-officer-roles_uk_5b048276e4b0784cd2af3d32

270. Birchall G. Outrage as 'Gender-Fluid' Credit Suisse Boss who Sometimes Wears a Wig to Work is Named Among Top 100 WOMEN in Business [Internet]. The Sun. 2018 [cited 2020 Mar 4]. Available from: https://www.thesun.co.uk/news/7322136/outrage-as-gender-fluid-credit-suisse-boss-who-sometimes-wears-a-wig-to-work-is-named-among-top-100-women-in-business/

271. Bayley L. Caitlyn Jenner Won Big at GLAMOUR's Woman of The Year Awards [Internet]. Glamour UK. 2015 [cited 2020 Apr 24]. Available from: https://www.glamourmagazine.co.uk/article/caitlyn-jenner-glamour-women-of-the-year-awards-america

272. Henderson L. The High Price of Being a Good Girl [Internet]. The Telegraph. 2014 [cited 2020 Apr 14]. Available from:

https://www.telegraph.co.uk/women/mother-tongue/10943285/The-high-price-of-being-a-good-girl.html

273. Duffy N. Planned Parenthood Expands Transgender Services, Infuriates Conservatives More [Internet]. PinkNews. 2018 [cited 2020 Mar 3]. Available from: https://www.pinknews.co.uk/2018/01/05/planned-parenthood-expands-transgender-services-infuriates-conservatives-more/

274. Hellen N. Terrified Patient Treated Like 'Transphobic Bigot'. The Times [Internet]. 2018 Jan 14 [cited 2020 May 1]; Available from: https://www.thetimes.co.uk/article/terrified-patient-treated-like-transphobic-bigot-bsfsgrv2p

275. Gallagher P. NHS Sorry to Woman After 'Nurse with Stubble' Tried to Take Smear Test [Internet]. i News. 2017 [cited 2020 Mar 9]. Available from: https://inews.co.uk/news/health/nhs-woman-transgender-nurse-smear-test-515660

276. Lees P. Fears Around Gender-Neutral Toilets are all in the Mind. The Guardian [Internet]. 2016 Dec 2 [cited 2020 Mar 23]; Available from: https://www.theguardian.com/commentisfree/2016/dec/02/fears-gender-neutral-toilets-women-trans-people-violence

277. Mullin G. Transgender Woman, 18, Sexually Assaulted Girl, 10, in Female Toilets in Morrisons [Internet]. The Scottish Sun. 2019 [cited 2020 Mar 31]. Available from: https://www.thescottishsun.co.uk/news/4002789/morrisons-sex-attack-girl-fife-transgender-katie-dolatowski/

278. Prestigiacomo A. 5 Times 'Transgender' Men Abused Women and Children in Bathrooms [Internet]. The Daily Wire. 2016 [cited 2020 Mar 29]. Available from: https://www.dailywire.com/news/5-times-transgender-men-abused-women-and-children-amanda-prestigiacomo

279. Kendall E. KFC 'Toilet Representative' Explains Gender Neutral Loos Mix Up [Internet]. SomersetLive. 2019 [cited 2020 Apr 16]. Available from:

https://www.somersetlive.co.uk/news/kfc-toilets-going-gender-neutral-3535116

280. Neale S. Gender-Neutral Bathroom Closed After High School Student Arrested for Sexual Assault [Internet]. Washington Examiner. 2020 [cited 2020 Mar 23]. Available from: https://www.washingtonexaminer.com/news/gender-neutral-bathroom-closed-after-high-school-student-arrested-for-sexual-assault

281. Seith E. Mixed-Gender Toilets have 'Negative Impact on Girls' [Internet]. Tes. 2019 [cited 2020 Mar 23]. Available from: https://www.tes.com/news/mixed-gender-toilets-have-negative-impact-girls

282. Petter O. Marks & Spencer Customer 'Outraged' Over Gender-Inclusive Fitting Rooms [Internet]. The Independent. 2019 [cited 2020 Apr 20]. Available from: https://www.independent.co.uk/life-style/marks-spencer-changing-rooms-gender-women-men-a9180391.html

283. Webber E. John Lewis Tells Customers to Use 'Whichever Fitting Room' [Internet]. Mail Online. 2019 [cited 2020 Apr 21]. Available from: https://www.dailymail.co.uk/news/article-7693141/John-Lewis-tells-customers-use-whichever-fitting-room-makes-feels-comfortable.html

284. Harley N. Topshop Announces Gender-Neutral Changing Rooms after Trans Customer was Refused Access to Female Cubicles. The Telegraph [Internet]. 2017 Nov 8 [cited 2020 Apr 21]; Available from: https://www.telegraph.co.uk/news/2017/11/08/topshop-announces-gender-neutral-changing-rooms-trans-customer/

285. Hayward S. Primark Sparks Backlash by Installing First Gender Neutral Changing Rooms [Internet]. The Mirror. 2019 [cited 2020 Apr 20]. Available from: https://www.mirror.co.uk/news/uk-news/primark-sparks-backlash-installing-first-14145532

286. Hosie R. Unisex Changing Rooms put Women at Danger of Sexual Assault, Data Reveals [Internet]. The Independent. 2018 [cited 2020 Mar 23]. Available from: https://www.independent.co.uk/life-style/women/sexual-assault-unisex-changing-rooms-sunday-times-women-risk-a8519086.html

287. Parveen N. Transgender Prisoner Who Sexually Assaulted Inmates Jailed for Life. The Guardian [Internet]. 2018 Oct 11 [cited 2020 Feb 24]; Available from: https://www.theguardian.com/uk-news/2018/oct/11/transgender-prisoner-who-sexually-assaulted-inmates-jailed-for-life

288. Safi M. Female Inmate Allegedly Coerced into Retracting Rape Accusations Against Transgender Inmate, Sues Prison [Internet]. 2020 [cited 2020 Mar 4]. Available from: https://dailycaller.com/2020/02/21/inmate-lawsuit-illinois-department-corrections-prison-janiah-monroe-transgender-rape-reports/

289. Murphy M. Discontinuation of Grant to Vancouver Rape Relief Shows Trans Activism is an Attack on Women [Internet]. Feminist Current. 2019 [cited 2020 Mar 6]. Available from: https://www.feministcurrent.com/2019/03/20/discontinuation-of-grant-to-vancouver-rape-relief-shows-trans-activism-is-an-attack-on-women/

290. Pazzano S. Predator Who Claimed to be Transgender Declared Dangerous Offender. Toronto Sun [Internet]. 2014 Feb 26 [cited 2020 May 10]; Available from: https://torontosun.com/2014/02/26/predator-who-claimed-to-be-transgender-declared-dangerous-offender/wcm/fc2c70f0-b1a1-41e2-85db-bec9d0012ce5

291. North A. Who can go to a Women's College? That Answer is Evolving. [Internet]. Vox. 2017 [cited 2020 Apr 24]. Available from:

https://www.vox.com/identities/2017/9/21/16315072/spelman-college-transgender-students-womens-colleges

292. Weaver M. Women-Only Cambridge College to Allow Students who 'Identify as Female'. The Guardian [Internet]. 2017 Oct 4 [cited 2020 Apr 17]; Available from: https://www.theguardian.com/education/2017/oct/04/women-only-cambridge-college-to-allow-students-who-identify-as-female-murray-edwards

293. Butler T. 10 Trans Athletes Explain Why it's Fair for Them to Compete [Internet]. PinkNews - Gay news, reviews and comment from the world's most read lesbian, gay, bisexual, and trans news service. 2019 [cited 2020 Feb 14]. Available from: https://www.pinknews.co.uk/2019/04/04/transgender-athletes-why-fair-compete/

294. BJJEE. Transgender MMA Fighter Who Broke Female Opponent's Skull. Are We Getting Too "Politically Correct" With Reality? [Internet]. Bjj Eastern Europe. 2018 [cited 2020 Mar 2]. Available from: https://www.bjjee.com/articles/transgender-mma-fighter-who-broke-female-opponents-skull-are-we-getting-too-politically-correct-with-reality/

295. Associated Press. Transgender Runners Finish One-Two in Connecticut High School Champs [Internet]. Mail Online. 2019 [cited 2020 Mar 2]. Available from: https://www.dailymail.co.uk/news/article-6743273/Transgender-runners-finish-one-two-Connecticut-high-school-champs.html

296. Harper J. Do Transgender Athletes have an Edge? I Sure Don't. Washington Post [Internet]. 2015 Apr 1 [cited 2020 Mar 9]; Available from: https://www.washingtonpost.com/opinions/do-transgender-athletes-have-an-edge-i-sure-dont/2015/04/01/ccacb1da-c68e-11e4-b2a1-bed1aaea2816_story.html

297. Ingle S. IOC Delays New Transgender Guidelines after Scientists Fail to Agree. The Guardian [Internet]. 2019 Sep 24 [cited 2020 Mar 6]; Available from: https://www.theguardian.com/sport/2019/sep/24/ioc-delays-new-transgender-guidelines-2020-olympics

298. LoMauro A, Aliverti A. Sex Differences in Respiratory Function. Breathe. 2018 Jun 1;14(2):131–40.

299. Moisse K. Going for the Gaunt: How Low Can an Athlete's Body Fat Go? [Internet]. Scientific American. 2010 [cited 2020 Mar 9]. Available from: https://www.scientificamerican.com/article/athlete-body-fat/

300. Geggel L. Why Do Men Run Faster Than Women? [Internet]. livescience.com. 2017 [cited 2020 Mar 3]. Available from: https://www.livescience.com/59289-why-men-run-faster-than-women.html

301. Shire E. Do Breasts Impede Athletic Performance? [Internet]. The Week. 2013 [cited 2020 Mar 9]. Available from: https://theweek.com/articles/462246/breasts-impede-athletic-performance

302. Hess A. Bustin' a Move [Internet]. ESPN.com. 2013 [cited 2020 Mar 13]. Available from: https://www.espn.com/espnw/article/9451835/female-athletes-biggest-opponents-their-own-breasts-espn-magazine

303. Vos T, Flaxman AD, Naghavi M, Lozano R, Michaud C, Ezzati M, et al. Years Lived with Disability (YLDs) for 1160 Sequelae of 289 Diseases and Injuries 1990-2010: A Systematic Analysis for the Global Burden of Disease Study 2010. The Lancet. 2012;380:2163–96.

304. BoysVsWomen.com. If Boys are Faster than Elite Female Athletes, Should Males Compete in Female Athletics? [Internet]. BoysVsWomen.com. [cited 2020 Mar 3]. Available from: http://www.boysvswomen.com

305. Trump Jr. D. Triggered: How the Left Thrives on Hate and Wants to Silence Us. New York: Center Street; 2019. 304 p.

306. Smith R. Chris Mosier Makes History as First Openly Trans Athlete to Compete in an Olympic Trial as Their True Gender [Internet]. PinkNews. 2020 [cited 2020 Mar 3]. Available from: https://www.pinknews.co.uk/2020/01/27/chris-mosier-trans-athlete-olympic-trials-history-race-walking-team-usa/

307. Liew J. The Prejudice of Those who Argue Against Trans, Intersex & DSD Athletes [Internet]. The Independent. 2019 [cited 2020 Mar 2]. Available from: https://www.independent.co.uk/sport/general/athletics/caster-semenya-news-gender-martina-navratilova-trans-cas-jonathan-liew-column-a8792861.html

308. BBC Sport. Doping in Sport: What is it and How is it Being Tackled? BBC Sport [Internet]. 2015 Aug 19 [cited 2020 Mar 19]; Available from: https://www.bbc.co.uk/sport/athletics/33997246

309. World Anti-Doping Agency. What is Prohibited [Internet]. World Anti-Doping Agency. 2017 [cited 2020 Mar 19]. Available from: https://www.wada-ama.org/en/content/what-is-prohibited

310. Special Olympics. Frequently Asked Questions [Internet]. SpecialOlympics.org. 2018 [cited 2020 Mar 15]. Available from: https://www.specialolympics.org/about/faq

311. International Committee of Sports for the Deaf. Audiogram Regulations [Internet]. Deaflympics.com. 2018 [cited 2020 Mar 15]. Available from: http://www.deaflympics.com/pdf/AudiogramRegulations.pdf

312. BBC News. 10 Things you Need to Know About the Paralympics. BBC News [Internet]. 2012 Aug 28 [cited 2020 Mar 19]; Available from: https://www.bbc.com/news/magazine-19341500

313. Williams J. How 'Woman' Became a Dirty Word [Internet]. Spiked! 2020 [cited 2020 Mar 5]. Available from: https://www.spiked-online.com/2020/03/04/how-woman-became-a-dirty-word/

314. Murphy M. Are We Women or Are We Menstruators? [Internet]. Feminist Current. 2016 [cited 2020 Mar 15]. Available from: https://www.feministcurrent.com/2016/09/07/are-we-women-or-are-we-menstruators/

315. Beale C. People are Mocking the Green Party Young Women's Invite to 'Non-Men' [Internet]. The Independent. 2016 [cited 2020 Apr 15]. Available from: http://www.independent.co.uk/news/uk/feminists-mock-green-party-young-womens-invite-to-non-men-a6987061.html

316. BBC News. Council Sorry for 'Transphobic' Women's Day Flags. BBC News [Internet]. 2020 Mar 3 [cited 2020 Apr 22]; Available from: https://www.bbc.com/news/uk-england-merseyside-51708961

317. Hall J. Cancer Research UK Responds to Claims That its New Campaign is 'Anti-Woman' [Internet]. indy100. 2018 [cited 2020 Mar 5]. Available from: https://www.indy100.com/article/cancer-research-uk-trans-inclusive-anti-woman-smear-test-cervix-campaign-8401981

318. Cancer Research UK. Testicular Cancer [Internet]. Cancer Research UK. 2017 [cited 2020 Mar 5]. Available from: https://about-cancer.cancerresearchuk.org/about-cancer/testicular-cancer

319. Cancer Research UK. Prostate Cancer [Internet]. Cancer Research UK. 2019 [cited 2020 Mar 5]. Available from: https://www.cancerresearchuk.org/about-cancer/prostate-cancer

320. Regan A. Should Women be Spelt Womxn? BBC News [Internet]. 2018 Oct 10 [cited 2020 Mar 5]; Available from: https://www.bbc.com/news/uk-45810709

321. Rovira Izquierdo C. Precarious, Invisible but Essential: Womxn Workers Sustaining Life in a Time of Crisis [Internet]. Oxfam. 2020 [cited 2020 May 10]. Available from: https://webcache.googleusercontent.com/search?q=cache:kfC-aNoYsX4J:https://views-voices.oxfam.org.uk/2020/05/precarious-invisible-but-essential-womxn-workers-sustaining-life-in-a-time-of-crisis/+&cd=1&hl=en&ct=clnk&gl=uk

322. Everyday Cissexism (@CissexismDaily) / Twitter [Internet]. Twitter. [cited 2020 Feb 12]. Available from: https://twitter.com/cissexismdaily

323. Khanna A. Nine out of Ten Wikipedians Continue to be Men: Editor Survey [Internet]. Wikimedia Blog. 2012 [cited 2020 Apr 14]. Available from: https://blog.wikimedia.org/2012/04/27/nine-out-of-ten-wikipedians-continue-to-be-men/

324. Burns K. I've Never Had a Period, but That Doesn't Mean I'm Not a Real Woman [Internet]. SheKnows. 2016 [cited 2020 Mar 15]. Available from: https://www.sheknows.com/health-and-wellness/articles/1122689/menstruation-matters-transgender/

325. O'Brien C. How your Period Positivity Might be Harming Others [Internet]. Ruby Cup. [cited 2020 Mar 28]. Available from: https://rubycup.com/blogs/news/how-your-period-positivity-might-be-harming-others

326. Brown M. Mom's Viral Post Celebrates That 'Some Women, Some Non-Binary People, & Some Men' Get Their Periods [Internet]. Parents. 2019 [cited 2020 Feb 22]. Available from: https://www.parents.com/news/moms-viral-post-celebrates-that-some-women-some-non-binary-people-some-men-get-their-periods-too/

327. Manning S. Trans Lobby Forces Always to Ditch Female Logo from Sanitary Towels [Internet]. Mail Online. 2019 [cited 2020 Mar 5]. Available from: https://www.dailymail.co.uk/news/article-7592413/Transgender-lobby-forces-ditch-female-logo-sanitary-towels.html

328. Yi D. Some Transgender Men Need Period Underwear Like This [Internet]. Mashable. 2015 [cited 2020 Mar 31]. Available from: https://mashable.com/2015/11/15/thinx-underwear-transgender/

329. Rutherford-Morrison L. Thinx Creates Period Underwear for Transgender Men [Internet]. Bustle. 2015 [cited 2020 Mar 17]. Available from: https://www.bustle.com/articles/124122-how-thinxs-period-underwear-for-transgender-men-is-creating-a-more-inclusive-period-experience

330. Hinchliffe E. Are Period Apps Gender-Inclusive? Not Quite, but They're Trying [Internet]. Mashable. 2017 [cited 2020 Apr 15]. Available from: https://mashable.com/2017/08/08/clue-period-apps-language/

331. Riedel S. Yes, Trans Women Can Get Period Symptoms [Internet]. The Establishment. 2016 [cited 2020 Mar 7]. Available from: https://theestablishment.co/yes-trans-women-can-get-period-symptoms-e43a43979e8c/

332. Crosta P. Menstrual Cramps: Causes and Management [Internet]. Medical News Today. 2017 [cited 2020 Apr 18]. Available from: https://www.medicalnewstoday.com/articles/157333

333. Bauer E. No, Men Taking Transgender Hormones Don't Get Periods [Internet]. The Federalist. 2018 [cited 2020 Apr 22]. Available from: https://thefederalist.com/2018/07/25/no-men-taking-transgender-hormones-dont-get-periods/

334. Montgomery J. Equality Institute: Don't Say 'Pregnant Women', as 'All Genders Can Fall Pregnant' [Internet].

Breitbart. 2018 [cited 2020 Mar 5]. Available from: https://www.breitbart.com/europe/2018/10/11/equality-institute-dont-say-pregnant-women-all-genderspregnant/

335. Braidwood E. LGBTQ Campaigners Say Trans Men in Ireland 'Will be Denied Abortion Access' [Internet]. PinkNews. 2018 [cited 2020 Mar 5]. Available from: https://www.pinknews.co.uk/2018/05/31/transgender-activists-call-for-gender-neutral-language-in-irelands-abortion-law-2/

336. Cretaz B de la. What It's Like to Chestfeed [Internet]. The Atlantic. 2016 [cited 2020 Apr 11]. Available from: https://www.theatlantic.com/health/archive/2016/08/chestfeeding/497015/

337. Reisman T, Goldstein Z. Case Report: Induced Lactation in a Transgender Woman. Transgender Health. 2018 Jan 1;3(1):24–6.

338. Burns K. Yes, Trans Women Can Breastfeed — Here's How [Internet]. them. 2018 [cited 2020 Apr 7]. Available from: https://www.them.us/story/trans-women-breastfeed

339. Food and Drug Administration. Domperidone IND Packet for Sponsors Treating Patients with Gastrointestinal Disorders [Internet]. Food and Drug Administration. 2019 [cited 2020 May 10]. Available from: https://www.fda.gov/media/100064/download

340. NHS. Domperidone: Anti-Sickness Medicine Used to Treat Nausea and Vomiting [Internet]. nhs.uk. 2020 [cited 2020 Apr 7]. Available from: https://www.nhs.uk/medicines/domperidone/

341. Booth R. Trans Man Argues Against Being Called Child's Mother at Appeal Court. The Guardian [Internet]. 2020 Mar 4 [cited 2020 Mar 6]; Available from: https://www.theguardian.com/society/2020/mar/04/transgender-man-appeals-decision-not-to-be-named-father

342. Oppenheim M. Trans Man Loses Legal Fight to be Called Father on Baby's Birth Certificate [Internet]. The Independent. 2020 [cited 2020 Apr 29]. Available from: https://www.independent.co.uk/news/uk/home-news/freddy-mcconnell-trans-man-father-mother-birth-certificate-baby-a9489751.html

343. Lyons I. Transgender Man Who Gave Birth Loses High Court Battle to Make his Child the First in the UK Without a Mother. The Telegraph [Internet]. 2019 Sep 25 [cited 2020 Mar 7]; Available from: https://www.telegraph.co.uk/news/2019/09/25/transgender-man-gave-birth-loses-high-court-battle-make-child/

344. Huffpost UK. Joan Of Arc And 9 Other 'Queer' Saints [Internet]. HuffPost UK. 2011 [cited 2020 Apr 15]. Available from: https://www.huffpost.com/entry/joan-of-arc-and-9-other-queer-saints_n_1129804

345. Michaelson J. Southern Baptist Convention: Trans People Don't Exist. The Daily Beast [Internet]. 2014 Jun 12 [cited 2020 Apr 15]; Available from: https://www.thedailybeast.com/articles/2014/06/12/southern-baptist-convention-trans-people-don-t-exist

346. Historic England. Trans and Gender-Crossing Histories [Internet]. Historic England. [cited 2020 Apr 16]. Available from: http://historicengland.org.uk/research/inclusive-heritage/lgbtq-heritage-project/trans-and-gender-crossing-histories/

347. The Question of Saint Joan of Arc's Sexuality and Gender [Internet]. The Saint Joan of Arc Center. [cited 2020 Apr 22]. Available from: http://stjoan-center.com/FAQ/question5.html

348. Howell C. Pragmatic Women Have Cross-Dressed Throughout History – but it Doesn't Make Them Transgender [Internet]. The Spectator. 2017 [cited 2020 Apr 16]. Available from: https://www.spectator.co.uk/article/pragmatic-women-have-

cross-dressed-throughout-history-but-it-doesn-t-make-them-transgender

349. Lewis A. Here's Why JK Rowling Uses Her Initials Instead of Her Name [Internet]. Cosmopolitan. 2017 [cited 2020 Apr 15]. Available from: https://www.cosmopolitan.com/uk/entertainment/a10287947/jk-rowling-initials-instead-real-name/

350. BBC News. Woman Loses Tribunal Over Transgender Tweets. BBC News [Internet]. 2019 Dec 19 [cited 2020 Mar 2]; Available from: https://www.bbc.com/news/uk-50858919

351. Mail on Sunday. Christian Maths Teacher Sues School for Religious Discrimination [Internet]. Mail Online. 2017 [cited 2020 Apr 11]. Available from: http://www.dailymail.co.uk/news/article-5163741/Christian-maths-teacher-sues-school-discrimination.html

352. BBC News. Teacher Faces Action Over 'Misgendering'. BBC News [Internet]. 2017 Nov 13 [cited 2020 Mar 3]; Available from: https://www.bbc.com/news/uk-england-oxfordshire-41966554

353. Adams S. Birth coach says only women have kids and is hounded from charity [Internet]. Mail Online. 2019 [cited 2020 Apr 16]. Available from: https://www.dailymail.co.uk/news/article-7643251/Charity-hounds-birth-coach-post-saying-women-children.html

354. Gerstmann E. Teacher Sues After Getting Fired For Refusing To Refer To Transgender Student With Male Pronouns [Internet]. Forbes. 2019 [cited 2020 Mar 20]. Available from: https://www.forbes.com/sites/evangerstmann/2019/10/03/virginia-school-district-fires-teacher-who-wouldnt-refer-to-transgender-student-using-male-pronouns/

355. Jackman J. Twitter Bans Misgendering and Deadnaming in Pro-Trans Move [Internet]. PinkNews. 2018 [cited 2020 Mar 11]. Available from:

https://www.pinknews.co.uk/2018/11/23/twitter-misgendering-deadnaming-trans/

356. 4thwavenow. WordPress Censors Gendertrender; Gallus Mag Responds. [Internet]. 4thWaveNow. 2018 [cited 2020 Mar 8]. Available from: https://4thwavenow.com/2018/11/17/wordpress-dumps-gendertrender-gallus-mag-responds/

357. Williams J. The Tide Beginning to Turn on Trans Lunacy? [Internet]. Spiked! 2019 [cited 2020 May 4]. Available from: https://www.spiked-online.com/2019/12/28/is-the-tide-beginning-to-turn-on-trans-lunacy/

358. Terfblocker. Block Together [Internet]. 2020 [cited 2020 Mar 1]. Available from: https://blocktogether.org/show-blocks/qqcYB_tb16JHW2hQG2fe2FCJ54pERR-JVOiQR2Le

359. Forsyth L. Mum Barred From Pub for Wearing T-Shirt 'in Case It Upsets Transgender People' [Internet]. The Mirror. 2019 [cited 2020 Apr 20]. Available from: https://www.mirror.co.uk/news/uk-news/mum-barred-pub-wearing-shirt-13821099

360. Parker C. Polo Lounge Clubber 'Ejected Over Anti-Trans Campaign T-Shirt'. The Times [Internet]. 2020 Jan 21 [cited 2020 May 2]; Available from: https://www.thetimes.co.uk/article/polo-lounge-clubber-ejected-over-anti-trans-campaign-t-shirt-xvvtd6stl

361. Bartosch J. The Silencing of Feminist Artists [Internet]. Spiked! 2019 [cited 2020 May 4]. Available from: https://www.spiked-online.com/2019/12/23/the-silencing-of-feminist-artists/

362. Edwards S. Mount Holyoke Cancels 'The Vagina Monologues' For Transgender Students [Internet]. Jezebel. 2015 [cited 2020 Feb 26]. Available from: https://jezebel.com/mount-holyoke-cancels-the-vagina-monologues-for-trans-1679845927

363. Dean-Bailey Y. All-Women's College Cancels 'Vagina Monologues' Because It's Not Feminist Enough [Internet]. Campus Reform. 2015 [cited 2020 May 4]. Available from: https://www.campusreform.org/?ID=6202

364. Romano A. Why We Can't Stop Fighting About Cancel Culture [Internet]. Vox. 2019 [cited 2020 Apr 20]. Available from: https://www.vox.com/culture/2019/12/30/20879720/what-is-cancel-culture-explained-history-debate

365. Zanotti E. J.K. Rowling Smeared as Transphobe, 'Canceled' After Saying Biological Sex 'Is Real' [Internet]. The Daily Wire. 2019 [cited 2020 Apr 15]. Available from: https://www.dailywire.com/news/j-k-rowling-smeared-as-transphobe-canceled-after-saying-biological-sex-is-real

366. Case S. Beyond the Hypatia Affair: Philosophers Blocking the Way of Inquiry [Internet]. Quillette. 2019 [cited 2020 Mar 7]. Available from: https://quillette.com/2019/09/06/beyond-the-hypatia-affair-philosophers-blocking-the-way-of-inquiry/

367. Brown University. Updated: Brown Statements on Gender Dysphoria Study [Internet]. 2019 [cited 2020 Feb 25]. Available from: https://news.brown.edu/articles/2019/03/gender

368. Tannehill B. 'Rapid Onset Gender Dysphoria' Is Biased Junk Science [Internet]. Advocate. 2018 [cited 2020 Feb 25]. Available from: https://www.advocate.com/commentary/2018/2/20/rapid-onset-gender-dysphoria-biased-junk-science

369. Tominey C, Walsh J. Trans Activists Fail to Block Research Suggesting Gender Dysphoria is 'Contagious'. The Telegraph [Internet]. 2019 Mar 19 [cited 2020 Apr 1]; Available from: https://www.telegraph.co.uk/news/2019/03/19/trans-activists-fail-block-research-suggesting-gender-dysphoria/

370. Gliske SV. A New Theory of Gender Dysphoria Incorporating the Distress, Social Behavioral, and Body-Ownership Networks. eNeuro [Internet]. 2019 Nov 1 [cited 2020 May 4];6(6). Available from: https://www.eneuro.org/content/6/6/ENEURO.0183-19.2019

371. Gliske S. Response to Retraction of My Paper on Gender Dysphoria [Internet]. Medium. 2020 [cited 2020 May 4]. Available from: https://medium.com/@sgliske/response-to-retraction-of-my-paper-on-gender-dysphoria-bc07df047c61

372. Society for Neuroscience. Retraction: Gliske, A New Theory of Gender Dysphoria Incorporating the Distress, Social Behavioral, and Body-Ownership Networks. eNeuro [Internet]. 2020 Mar 1 [cited 2020 May 4];7(2). Available from: https://www.eneuro.org/content/7/2/ENEURO.0149-20.2020

373. Marcus AA. Journal Retracts Paper on Gender Dysphoria After 900 Critics Petition [Internet]. Retraction Watch. 2020 [cited 2020 May 4]. Available from: https://retractionwatch.com/2020/04/30/journal-retracts-paper-on-gender-dysphoria-after-900-critics-petition/

374. Weale S. University 'Turned Down Politically Incorrect Transgender Research'". The Guardian [Internet]. 2017 Sep 25 [cited 2020 Feb 25]; Available from: https://www.theguardian.com/education/2017/sep/25/bath-spa-university-transgender-gender-reassignment-reversal-research

375. Jussim L. Rapid Onset Gender Dysphoria [Internet]. Psychology Today. 2019 [cited 2020 Mar 13]. Available from: https://www.psychologytoday.com/blog/rabble-rouser/201903/rapid-onset-gender-dysphoria

376. Quinn P. Why I Believe No-Platforming Germaine Greer Is the Only Option [Internet]. HuffPost UK. 2015 [cited 2020 Mar 10]. Available from: https://www.huffingtonpost.co.uk/payton-quinn/germaine-greer_b_8366838.html

377. Krasteva G. Oxford Professor Selina Todd Feminist Talk Cancelled [Internet]. Oxford Mail. 2020 [cited 2020 Apr 14]. Available from: https://www.oxfordmail.co.uk/news/18272672.oxford-professor-selina-todd-feminist-talk-cancelled/

378. BBC News. I Didn't Want to Wait to Be Hit, Says Professor. BBC News [Internet]. 2020 Jan 25 [cited 2020 Apr 16]; Available from: https://www.bbc.com/news/education-51248684

379. Williams J. Selina Todd and the Rise of Academic Mobs [Internet]. Spiked! 2020 [cited 2020 May 4]. Available from: https://www.spiked-online.com/2020/02/11/selina-todd-and-the-rise-of-academic-mobs/

380. Open Letter English Keynote [Internet]. 2020 [cited 2020 May 4]. Available from: https://docs.google.com/document/u/1/d/15ehzvwPnOLyM_HuZRDDKB4m5VWkXT2XcVXzSphSQsSU/mobilebasic

381. McVeigh K. Goldsmiths Cancels Free Speech Show by Comedian Kate Smurthwaite. The Guardian [Internet]. 2015 Feb 2 [cited 2020 Feb 25]; Available from: https://www.theguardian.com/culture/2015/feb/02/goldsmiths-comedian-kate-smurthwaite-free-speech-show-feminist-campaigners

382. Grove J. British University Calls off Conference Amid Protests From Transgender Activists [Internet]. 2019 [cited 2020 Mar 23]. Available from: https://www.insidehighered.com/news/2019/03/21/british-university-calls-conference-amid-protests-transgender-activists

383. Duffy N. NSPCC Scraps Debate on Trans Children After Complaints [Internet]. PinkNews. 2016 [cited 2020 Mar 16]. Available from: https://www.pinknews.co.uk/2016/10/13/nspcc-scraps-debate-on-trans-children-after-complaints/

384. Fisher O. Channel 4 Needs to Understand That My Gender Identity Is Not up for Debate [Internet]. i News. 2018 [cited 2020 Mar 8]. Available from: https://inews.co.uk/opinion/comment/genderquake-channel-4-germaine-greer-trans-511131

385. Daisy H. Hannah Daisy ☐☐☐ on Instagram: "When Is the Press Going to Wake up and Realise They're Publishing and Platforming People Who Are Actively Harming People? ☐☐Supporting…" [Internet]. Instagram. 2020 [cited 2020 Apr 9]. Available from: https://www.instagram.com/p/B9aVUHSB3Tt/

386. Murphy M. What If Your Identity Doesn't Matter at All? [Internet]. Feminist Current. 2020 [cited 2020 Apr 22]. Available from: https://www.feministcurrent.com/2020/03/22/what-if-your-identity-doesnt-matter-at-all/

387. Loggins K. As Hospitals Prepare for COVID-19, Life-Saving Trans Surgeries Are Delayed [Internet]. VICE. 2020 [cited 2020 Apr 11]. Available from: https://www.vice.com/amp/en_us/article/wxekyz/transgender-surgeries-delayed-coronavirus-hospitals

388. Parsons V. Trans People Are Seeing Surgeries Cancelled and Healthcare Deemed 'Non-Essential' During Coronavirus [Internet]. PinkNews. 2020 [cited 2020 Apr 11]. Available from: https://www.pinknews.co.uk/2020/03/23/coronavirus-trans-healthcare-gender-reaffirming-essential-surgery-cancelled-vice/

389. Whalen A. The Unexpected Way the Coronavirus Is Hurting Some Members of the Trans Community [Internet]. Newsweek. 2020 [cited 2020 Apr 11]. Available from: https://www.newsweek.com/trans-transgender-coronavirus-pandemic-covid-19-youth-students-trevor-project-1493527

390. Mooney C, Kaplan S, Kim MJ. Men Account for 70% of Coronavirus Fatalities in Italy [Internet]. The Independent. 2020 [cited 2020 Apr 20]. Available from: https://www.independent.co.uk/news/world/americas/coronavirus-death-toll-italy-south-korea-sex-update-cases-map-men-women-a9413271.html

391. Dusheck J. Women's Immune System Genes Operate Differently From Men's [Internet]. News Center. 2015 [cited 2020 Mar 4]. Available from: http://med.stanford.edu/news/all-news/2015/07/womens-immune-system-genes-operate-differently-from-mens.html

392. Brewin CR, Andrews B. False Memories of Childhood Abuse [Internet]. The Psychologist. 2017 [cited 2020 May 11]. Available from: https://thepsychologist.bps.org.uk/volume-30/july-2017/false-memories-childhood-abuse

393. French C. False Memories of Sexual Abuse Lead to Terrible Miscarriages of Justice. The Guardian [Internet]. 2010 Nov 25 [cited 2020 Apr 8]; Available from: https://www.theguardian.com/science/2010/nov/24/false-memories-abuse-convict-innocent

394. Bassett L. 45 Years Ago, a Nun Promised to Protect These Women. Now They're Searching for Her Killer. [Internet]. HuffPost UK. 2015 [cited 2020 Apr 8]. Available from: https://www.huffpost.com/entry/cesnik-nun-murder-maskell_n_7267532

395. Cheit RE. Legal Cases (53) [Internet]. Recovered Memory Project. 2010 [cited 2020 Apr 12]. Available from: https://blogs.brown.edu/recoveredmemory/case-archive/legal-cases/

396. Maran M. Did My Father Really Abuse Me? The Guardian [Internet]. 2010 Oct 8 [cited 2020 Apr 9]; Available from: https://www.theguardian.com/lifeandstyle/2010/oct/09/meredith-maran-father-abuse-false-memory

397. Tallmadge A. My Niece Believed She was Abused by a Satanic Cult. The Truth is Even Scarier. [Internet]. HuffPost. 2015 [cited 2020 Apr 6]. Available from: https://www.huffpost.com/entry/satanic-abuse-truth_n_5ac7dc6ee4b0337ad1e8169e

398. Milton J. Crucial Reforms to Allow Trans People to Self-Identify Allegedly Delayed by UK Equalities Minister Liz Truss [Internet]. PinkNews. 2019 [cited 2020 Mar 16]. Available from: https://www.pinknews.co.uk/2019/10/06/trans-liz-truss-gender-recognition-act-mail-on-sunday/

399. Scottish Legal News. Scottish Government Abandons Plans Over Gender Self-Identification Following Backlash [Internet]. Scottish Legal News. 2019 [cited 2020 Mar 19]. Available from: https://www.scottishlegal.com/article/scottish-government-abandons-plans-over-gender-self-identification-following-backlash

400. Martin T. Births, Deaths, Marriages and Relationships Registration Bill to be Deferred [Internet]. The Beehive. 2019 [cited 2020 Mar 15]. Available from: http://www.beehive.govt.nz/release/births-deaths-marriages-and-relationships-registration-bill-be-deferred

401. BBC News. Activist Loses Gender-Neutral Passports Challenge. BBC News [Internet]. 2020 Mar 10 [cited 2020 Apr 22]; Available from: https://www.bbc.com/news/uk-51823318

402. Duffy N. Republican Governor Just Signed Two of the Most Horrifically Transphobic Bills in American History Into Law [Internet]. PinkNews. 2020 [cited 2020 Apr 6]. Available from: https://www.pinknews.co.uk/2020/03/31/republican-governor-idaho-brad-little-trans-transphobia-law-coronavirus-hb509-hb500/

403. Strudwick P. A New Law Will End Gender Recognition. Now Trans People Are Speaking Out. [Internet]. BuzzFeed. 2020

[cited 2020 Apr 20]. Available from: https://www.buzzfeed.com/patrickstrudwick/coronavirus-hungary-trans-rights

404. Gall L. Hungary Seeks to Ban Legal Gender Recognition for Transgender People [Internet]. Human Rights Watch. 2020 [cited 2020 Apr 6]. Available from: https://www.hrw.org/news/2020/04/03/hungary-seeks-ban-legal-gender-recognition-transgender-people

405. Busel D. Government to Ban Gender Confirmation Surgery for Under-18s [Internet]. TalkRadio. 2020 [cited 2020 Apr 22]. Available from: https://talkradio.co.uk/news/government-ban-gender-confirmation-surgery-under-18s-20042233230

406. Holt A. NHS Gender Clinic 'Should Have Challenged Me More'. BBC News [Internet]. 2020 Mar 1 [cited 2020 Mar 3]; Available from: https://www.bbc.com/news/health-51676020

407. Holt A. NHS Use of Puberty Blockers Legal Challenge Begins. BBC News [Internet]. 2020 Jan 8 [cited 2020 Mar 8]; Available from: https://www.bbc.com/news/health-51033911

408. Reid S. Why Did the NHS Let Me Change Sex? Witness in Court Battle Speaks out [Internet]. Mail Online. 2020 [cited 2020 Mar 5]. Available from: https://www.dailymail.co.uk/news/article-7926675/Witness-court-battle-against-gender-clinic-reveals-happened-cry-help.html

409. Hurst G. Tavistock Clinic: My Daughter Can't Understand the Risk, Says Mother. 2019 Dec 10 [cited 2020 Mar 21]; Available from: https://www.thetimes.co.uk/article/tavistock-clinic-my-daughter-cant-understand-the-risk-says-mother-jr59vz0ck

410. RT International. UK Mom Sues Tavistock Children's Clinic Over 'Misleading' & 'Experimental' Gender Change Treatments [Internet]. RT International. 2019 [cited 2020 Mar

21]. Available from: https://www.rt.com/uk/470755-suit-tavistock-gender-change-clinic-kids/

411. NHS England. NHS England » Update on Gender Identity Development Service for Children and Young People [Internet]. NHS England. 2020 [cited 2020 Mar 21]. Available from: https://www.england.nhs.uk/2020/01/update-on-gender-identity-development-service-for-children-and-young-people/

412. Cason M. Senate Passes Bill Banning Transgender Meds for Minors [Internet]. Alabama.com. 2020 [cited 2020 Mar 7]. Available from: https://www.al.com/news/2020/03/alabama-senate-considers-bill-to-block-transgender-treatments-for-minors.html

413. The Guardian. South Dakota Lawmakers Vote to Jail Doctors for Treating Trans Teens. The Guardian [Internet]. 2020 Jan 30 [cited 2020 Mar 5]; Available from: https://www.theguardian.com/us-news/2020/jan/30/trans-teens-hormone-blockers-south-dakota-bill

414. Berry DS. Georgia Bill Would Make Child Transgender Surgeries, Drugs Illegal [Internet]. Breitbart. 2020 [cited 2020 Mar 23]. Available from: https://www.breitbart.com/politics/2020/03/07/georgia-bill-would-make-child-transgender-surgeries-drugs-illegal/

415. Lang N. Republicans Are Ready to Throw Doctors in Jail for Treating Trans Kids [Internet]. Vice. 2020 [cited 2020 Mar 22]. Available from: https://www.vice.com/en_us/article/g5x5jq/8-states-are-trying-to-make-the-medical-treatment-of-trans-kids-a-crime

416. Gillberg C. "Könsbytena på barn är ett stort experiment". Svenska Dagbladet [Internet]. 2019 Mar 13 [cited 2020 May 6]; Available from: https://www.svd.se/konsbytena-pa-barn-ar-ett-stort-experiment

417. Oxford A. Transgender Female Athletes Banned as Arizona House Approves HB 2706 [Internet]. azcentral. 2020 [cited

2020 Mar 15]. Available from: https://www.azcentral.com/story/news/politics/legislature/2020/03/03/transgender-female-athletes-banned-arizona-house-approves-hb-2706/4941634002/

418. Associated Press. Team USA Athlete Protests Transgender Bill at Idaho Rally [Internet]. Local News 8. 2020 [cited 2020 Mar 6]. Available from: https://localnews8.com/news/politics/idaho-politics/2020/03/04/team-usa-athlete-protests-transgender-bill-at-idaho-rally/

419. Beck C. Transgender Athlete Bill Stalls in House Committee [Internet]. https://www.waff.com. 2020 [cited 2020 Mar 6]. Available from: https://www.waff.com/2020/02/14/transgender-athlete-bill-stalls-house-committee/

420. Kelleher P. Republican Politician Introduces Law to Ban Trans Athletes From Playing on Teams That Match Their Gender Identity [Internet]. PinkNews. 2020 [cited 2020 Mar 22]. Available from: https://www.pinknews.co.uk/2020/01/03/republican-politician-introduces-law-ban-trans-athletes-playing-teams-gender-identity/

421. Staver A. Ohio Lawmakers Move to Ban Transgender Athletes From Girls and Women's Sports [Internet]. MSN. 2020 [cited 2020 Mar 22]. Available from: https://www.msn.com/en-us/news/us/ohio-lawmakers-move-to-ban-transgender-athletes-from-girls-and-womens-sports/ar-BB10nKeJ

422. Associated Press. Teen Runners Sue to Block Trans Athletes From Girls' Sports. The Guardian [Internet]. 2020 Feb 13 [cited 2020 Mar 8]; Available from: https://www.theguardian.com/us-news/2020/feb/13/transgender-athletes-girls-sports-high-school

423. Eaton-Robb P. US Justice Department: Don't Treat Trans Athletes as Girls [Internet]. WPEC. 2020 [cited 2020 Mar 27]. Available from: https://cbs12.com/news/nation-world/us-justice-department-dont-treat-trans-athletes-as-girls

424. Zeigler C. Powerlifting Bans All Trans Women From Competing as Women [Internet]. Outsports. 2019 [cited 2020 Mar 15]. Available from: https://www.outsports.com/2019/2/1/18204036/usa-powerlifting-trans-athlete-policy-jaycee-cooper

425. Save Women's Sports. Save Women's Sports [Internet]. [cited 2020 Mar 19]. Available from: https://savewomenssports.com/

426. Hope C. Women Must Be Guaranteed Female-Only Lavatories in Public Buildings, Says Minister. The Telegraph [Internet]. 2020 Feb 28 [cited 2020 Mar 15]; Available from: https://www.telegraph.co.uk/politics/2020/02/28/women-must-guaranteed-female-only-lavatories-public-buildings/

427. Owen G. Ban Male-Bod-ied Trans Women From Ladies' Toi-lets, Says Equal-ity Minister [Internet]. Mail Online. 2020 [cited 2020 Apr 6]. Available from: https://www.pressreader.com/uk/the-mail-on-sunday/20200329/282355451841159

428. Duffy N. Tory MP Jackie Doyle-Price Wants to 'Devise a Law' to Keep Trans Women out of Women-Only Spaces [Internet]. PinkNews. 2020 [cited 2020 Apr 6]. Available from: https://www.pinknews.co.uk/2020/03/10/tory-mp-jackie-doyle-price-law-equality-act-women-only-single-sex-space-trans-rights/

429. Woodcock A. LGBT+ Campaigners Concerned Over Government Plan to Protect Under-18s From 'Irreversible' Gender Decisions [Internet]. The Independent. 2020 [cited 2020 Apr 26]. Available from: https://www.independent.co.uk/news/uk/politics/lgbt-gender-government-liz-truss-transgender-rights-consultation-a9478901.html

430. Lyons I. CPS Pulls Its Hate Crime Guidance for Schools After 14-Year-Old Girl Mounted Legal Challenge. The Telegraph [Internet]. 2020 Apr 30 [cited 2020 May 1]; Available from: https://www.telegraph.co.uk/news/2020/04/30/cpspulls-hate-crime-guidance-schools-14-year-old-girl-mounted/

431. Hurst G, Ames J. Girl Forces U-Turn on Advice to Schools Over Trans Bullying. The Times [Internet]. 2020 Feb 5 [cited 2020 May 2]; Available from: https://www.thetimes.co.uk/article/girl-forces-u-turn-on-advice-to-schools-over-trans-bullying-2m5xz8nfz

432. The Economist. A Pushback Against Trans Activism in Britain. The Economist [Internet]. 2020 Jan 2 [cited 2020 Mar 8]; Available from: https://www.economist.com/britain/2020/02/01/a-pushback-against-trans-activism-in-britain

433. Safe Schools Alliance UK. Application for Judicial Review of Oxfordshire County Council's Trans Guidance Accepted [Internet]. Safe Schools Alliance UK. 2020 [cited 2020 Apr 20]. Available from: https://safeschoolsallianceuk.net/2020/04/18/application-for-judicial-review-of-oxfordshire-county-councils-trans-guidance-accepted/

434. BBC News. Court Action Over Oxfordshire County Council's Transgender Policy [Internet]. BBC News. 2020 [cited 2020 May 10]. Available from: https://www.bbc.co.uk/news/uk-england-oxfordshire-52439496

435. McLaughlin M. Staff Guidance Into Trans Patients on Women's Wards Is Under Review. The Times [Internet]. 2020 May 3 [cited 2020 Mar 8]; Available from: https://www.thetimes.co.uk/article/staff-guidance-into-trans-patients-on-womens-wards-is-under-review-cfq2c7nrf

436. Steinmetz K. President Trump Just Rolled Back Guidelines That Protected Transgender Students [Internet]. Time. 2017 [cited 2020 Mar 19]. Available from:

https://time.com/4679063/donald-trump-transgender-bathroom/

437. Berg K, Syed M. Under Trump, LGBTQ Progress Is Being Reversed in Plain Sight [Internet]. ProPublica. 2019 [cited 2020 Apr 20]. Available from: https://projects.propublica.org/graphics/lgbtq-rights-rollback

438. Simmons-Duffin S. 'Whiplash' of LGBTQ Protections and Rights, From Obama to Trump [Internet]. NPR.org. 2020 [cited 2020 Apr 12]. Available from: https://www.npr.org/sections/health-shots/2020/03/02/804873211/whiplash-of-lgbtq-protections-and-rights-from-obama-to-trump

439. Bennett R. Gavin Williamson Gives Universities Final Warning on Free Speech. The Times [Internet]. 2020 Jul 2 [cited 2020 Mar 15]; Available from: https://www.thetimes.co.uk/article/gavin-williamson-gives-universities-final-warning-on-free-speech-fhxrx92s6

440. Waugh P. Ministers Preparing Law to Protect Freedom of Speech at Universities [Internet]. HuffPost UK. 2020 [cited 2020 Mar 18]. Available from: https://www.huffingtonpost.co.uk/entry/gavin-williamson-new-law-freedom-of-speech-university-oxford_uk_5e63fa78c5b6670e72f90ef5

441. BBC News. Police's 'Transphobic' Tweets Probe Unlawful. BBC News [Internet]. 2020 Feb 14 [cited 2020 Mar 3]; Available from: https://www.bbc.com/news/uk-england-lincolnshire-51501202

442. Thoreson R. Trump Administration Takes Aim at Transgender Healthcare [Internet]. Human Rights Watch. 2019 [cited 2020 Apr 11]. Available from: https://www.hrw.org/news/2019/05/24/trump-administration-takes-aim-transgender-healthcare

443. Holden D. We Made a List of All the Anti-LGBT Stuff Trump Has Done as President [Internet]. BuzzFeed News. 2018 [cited 2020 Apr 20]. Available from: https://www.buzzfeednews.com/article/dominicholden/trump-lgbt-anti-actions-administration-pride-month

Index

20/20, 59
2016 Olympics, 99
2019 General Election, 80
Abortion, 87, 111, 129, 153
Action Trans Health Edinburgh, 82
ADHD, 53
Affordable Care Act, 6, 139
Alabama, 134, 135
Alabanza, Travis, 94
Always (sanitary towels), 109
Alzheimer's Disease, 131
American Civil Liberties Union, 75
American Psychological Association, 6
Amnesty International, 73
Anaemia, 98
Androphilic transsexuals, 18
Anne Evans, Mary, 113
Anorexia, 16, 21, 28
Anthony, Elan, 38–39
Anxiety, 17, 21, 53
Ara, Rachel, 118
Arizona, 135
Armstrong, Declan, 70–71, 71
Art, 118–19
Atkinson, CJ, 58
Australia, 67
Autism, 53, 57, 70, 71, 133, 134
Autistic. *See* Autism
Autogynephilia, 18–20, 27
Baroness Berridge, 136
Bath Spa University, 122
BBC, 39, 61, 147
BBC Trust, 147
Beatie, Thomas, 7

Bell, Kira, 133–34
Bellringer, James, 29
Benjamin, Harry, 6
Bhaskara, Milly, 108
Biden, Hunter, 88
Biden, Joe, 66, 81, 88
Bigender, 40
Bipolar Disorder, 21, 55, 92
Birmingham, University of, 29
Birth certificate, 66, 67, 68, 112
Birth control, 92, 101, 142, 153
Blair, Tony, 80
Blanchard, Richard, 18
Blanchard's transsexual types, 18
Blasphemy, 126
Blood clot, 34, 76
Bloomberg, Michael, 81, 82
Body fat, 97
Body masculinization surgery, 36
Bone density, 34
Bono, Chaz, 8
Boob job. *See* Breast Augmentation
Boys Don't Cry, 7
Boys vs Women, 99
Brain Sex, 22–24
Breast, 42, 62, 133
  and sport, 98
  Augmentation, 36
  Implant Illness, 36
  Reduction, 36
Breastfeeding, 36, 111–12
  Breastmilk, 112
Brexit, 125

Brighton and Hove Council, 56
Bronte, Charlotte, 113
Brown University, 20, 120, 131
Brown, Kay, 78
Bunce, Philip, 91
Burchill, Julie, 4
Butler, Judith, 125
Buzzfeed, 77
Caesarean, 91
California, 72, 93
Cambridge, University of, 96
Campomelic Dysplasia, 25
Can I Tell You About Gender Diversity?, 58
Canada, 67
Cancel Culture, 119
Cancer, 30, 34, 35, 104, 108
  breast, 36
  Breast Implant Associated Lymphoma, 35
  Breast screening, 90
  Cervical screening, 90, 103, 104
  Cervical smear, 93, *See* cervical screening
  Prostate, 103
  Screenings, 90
  Testicular, 103
Cancer Research, 103, 105, 116
Canterbury Christ University, 124
Cardiff, University of, 123
Cardiovascular disease, 30, 34
Caspian, James, 122
Celiac Disease, 110

Centre for Crime and Justice Studies, 124
Cervix, 103, 104, 116, 146, 153
Channel 4, 125
Chestfeeding. *See* Breastfeeding
Childbirth, 91, 98
Chromosome
  X, 104
  Y, 104
Chromosomes, 24
  XX, 25, 26
  XY, 24, 25, 26
Cis Privilege, 48, 49
Cissexism, 15, 105–6, 143
Civil Rights, 78–79
Clemmer, Cass, 109
Clue, 109
Colon, 35
Colorado, 134
Connecticut, 97, 135
Conservative Party, 80
Cooper, JayCee, 136
Coronavirus Pandemic, 128–29
Corradi, Richard, 16
Cotton ceiling, 85–86, 149
Court of Appeal, 132
COVID-19. *See* Coronavirus Pandemic
Coronavirus Pandemic, 15
Criado-Perez, Caroline, 104
Cross-sex hormones, 13, 26, 33–34, 74, 75, 82, 92, 110, 128, 134, 139
Crown Prosecution Service, 136
Cyrus, Mylie, 77

Deaflympics, 101
Democrat Party, 66, 81
    2020 Presidential Primaries, 82
Denmark, 67
Department for Communities and Local Government, 136
Department of Education, 137
Department of Health and Human Services, 139
Department of Justice, 135
Depression, 21, 31, 33, 53, 55, 133
Desisters. *See* Detransitioning
Detransitioning, 13, 38–39, 151
Diabetes, 34, 110
Digital Divide, 11–12
Dillon, Michael, 5
Domperidone, 111, 112
Doping, 101
Doyle-Price, Jackie, 136
Durham University, 40
Dyslexia, 153
Edge, Nina, 118
Edinburgh Science Festival, 103
Edinburgh University, 40
Egg (cell), 25, 74, 104, 112, 143
    freezing. *See* gamete freezing
Elbe, Lili, 5
Elliot, George, 113
Employment tribunal, 115
Endometriosis, 107
eNeuro, 122
Epilepsy, 55
Equal Access rule, 137
Equality Act (USA), 65–66
Equality Act 2010 (UK), 65, 115, 136
Equality and Human Rights Commission, 65, 74
Erection, 18, 35
European Court of Human Rights, 6, 66, 73
Everyday Feminism, 43, 48, 88
Facebook, 40, 84, 103, 117
Facial feminization surgery, 36
Fair Play for Women, 67, 146
Fallon, Fox, 96, 97
Fanshawe, Simon, 82
Farrow, Caroline, 70, 83, 85
Financial Times, 91
Fisher, Owl, 125
Fistula, 35
Florida, 134
Forstarter, Maya, 115, 119
Galileo, 123
Gallstones, 34
Gamete Freezing, 37–38
Gender Dysphoria, 6, 7, 13, 16, 17, 19, 20, 21, 22, 24, 26, 28, 29, 30, 31, 33, 36, 38, 39, 53, 54, 55, 58, 59, 62, 63, 66, 79, 117, 121, 122, 130, 132, 133, 141, 144, 151
    Delusion, 18
    Genes, 21
    Social Status, 22
Gender Identity Disorder. *See* Gender Dysphoria
Gender Recognition Act 2004, 66, 136

GenderTrender, 117
George, Greg, 71
Georgia, 134
Gillberg, Christopher, 135
Gillette Venus razors, 59
Girl Guides, 70
Glamor Magazine, 91
Glasgow, 118
Gliske, Stephen, 122
Goldsmiths, University of London, 84
Gonadal Dysgenesis, 24, 25
Good Morning Britain,, 70
Goodwin, Cliff, 78
Green Party, 103
Green, Jackie, 70
Green, Susan, 70
Greer, Germaine, 4, 47, 123
Guardian, 112, 126
Gymnastics, 99
Hachette, Jean, 94
Haematomas, 36
Haematosis, 36
Hambrook, Christopher, 96
Hannah Daisy, 126
Harrots, Daniel, 21
Hate crime, 12, 68–69, 71, 72, 73, 84, 124, 136
Hawaii, University of, 86
Hayden, Stephanie, 70
Hellen, Mark. *See* Kennedy, Natacha
Heyer, Walt, 38
High Court, 62, 137, 138
Hijras, 46
Hippocampus, 23
Historic England, 112
Honour killings, 3
Hubbard, Laurel, 96

Huffington Post, 77
Human Rights, 73–76
Hungary, 132
Hyde Park, 71
Hyde, Chris, 29
Hypatia, 120
Hysterectomy, 37, 107, 108
Iceland, 67
Idaho, 132, 135
Illinois, 95, 134
India, 46, 67
Indy100, 77
Infertility, 13, 25, 39, 74, 87, 107, 108, 144
Inflammatory Bowel Disease, 110
Intellectual disability, 57, 101
International Association for Athletics Federations, 97
International Women's Day, 103
Intestine, 34
Introducing Teddy, 57
In-vitro fertilization, 37, 74
IPSO, 147
Ireland, Republic of, 67
Ivy, Veronica, 96, 98
Jeffreys, Sheila, 12
Jenner, Caitlyn, 3, 7, 8, 91
Joan of Arc, 112, 113
John Lewis, 94
Johns Hopkins Hospital, 6, 16, 130
Jorgensen, Christine, 5
Kennedy, Natacha., 84
Kent, University of, 124
KFC, 93
Kidney disease, 110
Kłonkowska, Anna M., 22

Kokec, 46
Labour. *See* Childbirth
Labour Party, 80, 79–81
   All-Women Shortlists, 90
   Election performance, 80
   for Trans, 80
   Leader. *See* Starmer, Kier
   Leadership election, 80
   Rochester and Strood
     Branch, 90
   Students, 90
Le Fey, Leila, 74
Lees, Paris, 93
Lego, 44
Leicester, University of, 104
Lemay, Jacob, 81
Leo, 61–62
Leuprorelin. *See* Puberty
  blockers
Lewis, Helen, 63, 78
LGB Alliance, 80, 118, 146
LGB rights, 142
Liew, Jonathan, 100
Lineham, Graham, 85
Litigation, 84–85
Littman, Lisa, 20, 21, 120,
  121, 122
Liverpool, 72
Liverpool John Moore's
  University, 118
Lobotomy, 39
London, 104
Long-Baily, Rebecca, 80
Lupron. *See* Puberty blockers
Macclesfield, 118
MacLachlan, Maria, 71, 82
Madigan, Lily, 90, 116
Malicious Communications
  Act 1988, 69, 70

Malta, 67
Maran, Meredith, 131
Marks and Spencer, 94
Masochism, 18
Mastectomy, 36
Masturbation, 18
Mayer, Lawrence, 26
McCarthy-Calvert, Lynsey,
  116
McConnel, Freddie, 112
McHugh, Paul, 6, 29, 130, 132
Mckinnon, Rachel. *See*
  Veronica Ivy
Media, 7
Menstruation, 18, 56, 98, 107–
  10, 142
  pain, 98
Mermaids, 70
Mexico, 46
Michelle Remembers, 129
Miller, Harry, 138
Mills College, 96
Minnesota, 136
Minority stress, 22
Missouri, 134
Mixed Martial Arts, 96
Monroe, Jack, 77
Moody, Louise, 83, 85, 116
Moore, Suzanne, 90, 126
Mosier, Chris, 99
Mouncey, Hannah, 96
Mount Holyoke College, 96,
  118
Mraz, Jason, 46
Mum A, 133, 134
Mumsnet, 85
Munchausen Syndrome by
  Proxy, 63

Murder, 3, 77–78, 125, 126, 145
Murphy, Erin, 119
Murray Edwards College, 96
Muscle strength, 97
Muxes, 46
My Transsexual Summer, 7
Myers, Zoomer, 60–61
Nandy, Lisa, 80
National Police Chief's Council, 73
Necrosis, 35, 36
Nelson, Margaret, 69
Nepal, 67
Nettie Project, 26
Neuropathy, 25
New Hall Prison, 95
New Hampshire, 135
New York, 72
New York Times, 49
New Zealand, 67
NHS, 6, 28, 74, 92, 133, 134, 137
North Carolina, 26
North Wales Police, 71
Nose Job. *See* Rhinoplasty
NSPCC, 125
O'Brien, Casey, 107
O'Neill, Brendan, 66
Obama, 139
Oestrogen, 25, 33, 38, 59
　oestradiol, 25
OFCOM, 147
Ohio, 32, 66, 135
Oklahoma, 134
Olympics, 99, 101
Open University, 124
Ovaries, 24, 26
Oxfam, 104

Oxford (City), 72
Oxford Brookes University, 118
Oxford University, 123, 124
Oxfordshire County Council, 137
Pakistan, 67
Paralympics, 101
Parker, Posie, 117
Passports, 132
PCOS. *See* Polycystic Ovary Syndrome
Peanut goes for the Gold, 58
Penile inversion, 34
Penis, 7, 26, 34, 35, 57, 59, 72, 89, 95, 105
　neopenis, 35
Penny, Laurie, 77
Periods. *See* Menstruation
Phalloplasty, 35
Phobia, 17
Planned Parenthood, 92, 103
Polycystic Ovary Syndrome, 107
Polygender, 40
Pregnancy, 110
　and Sport, 99
　outcomes, 111
　Sex education, 152
　transmen, 7
　Transmen, 112
Primark, 95
Prison, 5, 12, 67, 68, 74, 95, 125, 131, 138
Pronouns, 1, 12, 14, 40, 44, 50, 51, 52, 57, 60, 61, 62, 72, 116
Prostate, 105

Puberty blockers, 34, 55, 58, 59, 63, 133, 134, 144
Pussyhats, 87
Quadriceps, 98
Quebec, 96
Queen Kristina of Sweden, 112
Rape, 2, 3, 95
Rapid-Onset Gender Dysphoria, 20–21, 120, 121, 120–21
Recovered memory craze, 129–32
Respiratory system, 97
Retraction Watch, 122
Rhinoplasty, 36
ROGD. *See* Rapid-Onset Gender Dysphoria
Rogers, Greg, 20
Rowling, JK, 113, 119
Sam (Doll), 58–59
Satanic ritual abuse, 130, 131
Saudi Arabia, 89
Savewomenssports.com, 136
Schizophrenia, 17, 21, 55
School
  Guidelines, 56, 57
  Sex education, 105
  Sports, 97
  Teacher, 115, 116
  Toilets, 94, 136, 137
Schools in Transition, 97
Scientific American, 24, 41
Scottish Nationalist Party, 125
Scottow, Kate, 70, 85
Sefton Council, 103
Self-Identification, 67–68
Seroma, 35
Serwotka, Mark, 81

Serwotka, Ruth, 81
Sex Change Regret. *See Detransitioning*
Sex reassignment surgery, 5, 6, 7, 13, 21, 24, 28, 29, 39, 49, 59, 75, 82, 84, 128
Sex Reassignment Surgery, 29
Shupe, James, 48, 75
Smith, Sam, 77
Snell, Hannah, 112, 113
Social media, 8, 9, 10, 11, 15, 20, 50, 51, 68, 69, 70, 78, 83, 108, 115, 117, 118, 119, 126, 147, 152, 153
South Dakota, 134
South Yorkshire Police, 73
Special Olympics, 101
Spelman College, 96
Sperm (cell), 37, 38, 74, 104, 112, 143
sperm (cell) freezing. *See* gamete freezing
Sport
  Transgender athletes, 101
Starmer, Kier, 81
Stonewall, 82
Strictures, 35
Suicide, 29–33, 55, 56, 75, 77, 83, 84, 125, 141, 144, 147
  in Children, 56
  of Leelah Alcorn, 32–33
  Rate, 31, 77
  Threats, 84
Sun, Simón(e) D, 24
Supreme Court, 112
Sutcliffe, Joshua, 115, 116
Sweden, 30, 73, 135
Swyer Syndrome. *See* Gonadal Dysgenesis

Talbot, Mary Ann, 112
Tampon, 98
Tampon tax, 114
Tatchell, Peter, 124
Tavistock and Portman Clinic, 20, 55, 56
Team USA, 99
Tennessee, 66, 135
TERF, 4, 82, 83, 88, 115, 117, 118, 123, 140
Terfblocker, 118
TERFs Out of Art, 118
Testicles, 25, 105
Testosterone, 25, 33, 36, 39, 58, 87, 97, 98, 99, 100, 133
The Courage to Heal, 129
The Crying Game, 7
The Daily Mail, 133
The Guardian, 90, 126
The Independent, 100
The Liberal Democrats, 80
The Matrix, 21
The Samaritans, 32, 83
The Sorrows of Young Werther, 31
The Transsexual Phenomenon, 6
The Vagina Monologues, 118
The White Pube, 118
Thinx, 109
Thornton, Sara, 73
TLC, 59
Todd, Selina, 123, 124
Together for Yes, 87
Toilets, 93–94, 106, 136, 146, 150
Top Surgery, 36
Topshop, 94
Toronto ,University of, 94

Trans Rights UK, 84
Trans Voices for Repeal, 87
Transgender Day of Remembrance, 77
Transracialism, 120
Trump Jr., Donald, 88, 99
Trump, Donald, 87, 137, 139
Truss, Liz, 136
Tumblr, 8, 32, 47
Turkey, 46
Tuvel, Rebecca, 120
Twitter, 70, 73, 81, 106, 116, 117
Two-spirit people, 42, 46
United Nations, 73
Urinary incontinence, 34
Uruguay, 67
USA Powerlifting, 135
Uterus, 26, 57, 103, 110, 112
Vagina, 18, 26, 57, 59, 82, 87, 103, 119
   Neovagina, 34, 35
Vaginoplasty, 34, 59
Van Meter, Quentin, 16
van Ness, Jonathan, 58
Vancouver Rape Relief, 95
Vice, 41
Violence, 41, 42, 71, 78
   Administrative, 67
   Against women, 2–3
   Toward feminists, 83
Virginia, 93
Vlaming, Peter, 116, 117
Vocal hyperfunction, 37
Voice Training, 36–37
von Goethe, Johann Wolfgang, 31
Vulva, 34, 87, 89
Wakefield, 95

Walton, Jessica, 57
Warren, Elizabeth, 81
Wellcome Collection, 104
Werther Effect, 31
West Yorkshire, 95
White, Karen, 95
Wikipedia, 106
Williamson, Gavin, 138
Windust, Jamie, 132
Wisconsin, 94
Wojtczak, Helena, 85
Wolf, Tara, 71, 82
Woman's Human Rights Campaign, 146
Woman's Place UK, 80, 81, 123, 146
Women
  Health, 92–93

Shelters, 82, 95–96, 137, 150
Socialization, 92
Women's March, 87
Womxn, 104
WordPress, 117
World Health Organization, 7
World Professional Association for Transgender Health, 28
WPATH. *See* World Professional Association for Transgender Health
Yaniv, Jessica, 84–85
York, University of, 116
Younger, James, 63
Zucker, Kenneth, 54, 117

Printed in Great Britain
by Amazon